Nationalism and the Postcolonial

Cross/Cultures

READINGS IN POST/COLONIAL
LITERATURES AND CULTURES IN ENGLISH

Edited by

Bénédicte Ledent
Delphine Munos

Co-founding editors

†Hena Maes-Jelinek
Gordon Collier
†Geoffrey Davis

VOLUME 214

ASNEL/GAPS Papers

ASNEL Papers appear under the auspices of the Gesellschaft
für Anglophone Postkoloniale Studien (GAPS)
Association for Anglophone Postcolonial Studies

Cecile Sandten GAPS President
Chemnitz University of Technology

VOLUME 24

The titles published in this series are listed at *brill.com/asne*

Nationalism and the Postcolonial

Edited by

Sandra Dinter and Johanna Marquardt

BRILL
RODOPI

LEIDEN | BOSTON

Cover illustration: Flags for sale on the 58th Republic day celebrations in India on 26th January, photograph by Nikhil Gangavane.

Library of Congress Cataloging-in-Publication Data

Names: Dinter, Sandra, editor. | Marquardt, Johanna, editor.
Title: Nationalism and the postcolonial / edited by Sandra Dinter and
   Johanna Marquardt.
Description: Leiden ; Boston : Brill | Rodopi, 2021. | Series: Asnel
   papers; vol.24 | Includes index.
Identifiers: LCCN 2021017460 (print) | LCCN 2021017461 (ebook) | ISBN
   9789004464278 (hardback) | ISBN 9789004464315 (ebook)
Subjects: LCSH: Commonwealth literature (English)–History and criticism. |
   Nationalism in literature. | Postcolonialism in literature. | Literature
   and society–Commonwealth countries–History–21st century.
Classification: LCC PR9080.5 .N38 2021 (print) | LCC PR9080.5 (ebook) |
   DDC 820.9/353–dc23
LC record available at https://lccn.loc.gov/2021017460
LC ebook record available at https://lccn.loc.gov/2021017461

Typeface for the Latin, Greek, and Cyrillic scripts: "Brill". See and download: brill.com/brill-typeface.

ISSN 0924-1426
ISBN 978-90-04-46427-8 (hardback)
ISBN 978-90-04-46431-5 (e-book)

Copyright 2021 by Koninklijke Brill NV, Leiden, The Netherlands.
Koninklijke Brill NV incorporates the imprints Brill, Brill Hes & De Graaf, Brill Nijhoff, Brill Rodopi, Brill Sense, Hotei Publishing, mentis Verlag, Verlag Ferdinand Schöningh and Wilhelm Fink Verlag.
All rights reserved. No part of this publication may be reproduced, translated, stored in a retrieval system, or transmitted in any form or by any means, electronic, mechanical, photocopying, recording or otherwise, without prior written permission from the publisher. Requests for re-use and/or translations must be addressed to Koninklijke Brill NV via brill.com or copyright.com.

This book is printed on acid-free paper and produced in a sustainable manner.

Contents

List of Tables and Figures   VII
Notes on Contributors and Editors   VIII

Nationalism and the Postcolonial: An Introduction   1
  Sandra Dinter

PART 1
The Languages of Nationalism

1 The Nationalist Ideology of Monolingualism in Postcolonial Theory   23
   Michael Westphal

2 Talking Kenya*n: Dynamic Practices for a Heterogeneous Nation   40
   Natascha Bing

3 The Hindi Language and the Imagination of the Indian Nation: Ramchandra Shukla's Construction of Indian Civilization   57
   Prachi Gupta

PART 2
The Songs and Sounds of Nationalism

4 Singing the Postcolonial Independent in Trinbagonian Calypso   75
   Arhea Marshall

5 Singing the Nation: The Condition of Englishness in the Lyrics of PJ Harvey and Kate Tempest   92
   Sina Schuhmaier

PART 3
Nationalisms in Postcolonial Popular Culture

6   Pop Culture: A Vehicle of State Nationalism in India   111
     Idreas Khandy

7   Meet the 'Holy Family': From Multicultural Australia to Enforced Reconciliation in Baz Luhrmann's *Australia* (2008)   131
     Hanna Teichler

8   Intersections of Race, Sexuality, and National Identity in BioWare's *Mass Effect*   149
     Theresa Krampe

PART 4
Nationalisms in Postcolonial Literatures

9   Blind Spots: Nationalism and the Photographic Gaze in Teju Cole's *Every Day Is for the Thief*   169
     Ralf Haekel

10 Emotional Nationalism in the New Nigerian Novel   186
     Hannah Pardey

11 The British Empire and the 'Laureate of Its Demise': Postimperial Nostalgia in Jane Gardam's Old Filth Trilogy   204
     Lukas Lammers

12 'Bastardizing' National Belonging: Derek Walcott and Joseph Conrad   223
     Kathrin Härtl

Index   239

Tables and Figures

Tables

2.1   Transcription Conventions (GAT 2)   54
4.1   The Independence Calypso Contest 1962 – calypsonians, their entries, and the 2012 re-enactment calypsonians   82

Figures

9.1 and 9.2   Photographs from Teju Cole's *Every Day Is for the Thief*   178

Notes on Contributors and Editors

Natascha Bing
holds an MA in African Studies and Political Science from Johannes Gutenberg University Mainz, Germany. In 2017, she completed her PhD at the Institute of African Studies at Leipzig University where she worked as a research associate and lecturer. In her dissertation, she analysed linguistic practices in the postcolonial and heterogeneous setting of Kenya's capital Nairobi. Recently, Natascha Bing extended her research towards the analysis of postcolonial linguistics and humanitarian assistance in an urban context, particularly in everyday practices in dynamic and heterogeneous settings.

Sandra Dinter
is a postdoctoral researcher and lecturer in English Literature and Culture at Friedrich-Alexander-University Erlangen-Nürnberg in Germany. Her research interests include representations of gender and space, adaptation studies, literary and cultural theory, (neo-)Victorian Studies, and narrative fiction about and for children. Currently, she is researching female pedestrianism in nineteenth-century British culture and literature. She is the author of *Childhood in the Contemporary English Novel* (Routledge, 2019) and co-editor of *Transdisciplinary Perspectives on Childhood in Contemporary Britain: Literature, Media and Society* (Routledge, 2018).

Prachi Gupta
is a doctoral student at the Centre for Political Studies at Jawaharlal Nehru University in New Delhi, India. The title of her PhD thesis is "Language, Religion and the Nation: A Critical Analysis of the Works of Ramchandra Shukla and Hazari Prasad Dwivedi."

Ralf Haekel
is Professor of British Literature at Leipzig University, Germany. His main research interests are Romantic Studies, Early Modern Drama and Theatre, Irish Studies, and Literary Media Studies. In 2003, he received his PhD from Free University Berlin and, in 2013, his Habilitation from Göttingen University. His publications include the monograph *The Soul in British Romanticism: Negotiating Human Nature in Philosophy, Science and Poetry* (WVT, 2014) and the co-edited collection *Community, Seriality, and the State of the Nation: British and Irish Television Series in the 21st Century* (Narr, 2019). Ralf Haekel is editor of the *Handbook of British Romanticism* (De Gruyter, 2017).

Kathrin Härtl

studied English and German Literature at LMU Munich where she completed her studies in 2011. Since then, she has been working in the English Department of LMU Munich. In 2019, she published her first book *The Common Bond of the Sea: Derek Walcott and Joseph Conrad* (Fink). Currently, she is a postdoctoral researcher in the research unit "Philology of Adventure" funded by the German Research Foundation. Her research focuses on Victorian, modernist, and postcolonial adventure fiction.

Idreas Khandy

is currently enrolled in the PhD programme in Politics at Lancaster University in the United Kingdom where he focuses on Kashmiri nationalism. His research interests include pop culture, social movements, capitalism, and the future of the nation-state.

Theresa Krampe

holds an MA in National and Transnational Studies from Münster University, Germany. Her MA thesis, parts of which have been published in *Game Studies* (2018), focuses on identity politics in role-playing games from a queer game studies perspective. Since 2018, she has been a doctoral candidate at the International Graduate Centre for the Study of Culture (GCSC) in Gießen where she researches forms of metareference in videogames.

Lukas Lammers

is Assistant Professor at Free University Berlin, Germany, where he teaches English literature and cultural studies. His research focuses on historical fiction, questions of cultural memory and identity, early modern drama, World War II, and processes of decolonisation. His monograph *Shakespearean Temporalities* was published with Routledge in 2018. He is co-editor of *Shakespeare Seminar* and regularly reviews performances for the *Shakespeare Jahrbuch*.

Johanna Marquardt's

research concerns Irish literature of the mid-twentieth century, particularly Brian O'Nolan's literary and journalistic work and its production and reception contexts. She holds a degree in English literature and linguistics, political science, and didactics from Leibniz University, Hanover, and teaches English literature and cultural studies with a focus on Ireland at Johannes Gutenberg University Mainz, Germany.

Arhea Marshall

is a PhD candidate in Anglophone Literary Cultures and Global South Studies at the University of Tübingen and Konrad Adenauer fellowship holder in Germany. She was born and raised in Trinidad, obtained her Bachelor of Arts in German Studies and Environmental Studies at Bowdoin College (Brunswick, ME) and her Master of Arts in English Literatures and Cultures at the University of Tübingen. Her current dissertation research focuses on archives of perceived change from independence into the postcolonial, specifically in Trinidad and Tobago through calypso lyrics. Her research interests include the Global South and the Caribbean, gastropoetics in literary theory, archives, collective memory, cultures of memorialisation and celebration, as well as entanglements between ideas of nature and culture.

Hannah Pardey

is a research assistant and doctoral candidate at the University of Hanover, Germany. She teaches British literatures and cultures from the sixteenth to the twenty-first century with a strong focus on postcolonial literatures in English and theories and methods of literary studies. Her master's thesis "Historiographic Metafiction from the Nigerian Diaspora" received the GAPS Graduate Award (complimentary prize) in 2016. Her dissertation project, "Postcolonial Middlebrow: The New Nigerian Novel," concerns the conditions of production, distribution, and reception of recent Nigerian fictions.

Sina Schuhmaier

is an academic staff member and doctoral student at the University of Mannheim's chair of English Literary and Cultural Studies. In her doctoral thesis, she examines a range of contemporary song lyrics centred on, and generally critical towards, the English nation. She investigates the conceptions of nation and national identity articulated in these lyrics, the positionings of national and cultural identity assumed and rejected, and the wider context of British popular music and the nation, considered through the lenses of cultural and postcolonial studies. Further research interests comprise contemporary British television drama, Black British literature, and literature and economy. She has published on BBC Two's *Peaky Blinders* and is currently co-editing a volume on contemporary literature and recent critiques of capitalism, *Literarische Perspektiven auf den Kapitalismus: Fallbeispiele aus dem 21. Jahrhundert* (Narr Francke Attempto, 2021).

Hanna Teichler

holds a PhD from the Department of Anglophone Literatures and Cultures, Goethe University Frankfurt, and an MA degree in English, French, and Portuguese philology. She works as a postdoctoral researcher at the Department of Anglophone Literatures and Cultures at Goethe University, Frankfurt, Germany. Her first monograph titled *Carnivalizing Reconciliation* will appear with Berghahn in 2021. Hanna Teichler is the co-editor (with Rebekah Vince) of the new book series *Mobilizing Memories* and the *Handbook Series in Memory Studies* (Brill Publishing) and a member of the MSA Executive Committee, the Frankfurt Memory Studies Platform, and GAPS.

Michael Westphal

is a postdoctoral researcher at the Chair of Variation Linguistics at the English Department of the University of Münster, Germany, where he received his PhD in 2016. He also studied and conducted research at the University of the West Indies in Mona, Kingston, Jamaica. Michael Westphal is the author of *Language Variation on Jamaican Radio* (Benjamins, 2017). He is currently working on his postdoctoral project "Question Tags Across Englishes: A Variational Pragmatic Analysis." His further research interests include (postcolonial) varieties of English with a focus on the Caribbean, the sociolinguistics of globalisation, language attitudes, variational pragmatics, and language in the media.

Nationalism and the Postcolonial

An Introduction

Sandra Dinter

1   Points of Departure: From Populist Nationalism to 'Coronationalism'

Multiculturalism, cosmopolitanism, globalisation, and transnationalism were some of the big buzzwords of the 1990s and 2000s. After the rise of populist nationalism in the 2010s, they increasingly appear as the remnants of a bygone era that even their most outspoken sceptics may look back upon with nostalgia. Multiculturalism signalled a spirit of optimism and inclusivity that was declining as more and more populist nationalists rose to power and xenophobic movements gained support around the globe. One of the first memorable events heralding this shift was the election of Narendra Modi of the Bharatiya Janata Party as Prime Minister of India in May 2014. As Pankaj Mishra writes, back in 1951 when India held its first general election, it would have been unlikely "that a figure such as Narendra Modi, the Hindu nationalist former chief minister of Gujarat accused … of complicity in crimes ranging from anti-Muslim pogrom in his state in 2002 to extrajudicial killings, and barred from entering the United States, came to occupy India's highest political office" (196). Like the numerous populist nationalists who ascended to influential political offices in other countries after him, Modi was not brought to power by a few extremists but democratically elected with a comfortable majority (198). Five years later, he was re-elected despite the massive spread of violence against Muslims in India. Populist nationalism, Modi's case suggested, was not only tolerated but desired by large sections of society.

While populist nationalism had, of course, existed before, it had moved from the fringes into mainstream politics in various countries of the Global South and the Global North in a remarkably short period of time (Bergmann 13–4). In 2016, two further landmarks of populist nationalism urged newsreaders around the world to hold their breath: the Brexit referendum in the United Kingdom and the election of Donald Trump as President of the United States of America. Although the outcome of the referendum, as close as it was, can be traced back to various factors, many of which had more to do with domestic issues than the country's EU membership, it was a symptom of the British (or, rather, English) nation's inability to come to terms with its altered position in a postcolonial world.[1] The decision to leave the European Union, as Craig Calhoun argues, was essentially "a vote against multiculturalism and for English nationalism" (60). The referendum was an occasion for the populist nationalists involved in the Leave campaign to create and disseminate a distinct self-image of the nation. According to Caroline Koegler, Pavan Kumar Malreddy, and Marlena Tronicke, this was "a victim-like, sacrificial, and defensive position, giving ample opportunity for constructing the country as having to fend off unjust, inferiorizing 'onslaughts' of EU bureaucrats, and abject invasions of European immigrants" (586).[2] These "parts of the Brexit debate," they point out, were "narcissistically invested in hierarchical, controlling relationships ('take back control'), rather than more balanced, inclusive, and socially just models of cooperation" (587). Therefore, Brexit sealed, if perhaps not the end, at least a decisive turn away from transnational collaboration to a pre-WWII model of state nationalism.

Similar observations can be made about the politics and rhetoric of Donald Trump in the United States. Just as the Leave campaign and parts of the Conservative Party in the UK saw their nation's cultural, political, and economic integrity threatened by an international organisation and its maxim of free movement, "Donald Trump's vision of national greatness built on an 'America First' platform, blaming foreigners and minorities for many of the country's current problems, reverting to a manufacturing base built on protectionism and tariff walls" (Stone and Rizova 33). One of Trump's most powerful tools was his language. While his nationalist and xenophobic rhetoric along with his refusal to condemn white supremacists offended his opponents, its constant reiterations on TV and social media normalised racism and scapegoating. As John Stone and Polly Rizova specify, Trump's speeches deliberately invoke stereotypes and hatred,

> blaming immigrants from south of the border as the source of 'muggers and rapists' requiring the building of a huge wall to keep out this threat to the American way of life. Refugees fleeing the chaos of Syria and other parts of the Middle East are seen as potential Islamic terrorists intent on continuing the murderous activities of Osama bin Laden and ISIS. The

---

1 This sentiment has been examined in depth by Paul Gilroy in *Postcolonial Melancholia* (2005) and Fintan O'Toole in *Heroic Failure: Brexit and the Politics of Pain* (2018) and *The Politics of Pain: Postwar England and the Rise of Nationalism* (2019).
2 Paying attention to racial and racist dimensions of this stance in the Brexit debate, James Rhodes and Natalie-Anne Hall suggest that the Leave campaign and the UK Independence Party promoted narratives of white victimhood (292).

> attacks on traditional allies, as well as trading partners, are interpreted as a necessary measure to prevent the evil exploitation of American generosity among friend and foe alike. (37)

Part of Trump's success, as well as of other contemporary populist nationalists, is his use of social media and its algorithms. As Christian Fuchs suggests, "[s]ocial media platforms such as Facebook, Twitter, and YouTube have become important spheres of political communication that have added a new level of communication to traditional media of the public sphere such as newspapers and television" (12) and "[f]ar-right movements, groups, parties, and individuals are among the most widely followed social media profiles" (13). Trump was not the only leader to deploy these channels. He joined established nationalist populists like Viktor Orbán in Hungary, Recep Tayyip Erdoğan in Turkey, Nicolás Maduro in Venezuela, and Rodrigo Duterte in the Philippines, and may have paved the way for the election of Jair Bolsonaro as President of Brazil in 2018 and Boris Johnson as Prime Minister of the United Kingdom in 2019. Moreover, Trump shares views with the many far-right movements and organisations that rose to popularity in the 2010s, such as Reclaim Australia and One Nation in Australia, Alternative für Deutschland in Germany, and the Rassemblement National (formerly Front National) in France.

The politicians and movements above are representative of populist nationalism insofar as they all claim

> to defend the interest of the working classes – or special groups that it defines as 'the people' – while at the same time protecting the national interests and 'the nation' incarnated in groups characterized by a certain culture, ethnicity, or background. ... In the twenty-first century one of PN's [populist nationalism's] main enemies is foreign influence and it is thus anti-globalization, arguing for a defense of national culture, values, or ethnicity against immigrants and what it perceives as foreign interference in the affairs of the nation. (López-Alves and Johnson 7)

While Modi's Hindu nationalism discriminates in terms of religion, Trump's nationalism does so with respect to race, addressing primarily white Americans. As Fernando López-Alves and Diane E. Johnson explain, "virtually all populisms are nationalistic, but not all nationalisms are populistic" (7). Populist nationalism is therefore only one variant of numerous forms of nationalism, many of which operate more discreetly than Modi's, the Brexiteers', and Trump's, and some of which assume even more drastic shapes in dictatorships. Accordingly, this volume includes discussions of various nationalisms.

The events outlined above initiated the idea to put together an edited collection on nationalism and the postcolonial. They kept us and our authors preoccupied when we sent out their submissions for peer review in early 2019. Little did we know that this rise of populist nationalism was to be complemented by an unexpected global upsurge of nationalism in the second half of 2020 while we were in the final round of editing this collection. By March, the COVID-19 epidemic in Wuhan, China, had turned into a pandemic taking its toll on virtually all continents. Although various pandemics had afflicted humanity before, it was the first time that a health crisis "involved worldwide lockdowns, cessation of normal activities and massive state-sponsored and state-controlled mitigation" (Woods et al. 5). As the numbers of positive cases in individual countries were recorded in charts and maps, it quickly became apparent that "several of the countries with the highest COVID-19 infection rates ... [were] led by populist nationalist leaders – including the United States, Brazil and the United Kingdom" (10). These numbers suggested that populist nationalism, instead of putting its nation's wellbeing first as promised, actually harmed its citizens.

But this was only one of the ways in which nationalism entered the picture. Even the countries whose leaders were not considered populist nationalists employed isolation as an immediate measure to contain the virus. Across all political camps, presidents and prime ministers around the globe presented themselves as firm leaders of their afflicted nations, closing their borders, banning international travel, and, where possible, organising emergency return flights for their citizens abroad, often by the use of executive orders. Political acts of transnational solidarity and collaboration remained the exception rather than the rule since sympathy was to be devoted to fellow nationals first. By April, it seemed all the more as if the era of globalisation had come to a halt and rigorous nation-states provided the political foundation of the 'new normality' that many journalists saw emerging in the wake of the pandemic. It did not take long for scholars to pick up on the neologism 'coronationalism' (e.g. Bieber; van Uden and van Houtum) to make sense of this new context and form of nationalism. Indeed, the coronavirus crisis made us experience more consciously than before the basic principles, rituals, and consequences of nationalism, just as much as it confronted us with its manifold entanglements with (neo)colonialist structures, some of which shall briefly be charted here.

Every nationalism is inevitably an exclusive ideology operating on the basis of " 'cultural' factors [such] as religious beliefs or language, or notions of shared biological substance, or of inherited historical experiences, but ... also ... more abstract qualities such as core values (e.g. egalitarianism, liberty, democracy)" (Hearn 11). As such, nationalism always relies on 'Others' inside and outside its borders (Rhodes and Hall 285; Valluvan and Kalra 2395). What makes coronationalism stand out is that "the actual enemy is invisible" (Goode et al. 13). As Annelies van Uden and Henk van Houtum state, the virus is an unusual antagonist because it threatens all nations across the globe equally, being "blind for national borders, skin colour, power positions, descent or richness, and as such is a-political" (338). This scenario reveals once again the power of nationalist language. Many leaders – not just the populist nationalists – have used militarist language to construct the invisible and apolitical virus as a conventional Other. As Yasmeen Serhan observes, along with Xi Jinping, Donald Trump, and Boris Johnson, Emmanuel Macron and Italy's special commissioner for the coronavirus emergency, Domenico Arcuri, have repeatedly used war metaphors to refer to the coronavirus (n. pag.). Serhan posits that "while wartime imagery can promote national cohesion, it can also breed fear, which can in turn drive anxiety and panic" (n. pag.). In so doing, militarist language can distract from the fact that the entire world population is affected by the virus and that it demands transnational solutions to be eliminated. In addition to linguistically declaring war on the pandemic, Donald Trump applied his xenophobic register to the virus. Florian Bieber recounts that in deliberate opposition to the neutral acronym COVID-19 chosen by the World Health Organization, "[t]he Trump administration has adopted the term *Chinese virus* to link the pandemic to China and also externalize responsibility for the spread" (6, emphasis in original). Eva Nossem explains that "the practice of naming in this specific case can be understood as a linguistic practice of (re-) bordering ... The disease is assigned to a specific location outside of one's own borders and thus created as something foreign, which is then seen as a threat to the nation" (5). Yet scapegoating can, of course, also operate within the nation, and this has happened in the pandemic. As Bieber notes, the Bharatiya Janata Party and the media in India, for example, "have singled out Muslims as 'super-carriers'" (6) of the virus. Precisely this xenophobic rhetoric, Bieber goes on to argue, has led to a further increase of reported instances of discrimination and harassment against minority groups since the beginning of the pandemic (6). To postcolonial scholars, such strategies of Othering are all too familiar.

Just as much as coronationalism reinforces borders and excludes and blames its Others, internally it relies on rituals and representations of nation-building that accommodate the circumstances of the pandemic. To use the words of Benedict Anderson, in the times of COVID-19, nations require new ways of 'imagining' themselves as communities that share the fate of staying home during a lockdown or keeping apart in public settings. At a time when social distancing makes many of the established ceremonies of nation-building like festivities, national holidays, and singing national anthems impossible and international sporting events like the Olympic Games had to be cancelled, rituals beyond occasional addresses to the nation by heads of states are necessary so that individuals can profess their belonging to and solidarity with their nation. According to J. Paul Goode, David R. Stroup, and Elizaveta Gaufman, one case in point was the Clap for Our Carers initiative in the United Kingdom (4), which set a day and time for the entire nation to applaud their essential workers collectively outside their doorsteps or behind open windows, particularly those in the National Health Service. As Goode and his colleagues state, such events fulfilled multiple purposes, such as "produc[ing] feelings of national solidarity and common belonging that provide ontological security" and "justifying (or perhaps even rejecting) the changes wreaked by the virus on the course of everyday life. By standing up to applaud for care workers, participants sought to recognize, validate, and participate in the efforts to beat the virus and restore normality" (4–5). The circulation of images of neighbours clapping together across the internet underscored this solidarity and may fuel future myths of the nation. As Marco Antonsich argues, such rituals, which could be found in many parts of the world, created "an atmosphere of national affect [that] brought people together, confirming how the nation is something to celebrate, identify with and hold on to in times of uncertainty" (n. pag.). Such moments indicate that nationalism is always an ambivalent phenomenon, "a twin-headed force" (15), as Gregory Jusdanis puts it. Just as much as it can force and harm, it can also unite. In the words of Bill Ashcroft, Gareth Griffiths, and Helen Tiffin, nationalism is "an extremely contentious site, on which ideas of self-determination and freedom, of identity and unity collide with ideas of suppression and force, of domination and exclusion" (136). In *Why Nationalism* (2019), Yael Tamir makes a strong case for the benefits of (non-populist) nationalism:

> In seeking to build a more decent social and political regime, one that provides all citizens better protection and better life chances, it is important to remember that no institution did it better than the nation-state. International organizations are playing a growing role in a wide range of spheres ... yet none is able to replace the state in its most important social and democratic roles: allowing individuals to be self-governing, meeting the political challenge of 'no taxation without representation,' and developing distributive tools and a social support system for those who need it. (31)

It is therefore not surprising that nationalism has been flourishing more than ever during a public health crisis and that even many opponents may now recognise its usefulness.

Yet despite its capability to provide consolation and effective governance, the question of whether coronationalism is successful relies to a great extent on economic and technological resources. Ultimately, this means that the pandemic has and will continue to affect the countries of the Global South more severely than those of the Global North. According to Gurminder K. Bhambra, "[t]he inequalities that sit at the heart of our societies have been highlighted during the pandemic" (19). She identifies this global disparity in resources as "a consequence of European (and US) colonial and imperial histories" (22). In other words, the COVID-19 crisis unfolds in conjunction with the residual structures of colonialism.[3] The former colonial powers have a wider scope of addressing the crisis economically, logistically, and scientifically, even if many of them are hotspots of the pandemic. In Nossem's view,

> [t]he coronavirus, spread by the rich (who travelled their globalized world), will hit worst the poor (especially if with restricted mobility) ... The rich have ... far better opportunities of shielding themselves from the virus, the poor are exposed to it without protection. The three commandments preached in the news all over the world now – stay home, keep distance, wash hands – are only feasible for a limited portion of humankind while the rest maybe does not have a home, maybe lives in circumstances where it is impossible to keep distance, and maybe has no access to clean water. (9–10)[4]

The legacies of colonialism determine how well nation-states can hold the virus at bay and keep their economies running at the same time, but they will also be vital once a vaccine is available. Although private companies conduct most vaccine studies, the race for the discovery of the right vaccine candidate signifies a competition among nation-states. Not only may one nation pride itself on a spectacular scientific discovery in case the successful company

---

3 For one of the first basic considerations of how postcolonial theory can inform the analysis of COVID-19 pandemic politics, see Kwok.
4 Nossem mentions refugees as a particularly vulnerable group in the pandemic (8), while Bhambra also pays attention to the role of migrant workers who often leave their home countries for economic reasons and work in health services in the Global North. According to Bhambra, this labour movement leads to another "colonial drain" (22) in terms of medical expertise that affects primarily postcolonial nations.

or research centre happens to be located within its national bounds, but it may also reserve large shares of the vaccine for its own population by placing advance orders with this company. As an article in *The Indian Express* reported in August 2020, the United States, the United Kingdom, Japan, and the European Union alone had invested billions of dollars in major vaccine manufacturers although it was not even clear if their products were working (De n. pag.). Thomas J. Bollyky and Chad P. Bown propose that such a "vaccine nationalism" could have disastrous ramifications in a world that remains marked by inequality:

> Without global coordination, countries may bid against one another, driving up the price of vaccines and related materials. Supplies of proven vaccines will be limited initially even in some rich countries, but the greatest suffering will be in low- and middle-income countries. Such places will be forced to watch as their wealthier counterparts deplete supplies and will have to wait months (or longer) for their replenishment. In the interim, health-care workers and billions of elderly and other high-risk inhabitants in poorer countries will go unprotected, which will extend the pandemic, increase its death toll, and imperil already fragile health-care systems and economies. (97)[5]

Although it is impossible to predict whether coronationalism will be a thing of the past or indeed a new normality once the pandemic comes to an end, John Allen is right in presuming that

> [a]s it has always been, history will be written by the 'victors' of the COVID-19 crisis. ... Inevitably, those nations that persevere – both by virtue of their unique political and economic systems, as well as from a public health perspective – will claim success over those who experience a different, more devastating outcome. To some, this will appear as a great and definitive triumph for democracy, multilateralism, and universal health care. To others, it will showcase the clear 'benefits' of decisive, authoritarian rule. (n. pag.)

---

5   To prevent such an outcome, the World Health Organization launched COVAX, a global initiative to ensure that participating countries have equitable access to vaccines regardless of their financial and technological resources (Berkley n. pag.). However, as of November 2020, Russia and the United States had not joined the COVAX platform, and it remains unclear whether the countries in the programme will adhere to its rules.

The rise of populist nationalism and coronationalism are only two recent cases to counter the neat teleology which presumes that the eras of nationalism and colonialism were overcome in favour of a postcolonial and transnational world order. As Jusdanis has observed, nationalism is resilient, having "reproduced itself around the world as have few ideologies" (18). Since its inception, nationalism has never been away and will, in whatever form, most likely accompany us in a post-COVID world.

2   Postcolonial Studies and Studies of Nationalism

Acknowledging that nationalism continues to be a reality in postcolonial times, this collection seeks to interrogate and illustrate how the perspective of postcolonialism can inform the study of nationalism and vice versa. Nationalism has been defined in many ways, usually, though not exclusively and consistently, as a conglomerate of discourse, ideology, identity, bureaucracy, and territory which all have the "aim of declaring and maintaining political sovereignty" (Jusdanis 18). Since the 1980s, major publications in nationalism studies, among them Benedict Anderson's *Imagined Communities: Reflections on the Origin and Spread of Nationalism* (1983), Étienne Balibar's *Race, Nation, Class: Ambiguous Identities* (1991), Homi Bhabha's edited collection *Nation and Narration* (1990), Michael Billig's *Banal Nationalism* (1995), Ernest Gellner's *Nations and Nationalisms* (1983), Eric Hobsbawm's *Nations and Nationalism since 1780* (1990), and Anthony D. Smith's *The Ethnic Origins of Nations* (1986), have established "that the idea of the nation is an invention … and that it will need to be narrated and performed into existence" (Closs Stephens 7). With this constructivist paradigm, the study of nationalism shares basic premises with postcolonial studies, which is similarly intent on contesting essentialisms. More specifically, Ashcroft, Griffiths, and Tiffin propose that in the constructivist paradigm it is presumed that

> nations are not 'natural' entities, and the instability of the nation is the inevitable consequence of its nature as a social construction. This myth of nationhood, masked by ideology, perpetuates nationalism, in which specific identifiers are employed to create exclusive and homogenous conceptions of national traditions. Such signifiers of homogeneity always fail to represent the diversity of the actual 'national' community for which they purport to speak, and, in practice, usually represent and consolidate the interests of the dominant power groups within any national formation. (135)

This definition points to two contexts in which the perspective of postcolonialism is not only valuable but central to the examination of nationalisms: diversity and migration. With their insistence on homogeneity, many forms of Western nationalism, for instance, have marginalised, if not excluded, postcolonial subjects. Contemporary Britain is once again a case in point. Shailja Sharma delineates that "[i]n Britain, no coherent national identity replaced the imperial one" (109). Even if ethnic minorities, for instance, may have attained British citizenship, they have not been fully incorporated into narratives and performances of nationhood. Sivamohan Valluvan rightly notes that at the same time "[a]nxieties are written upon the figure of the migrant, a figure who is articulated via multiple guises – as the labour migrant, a refugee, as asylum seeker and, less frequently, the rapacious, uncouth foreign capitalist" (5). The methodological and theoretical repertoire of postcolonial studies can unpack and foreground these dynamics of nationalism and their consequences, be it in the forms of representations of the nation and its Others or policies of nation-states.

Yet despite such parallels and some scholars having approached the topic of nationalism from the perspective of postcolonialism, as is evident in major studies like Neil Lazarus's *Nationalism and Cultural Practice in the Postcolonial World* (1999), Shalini Puri's *The Caribbean Postcolonial: Social Equality, Post-Nationalism, and Cultural Hybridity* (2004), or Srirupa Roy's *Beyond Belief: India and the Politics of Postcolonial Nationalism* (2007), much remains to be done in this realm. Charles Leddy-Owen, for example, points to the homogenous reception of theories of nationalism in postcolonial studies, arguing that "[i]t is rare for studies concerned with postcolonialism, or racism more generally, to cite scholars of nationalism – other than, occasionally, Anderson" (275). Furthermore, in contrast to postcolonial studies, a field that routinely engages with cultural and literary phenomena, Tim Nieguth makes clear that "the literature on nationalism has paid relatively little attention to popular culture" (2). These are two discrepancies that this collection aims to address by putting anglophone postcolonial studies and nationalism studies into dialogue.

One strength of postcolonial studies is that it asserts more demandingly than studies of nationalism the fundamental point that the rise of nation-states in nineteenth-century Europe – which still ranks as the historical heyday of nationalism – would have been impossible without colonialism and imperialism. Robert J. C. Young explains that

> the way that European colonialism and the growth of its empires used to be characterized implicitly suggests that 'Europe' was an already constituted continent of nations which expanded its borders by acquiring

> colonial territories. This is far from the case. Europe developed into its current form through the process of amassing colonies: colonialism was a central element in the formation and construction of the European nation-states. It was a symbiotic process in which each formed a part of the other. Where chances of proximate physical expansion of individual countries were unavailable, colonies and the establishment of an overseas empire offered the same advantages as a larger land empire: increased trade, revenue, wealth, and power. (66)

While this insight may be common currency in postcolonial studies, it remains as yet largely underexplored in studies of nationalism. Furthermore, a postcolonial perspective can also enrich scholarly debates about the current wave of populist nationalism. As Koegler and her colleagues remark with respect to Brexit, even if it "is not a bona fide postcolonial event ... it represents a moment when anxieties about harnessing and unleashing colonially engineered power structures and cultural hierarchies crystallized" (585). In other words, the current wave of populist nationalism did not come out of the blue; rather, it attests to the fact that the discursive and institutional frameworks established by colonialism and imperialism remain powerful entities in contemporary nationalisms.

Another way in which nationalism and postcolonialism intersect is in the shape of anti-colonial nationalism. Whereas the nationalism of former colonial powers today conjures up images of war, violence, and genocides, nationalism assumes other and, ultimately, more positive meanings with respect to postcolonial nations. Tamir notes that albeit "discredited in the West," nationalism kept "its liberating power in the developing world and was the engine behind postcolonial movements" (15). For example, when former colonies of the UK such as India, Ghana, and Jamaica gained independence in the twentieth century, nationalism functioned as a vehicle of decolonisation. In this shape, nationalism was not only a necessary means to exercise "the right to determine their own political existence" (Young 82) and create state apparatuses, but also a mechanism to forge, spread, and celebrate 'new' postcolonial national identities through cultural practices, holidays, radio and television broadcasting, music, art, education, and many other instruments. A positive side effect of this transformation was the increasing (if by no means completed) recognition of the rights of indigenous peoples in countries like Australia and New Zealand. In its anti-colonial form, nationalism is often seen as a legitimate, even welcome, development. Such views also prevail in current discussions of regional nationalisms and independence movements. A case in point is devolution in the United Kingdom, which has given more opportunities for self-governance to Northern Ireland, Wales, and Scotland, as well as the Scottish independence referendum held in 2014. Such forms of nationalism rarely cause the anxieties that populist nationalism has been met with. Quite on the contrary, after the Brexit referendum, many European neighbours had sympathy with the Scottish National Party and its initiative to hold a second independence referendum, which could put an end to the United Kingdom as we know it today.

Although nationalism's potential to counter colonial oppression should not be underestimated, such a liberation narrative can easily oversimplify the intricacies of postcolonial nationalisms. Laura Chrisman hesitates to view the nation-state and nationalism as concepts originating exclusively in Western Europe, suggesting that "[h]istorically neither the political unit of the nation-state nor the concept of nationalism was necessarily alien to colonized countries" (184) and that "[t]he effect of presenting the nation-state, and the practice of nationalism as a permanently 'derivative discourse' is to deny the capacity of colonized and formerly colonized peoples to transform structures of thought and governance" (185). Similarly, Young reminds us not to ignore the social hierarchies and inequalities that have always existed within postcolonial nations. Nationalism may have been a unifying force on the state level but also came with privileges for the elite that was intent on securing its hegemonic position (138). Finally, the former imperial powers continue to dominate world politics today, for example, in crucial institutions like the United Nations, whose rules postcolonial nation-states must follow, although they have not been granted permanent veto rights.

While the perspective of postcolonial studies should therefore include the empowering potentials of postcolonial nationalism, it always needs to consider the other side of the coin. As the case of Modi in India suggests, postcolonial nationalism is never innocent and can become just as exclusionary and oppressive as the nationalisms it originally opposed. The same applies to the cultural and literary phenomena examined in postcolonial studies, which can resist and reflect upon nationalism just as much as they can serve as overt or latent extensions of it. The contributions in this collection will shed light on these manifold faces of (post)colonial nationalisms.

3   This Collection

This volume contains essays selected and expanded from papers presented at the twenty-ninth annual conference of the Association for Anglophone Postcolonial Studies (GAPS) that took place on 10–12 May 2018 in Mainz, Germany. Under the heading of "Nationalism and the Postcolonial" the conference brought together over one hundred participants from Austria, Canada, Germany, Nigeria, Poland, India, Spain, Switzerland, the United Kingdom, and the United States. Sixteen panels examined forms, representations, and consequences of nationalisms in a variety of media, politics, and cultural practices across Africa, Australasia, Europe, North America, and South Asia. The speakers explored manifestations of nationalisms in autobiography, romance fiction, the historical novel, nonfiction, drama, poetry, computer games, calendar art, photography, music, cinema, journalism, teaching scenarios, independence celebrations, immigration policies, and political speeches.

This programme was complemented by three keynote lectures and a creative performance. The first keynote speaker, Bruce Berman (Department of Political Studies, Queen's University at Kingston), opened the conference with a historical take on nationalism in his talk "Ethnic Nationalism and the Global Crises of Capitalist Modernity." Berman reconstructed how the academic understanding of ethno-nationalism in Africa has transformed significantly since the 1980s from a primordialist stance imbued with cultural stereotypes to an intersectional constructivism that acknowledges the plurality, fluidity, and complexity of sub-Saharan communities. Furthermore, Berman traced how global crises of modernity, the two world wars and the financial crisis of 2008, continue to shape ethnic nationalisms in sub-Saharan Africa today. In the second keynote lecture titled " 'That Place of Bubbling Trepidation': Reflections on Nations and the Transnational Turn," Laura Chrisman (Department of English, University of Washington) remained on the African continent, investigating the ambivalent ways in which writers commonly known as Afropolitans re-engage with nationalism and nationhood in the light of the continuing economic dominance of the United States over postcolonial nations. Drawing on NoViolet Bulawayo's novel *We Need New Names* (2013) and its portrayal of Zimbabwe as her main case study, Chrisman suggested that these authors see the necessity and appeal of nationalism but also recast it so that it includes diasporas and transnational alliances. The third keynote speaker, Nikita Sud (Department of International Development, University of Oxford), combined historical and contemporary perspectives in her lecture "Indian Nationalisms as Encountering and Othering." Sud began by theorising early nationalism in India as a product of encountering and othering colonial, enlightenment Britain, arguing that it attempted to build a new nation by using secularism to unite a multi-religious society. According to Sud, the subsequent rise of religious nationalism came with new forms of encountering and othering. Today, as Hindu nationalism prevails as the political ideology of the ruling classes in India, it paradoxically relies on the electoral support of a range of its non-Hindu 'Others' to survive in a democratic system. On the third day of the conference, British-Nigerian playwright Oladipo Agboluaje complemented the academic keynotes with a creative performance that involved the conference participants as his chorus. At the centre of his performance stood the educational aspirations and obstacles of a young Nigerian heroine. Agboluaje also reflected upon his work as a 'postcolonial' playwright in London, which requires many theatres to confirm positive clichés to be successful.

The essays included in this collection display the conference's broad geographical and cultural scope, its thematic diversity, and its interdisciplinarity. Their authors scrutinise figurations of past and present nationalisms in or associated with Australia, Canada, England, India, Jamaica, Kenya, Nigeria, Saint Lucia, and Trinidad and Tobago. They assemble vantage points from literary and cultural studies, game studies, film studies, linguistics, and political science, illustrating throughout how postcolonial nationalisms intersect with hierarchies emerging from race, gender, class, and religion. Their contributions illustrate that different kinds of nationalism can exercise disruptive as well as stabilising forces on countries and societies, demonstrating the versatility of the concept and pointing towards the reasons for its persistence on the world stage.

The chapters are grouped into four sections. Section one, "The Languages of Nationalism," attests to the fact that nationalism is often based on and disseminated through language. In the volume's opening chapter, "The Nationalist Ideology of Monolingualism in Postcolonial Theory," Michael Westphal offers a metaperspective on his discipline by highlighting a methodological bias in linguistic theory-making. Westphal proposes that linguistics not only analyses nationalism but, just as often, whether consciously or not, serves as an extension of it. More specifically, he argues that models of postcolonial Englishes perpetuate the ideology of monolingualism, i.e. the notion that a nation is united by one language. Providing insights into the multilingual speech communities of Kenya and Jamaica, Westphal calls for theory-making beyond the paradigm of monolingualism. The next chapter, Natascha Bing's "Talking Kenya*n: Dynamic Practices for a Heterogeneous Nation," similarly questions concepts of linguistic and national homogeneity. Although Kiswahili and English are Kenya's two official languages in the constitution, Bing illustrates that over sixty languages are spoken in the country. Drawing on her fieldwork in Kenya in the run-up to the general elections in 2013, Bing suggests that while politicians perpetuate images of a homogeneous Kenya, her interviewees switch and combine languages flexibly and welcome their nation's diversity. Bing introduces the term 'Vi-Swahili' to take account of these fluid linguistic practices, which, she maintains, can be interpreted as an expression of an emerging pluralist 'Kenya*n' national identity. The final chapter of the first section, Prachi Gupta's "The Hindi Language and the Imagination of the Indian Nation: Ramchandra Shukla's Construction of Indian Civilization," considers entanglements of nationalism and language in India, a country which has even more official languages than Kenya. Hindi, Gupta explains, had been promoted as a potential 'national' language long before independence came. Gupta uses the writings of literary critic and political thinker Ramchandra Shukla (1884–1941) to investigate the ideological origins and implications of the imagination of one Indian nation that speaks and writes Hindi. In the light of current language policies in the Hindi-speaking belt, Shukla's early vision of an Indian civilisation unified by Hindi is surprisingly topical.

"The Songs and Sounds of Nationalism," the following section, expands Westphal, Bing, and Gupta's focus on spoken language to song lyrics. In their contributions, Arhea Marshall and Sina Schuhmaier demonstrate that music is a crucial medium to envision, celebrate, and criticise nations in the postcolonial era. Taking us back to the early 1960s in her chapter "Singing the Postcolonial Independent in Trinbagonian Calypso," Marshall examines songs from the Trinbagonian Independence Calypso Contest, demonstrating how calypso functioned as a cultural practice through which a 'new' postcolonial nation could literally sing itself independent from colonial rule. Marshall uncovers the rhetoric and imagery calypsonians employ in their songs to create new visions of their home and nation, reminding us that rather than only looking at nationalism as a political phenomenon, we must also recognise the cultural work it entails. Schuhmaier's chapter "Singing the Nation: The Condition of Englishness in the Lyrics of PJ Harvey and Kate Tempest" moves on to the period before the Brexit referendum in England. Situating Harvey's song "The Last Living Rose" (2011) and Tempest's "Europe Is Lost" (2016) in the tradition of the 'Condition of England' genre, Schuhmaier deconstructs the singers' portrayals of their nation, proposing that they both diagnose a state of collective postcolonial melancholia in England. Yet, as Schuhmaier observes further, in Harvey's case, this critique has clear limits. While Tempest integrates alternative modes of national identity into her vision of English nationhood, Harvey, by relying on pastoral tropes, falls back into conventional conceptions of Englishness, indicating that even texts that position themselves as counterhegemonic interventions may contain nationalist subtexts.

Section three, "Nationalisms in Postcolonial Popular Culture," focuses on nationalisms in cinema, television, and videogames. Idreas Khandy's chapter "Pop Culture: A Vehicle of State Nationalism in India" elucidates how the Indian state uses popular media to disseminate nationalism. With reference to Hindi films and soundtracks since the second half of the twentieth century, Khandy argues that such cultural representations have naturalised and enforced a view of the Indian nation as exclusively Hindu. Khandy prompts that this nationalism, not least in its recent manifestations under the Modi government, has fuelled violence and hatred across the country. Hanna Teichler stays in the realm of film in her contribution "Meet the 'Holy Family': From Multicultural Australia to Enforced Reconciliation in Baz Luhrmann's *Australia* (2008)." Placing Luhrmann's epos *Australia* in the context of the country's attempt in the twenty-first century to come to terms with its history of the forced removal and re-education of Aboriginal people, Teichler deconstructs the film's vision of a reconciled multicultural Australian nation. By recasting the Australian nuclear family, the film attempts to depart from prior narratives of the Australian nation, but, running counter to its own aspirations, ultimately affirms colonial hierarchies and stereotypes. Theresa Krampe documents a similar dynamic in contemporary videogames by the Canadian game developer BioWare. Her chapter "Intersections of Race, Sexuality, and National Identity in BioWare's *Mass Effect*" looks at what comes across as an exceptionally diverse cast of characters in the *Mass Effect* game trilogy. The games' endorsement of pluralism, Krampe suggests, stands out in the current landscape of videogames, and can be read as an invocation of a distinctly modern and inclusivist Canadianness. Yet, on closer inspection, even this deliberately progressive, almost utopian, agenda comes with vestiges of heteronormativity, imperialism, and nationalism.

The fourth and final section, "Nationalisms in Postcolonial Literatures," considers different engagements with nationalism in literary texts from the twenty-first century as well as the early twentieth century. Ralf Haekel's chapter "Blind Spots: Nationalism and the Photographic Gaze in Teju Cole's *Every Day Is for the Thief*" inquires how Nigerian-American author Cole undermines his narrator's Western colonialist point of view that comes to the fore when he visits the Nigerian National Museum in Lagos. Concentrating on the novel's self-conscious mixing of various literary modes and its self-referential use of photography, Haekel asserts that Cole questions essentialist concepts of alterity that so many nationalisms rely on, showing us instead that such concepts are always mediated. The following chapter by Hannah Pardey is also concerned with literature based in Nigeria. In "Emotional Nationalism in the New Nigerian Novel," Pardey investigates how audiences from all over the globe respond to the national conflicts depicted in contemporary Nigerian novels. Employing Chimamanda Ngozi Adichie's *Half of a Yellow Sun* and Helon Habila's *Measuring Time* as her case studies, Pardey establishes the term 'emotional nationalism' to capture modes of realism that encourage readers to be emotionally involved with fictional postcolonial nations and to respond to them in certain ways in online reviews on Amazon and Goodreads. Pardey provides an insight into how imagined communities operate in an increasingly digitalised age. Lukas Lammers follows with his contribution "The British Empire and the 'Laureate of Its Demise': Postimperial Nostalgia in Jane Gardam's Old Filth Trilogy," in which he reads Gardam's historical novels as articulations of postcolonial melancholia. Lammers uncovers a problematic dynamic at the heart of the trilogy which laments the end of the British Empire. He scrutinises, for example, how Gardam presents her protagonists, all representatives of colonial Britain, as victims of imperialism – a narrative all too familiar from the debates surrounding Brexit. The nineteenth-century nationalism that has so often been declared to be a thing of the past, Lammers persuasively argues, thus resurfaces in Gardam's fiction. In the closing chapter of the section and volume, Kathrin Härtl examines Derek Walcott's complex vision of the nation-state and national literature in the Caribbean that he develops in his poetry, particularly in *White Egrets* (2010). Her piece "'Bastardizing' National Belonging: Derek Walcott and Joseph Conrad" argues that Joseph Conrad, whom Walcott unapologetically calls a "bastard" in his poetry, functions as a metonym capturing Walcott's concept of Caribbean literature that oscillates ambivalently between an indebtedness to and liberation from English colonial literature.

Works Cited

Allen, John et al. "How the World Will Look After the Coronavirus Pandemic." *Foreign Policy*, 20 Mar. 2020, www.foreignpolicy.com/2020/03/20/world-order-after-coroanvirus-pandemic/. Accessed 28 Oct. 2020.

Anderson, Benedict. *Imagined Communities: Reflections on the Origin and Spread of Nationalism*. 1983. Verso, 2006.

Antonsich, Marco. "Did the COVID-19 Pandemic Revive Nationalism?" *OpenDemocracy*, 22 July 2020, www.opendemocracy.net/en/pandemic-border/did-covid-19-pandemic-revive-nationalism/. Accessed 28 Oct. 2020.

Ashcroft, Bill et al. *Post-Colonial Studies: The Key Concepts*. 2nd ed. Routledge, 2007. doi: 10.4324/9780203933473.

Balibar, Étienne. *Race, Nation, Class: Ambiguous Identities*. Verso, 1991.

Bergmann, Eirikur. *Neo-Nationalism: The Rise of Nativist Populism*. Palgrave Macmillan, 2020. doi: 10.1007/978-3-030-41773-4.

Berkley, Seth. "COVAX Explained." *Gavi: The Vaccine Alliance*, 3 Sept. 2020, www.gavi.org/vaccineswork/covax-explained. Accessed 28 Oct. 2020.

Bhabha, Homi, ed. *Nation and Narration*. Routledge, 1990.

Bhambra, Gurminder K. "COVID-19, Europe, Inequality and Global Justice." *12 Perspectives on the Pandemic: International Social Science Thought Leaders Reflect on COVID-19*, De Gruyter, 2020, pp. 18–24.

Bieber, Florian. "Global Nationalism in Times of the COVID-19 Pandemic." *Nationalities Papers*, 2020, pp. 1–13. doi: 10.1017/nps.2020.35.

Billig, Michael. *Banal Nationalism*. 1995. SAGE, 2009.

Bollyky, Thomas J., and Chad P. Bown. "The Tragedy of Vaccine Nationalism: Only Cooperation Can End the Pandemic." *Foreign Affairs*, vol. 99, no. 5, 2020, p. 96–109.

Bulawayo, NoViolet. *We Need New Names*. Chatto & Windus, 2013.

Calhoun, Craig. "Populism, Nationalism and Brexit." *Brexit: Sociological Responses*, edited by William Outhwaite, Anthem P, 2017, pp. 57–76.

Chrisman, Laura. "Nationalism and Postcolonial Studies." *The Cambridge Companion to Postcolonial Literary Studies*, edited by Neil Lazarus, Cambridge UP, 2004, 183–98. doi: 10.1017/CCOL0521826942.010.

Closs Stephens, Angharad. *The Persistence of Nationalism: From Imagined Communities to Urban Encounters*. Routledge, 2013. doi: 10.4324/9780203575383.

De, Abhishek. "Explained: Vaccine Nationalism, and How It Impacts the Covid-19 Fight." *The Indian Express*, 23 Aug. 2020, www.indianexpress.com/article/explained/what-is-vaccine-nationalism-how-does-it-impact-the-fight-against-covid-19-6561236/. Accessed 28 Oct. 2020.

Fuchs, Christian. *Nationalism on the Internet: Critical Theory and Ideology in the Age of Social Media and Fake News*. Routledge, 2019. doi: 10.4324/9780429343476.

Gellner, Ernest. *Nationalism*. 1988. Weidenfeld & Nicolson, 1997.

Gilroy, Paul. *Postcolonial Melancholia*. Columbia UP, 2005.

Goode, J. Paul et al. "Everyday Nationalism in Unsettled Times: In Search of Normality during Pandemic." *Nationalities Papers*, 2020, pp. 1–25. doi: 10.1017/nps.2020.40.

Hearn, Jonathan S. *Rethinking Nationalism: A Critical Introduction*. Palgrave Macmillan, 2006.

Hobsbawm, Eric. *Nations and Nationalism since 1780*. Cambridge UP, 1990.

Jusdanis, Gregory. *The Necessary Nation*. Princeton UP, 2001.

Koegler, Caroline et al. "The Colonial Remains of Brexit: Empire Nostalgia and Narcissistic Nationalism." *Journal of Postcolonial Writing*, vol. 56., no. 5, 2020, pp. 585–92. doi: 10.1080/17449855.2020.1818440.

Kwok, Henry. "Beyond the Anti-racist Reason: A Postcolonial Perspective on Pandemic Politics." *Health Sociology Review*, vol. 29, no. 2, 2020, pp. 122–30. doi: 10.1080/14461242.2020.1785320.

Lazarus, Neil. *Nationalism and Cultural Practice in the Postcolonial World*. Cambridge UP, 1999.

Leddy-Owen, Charles. "Nationalism, Postcolonial Criticism and the State." *Routledge International Handbook of Contemporary Racisms*, edited by John Solomos, Routledge, 2020, pp. 273–83.

López-Alves, Fernando, and Diane E. Johnson. "The Rise of Nationalism in Comparative Perspective: Europe and the Americas." *Populist Nationalism in Europe and the Americas*, edited by Fernando López-Alves and Diane E. Johnson, Routledge, 2019, pp. 3–18.

Mishra, Pankaj. "Indian Nationalism: The Most Recent Turn." *Asian Nationalisms Reconsidered*, edited by Jeff Kingston, Routledge, 2016, pp. 196–206.

Nieguth, Tim. "Popular Culture and Quotidian Nationalism." *Nationalism and Popular Culture*, edited by Tim Nieguth, Routledge, 2020, pp. 1–16.

Nossem, Eva. "The Pandemic of Nationalism and the Nationalism of Pandemics." *UniGR-CBS Working Paper*, vol. 8, 2020, pp. 1–14. doi: 10.25353/ubtr-xxxx-1073-4da7/.

O'Toole, Fintan. *Heroic Failure: Brexit and the Politics of Pain*. Head of Zeus, 2018.

O'Toole, Fintan. *Politics of Pain: Postwar England and the Rise of Nationalism*. Liveright, 2019.

Puri, Shalini. *The Caribbean Postcolonial: Social Equality, Post-Nationalism, and Cultural Hybridity*. Palgrave Macmillan, 2004. doi: 10.1057/9781403973719.

Rhodes, James, and Natalie-Anne Hall. "Racism, Nationalism and the Politics of Resentment in Contemporary England." *Routledge International Handbook of Contemporary Racisms*, edited by John Solomos, Routledge, 2020, pp. 284–99.

Roy, Srirupa. *Beyond Belief: India and the Politics of Postcolonial Nationalism*. Duke UP, 2007. doi: 10.1215/9780822389910.

Serhan, Yasmeen. "The Case against Waging 'War' on the Coronavirus." *The Atlantic*, 31 Mar. 2020, www.theatlantic.com/international/archive/2020/03/war-metaphor-coronavirus/609049/. Accessed 20 Oct. 2020.

Sharma, Shailja. *Postcolonial Minorities in Britain and France: In the Hyphen of the Nation-State*. Manchester UP, 2016. doi: 10.7228/manchester/9781784993993.001.0001.

Smith, Anthony D. *The Ethnic Origins of Nations*. Blackwell, 1986.

Stone, John, and Polly Rizova. "From Obama to Trump: The Dialectics of Race and Nationalism in Contemporary America." *The Wiley Blackwell Companion to Race, Ethnicity, and Nationalism*, edited by John Stone et al., Wiley Blackwell, 2020, pp. 29–42. doi: 10.1002/9781119430452.ch2.

Tamir, Yael. *Why Nationalism*. Princeton UP, 2019.

van Uden, Annelies, and Henk van Houtum. "Beyond Coronativism: The Need for Agape." *Tijdschrift voor Economische en Sociale Geografie*, vol. 111, no. 3, 2020, pp. 333–46. doi: 10.1111/tesg.12438.

Valluvan, Sivamohan. *The Clamour of Nationalism: Race and Nation in Twenty-First-Century Britain*. Manchester UP, 2019.

Valluvan, Sivamohan, and Virinder S. Kalra. "Racial Nationalisms: Brexit, Borders and Little Englander Contradictions." *Ethnic and Racial Studies*, vol. 42, no. 14, 2019, pp. 2393–412. doi: 10.1080/01419870.2019.1640890.

Woods, Eric Taylor, et al. "COVID-19, Nationalism, and the Politics of Crisis: A Scholarly Exchange." *Nations and Nationalism*, 2020, pp. 1–19. doi: 10.1111/nana.12644.

Young, Robert J. C. *Empire, Colony, Postcolony*. Wiley Blackwell, 2015.

PART 1

The Languages of Nationalism

CHAPTER 1

The Nationalist Ideology of Monolingualism in Postcolonial Theory

Michael Westphal

1   Introduction

> A language is a dialect with an army and a navy.

This famous linguistic adage, attributed to sociolinguist Max Weinreich, highlights that the distinction between a language and a dialect is not a linguistic matter but is determined by social and political conditions. The quote encapsulates the close relationship between languages and nation-states in a humorous way.

Nation-states (or countries), i.e. sovereign units of political organization, are linked to nations, i.e. socially constructed political communities that are imagined by people who perceive themselves as members (Anderson 5–7). Nation-states and nations are relatively recent phenomena in human history, as they started to emerge in late eighteenth-century Europe. Connected to the rise of nation-states is an ideology of a national identity which is autonomous and coherent, represented by (imagined) common cultural norms and values, in the European case by a shared ethnicity, and a mutual uniform language (Edwards 175–224).

Germany – from the eighteenth century until today – is a prime example of the rise and continuation of a nationalist ideology of monolingualism, summarized in 'one nation, one language.' In response to the French (linguistic) hegemony in Europe, German Romanticists forged a strong, even mythical, connection between one common homogenous German language and a German nation (208–11). In 1772, Johann Gottfried Herder asked rhetorically, "Has a nation anything more precious than the language of its fathers?" (qtd. in Edwards 205). To him, language unites all cultural aspects of a nation:

> What a treasure language is when kinship groups grow into tribes and nations. Even the smallest of nations … cherishes in and through its language the history, the poetry, and songs about the great deeds of its forefathers. The language is its collective treasure. (qtd. in Edwards 209)

This nationalist ideology of monolingualism is shared by Wilhelm von Humboldt. In 1797, he wrote that "absolutely nothing is so important for a nation's culture as its language" and that the "language is the spiritual exhalation of the nation" (qtd. in Edwards 205). In his 1808 "Addresses to the German Nation," Johann Gottlieb Fichte argued that the German nation is united by a common language and hence a common way of thinking. To him, language is essential for defining a nation:

> The first, original, and truly natural boundaries of states are beyond doubt their internal boundaries. Those who speak the same language are joined to each other by a multitude of invisible bonds by nature herself ... they belong together and are by nature one and an inseparable whole. (qtd. in Joseph 110)

The discourse of what defines 'the German nation' in the twenty-first century has evolved far from this ethno-linguistic nationalism, which assumes a natural division between different nations, languages, and ways of thinking. However, the ideology of 'one nation, one language' is still central to debates about national identity today. A case in point is the debate about the so-called German *Leitkultur* (leading culture), i.e. an imagined dominant culture to which everyone should adhere, which has been included in the basic political program of the Christian Social Union (CSU) since 2007. The CSU defines this leading culture through "language, history, traditions, and Christian-occidental values" (41–3). This concept of a German leading culture has been strongly criticized. However, while there is an awareness that traditions are diverse and Christian-occidental values are not conceptualized in the same way by all people in Germany, the idea of the language being the main cultural unifier of a nation has not been challenged. For example, Aydan Özoğuz, the German Federal Government Commissioner for Migration, Refugees, and Integration from 2013 to 2017, stated that due to the current cultural diversity in Germany it is impossible to identify a specific German culture beyond the German language (n. pag.). Thus, the ideological link between one German language and the nation is usually not questioned.

This nationalist ideology of 'one nation, one language' implies that a nation's language is one homogenous entity. Thus, the term 'language' is not used as an umbrella term that includes all regional, ethnical, or social varieties of a language but just denotes the standard variety of a language, such as Standard German or Standard English. A standard variety is just one variety out of many of a language. According to Einar Haugen's model of standardization, this variety is selected as the norm; its form is codified in grammar books and lexicons to suppress variability; it is elaborated to achieve maximal variation in its functions in society; and the community has to accept it as the norm. This process leads to a standard language ideology: the standard variety is seen as the only correct, prestigious, and legitimate variety, while all other varieties are devalued as incorrect, stigmatized, and illegitimate (Milroy 532–48). Ultimately, the standard variety is equated with the language as a whole (539). To Haugen, linguistic standardization is linked to nationalism in the modern world: "Nations and language become inextricably intertwined. Every self-respecting nation has to have a language. Not just a medium of communication or a dialect, but a fully developed [i.e. standardized] language. Anything less marks it as underdeveloped" (344–5).

The ideology of 'one nation, one (standard) language' is tied to the rise of nationalism in Europe in the eighteenth century and continues to play a key role in nationalist thinking today. As has been shown for Germany, language has become the lowest common denominator of a nation. However, this ideology is not restricted to Europe. Nation-building in multilingual postcolonial countries often seeks to develop one language as a common national language (Wright 78–111). A case in point is the development of Swahili as a national language in Tanzania after independence in 1964 (85–95). Postcolonial language planning in Tanzania rejected English as the colonial language and instead selected Swahili, which had already been used as a lingua franca in East Africa, as its anti-colonial national language. Particularly the administration under the country's first Prime Minister, Julius Nyerere, put tremendous effort into the codification and elaboration of Swahili. For Nyerere, Swahili was a major tool for the transformation of Tanzania's ethnically diverse population "into a cohesive and stable nation" (qtd. in Bunting n. pag.). Thus, Tanzania's anti-colonial language planning program was influenced by a European nationalist ideology of monolingualism.

In this chapter, I argue that the European nationalist ideology of monolingualism ('one nation, one language') has not only spread globally but also transcends into theories on postcolonial Englishes. For this analysis of underlying nationalist ideologies in postcolonial theory-making, I focus on the two most well-known models that are used to discuss the status and development of postcolonial Englishes: Braij Kachru's model of World Englishes and Edgar Schneider's Dynamic Model of Postcolonial Englishes. On the one hand, this analysis is inspired by Dick Smakman and Patrick Heinrich's *Globalizing Sociolinguistics* program, which challenges the Western dominance in sociolinguistic theory-making. On the other hand, my analysis is part of a wider criticism of "methodological nationalism," which Andreas Wimmer and Nina Glick-Schiller define as "the assumption that the nation/state/society is the natural social and political form of the modern world" (301). They take an interdisciplinary perspective and identify this bias in mainstream social sciences (e.g. economics, history, and migration studies). Britta Schneider takes up this approach and highlights the recurring bias of methodological nationalism in different areas of linguistics, including variationist sociolinguistics, creole studies, and the World Englishes paradigm. The latter conceptualizes the heterogeneity of English worldwide as national Englishes, often using British and American English as benchmark varieties and thus reproducing symbolic hierarchies. B. Schneider's main point of criticism is that the nationalist bias in the major approaches in economics, history, and migration studies ignores multilingualism and the complexities of sociolinguistic variation beyond categorical distinctions along national lines or binaries of standard vs. non-standard. B. Schneider then presents examples of language use that are difficult to capture along national lines, such as the integration of English in the linguistic landscape of Berlin or the transnational music culture of salsa. B. Schneider's discussion takes a bird's eye view on English worldwide without going into detail on specific theories or taking into account the language users' perspective.

My approach focuses on the major frameworks of World/postcolonial Englishes by Kachru and E. Schneider: I first present each model and then discuss the inherent nationalist and monolingual bias. Subsequently, I take a bottom-up perspective on postcolonial Englishes by illustrating the linguistic reality and language attitudes of actual speakers of these varieties and contrasting them with the nationalist ideology of monolingualism underlying the two theories discussed in the preceding section. This approach counteracts most theory-making, which takes a bird's eye view that is seemingly objective but ignores local complexities and the speakers' perspectives. I present findings from language attitude research for two linguistically diverse postcolonial speech communities: Kenya and Jamaica. Both are former British colonies, where English functions as an official language but is not learned as a first language by the majority of the population. However, Kenya's and Jamaica's linguistic ecologies differ and provide good case studies for the dynamics of English in multilingual and -dialectal contexts. In the last section, I discuss how the insights from this bottom-up perspective should be considered in future theory-making and I call for an extension of Ngũgĩ wa Thiong'o's *Decolonising the Mind* agenda to overcome nationalist ideologies of monolingualism in postcolonial theory.

2   Methodological Nationalism in Models of Postcolonial Englishes

The global spread of English through British colonialism and the rise of the USA as a world power has led to the emergence of a vast array of different varieties of English: non-native speakers have made English their own and many nation-states that were former British (and American) colonies have made English (one of) their official language(s). Indian linguist Kachru was most influential to emphasize this global heterogeneity of English in his model of World Englishes. By adding the plural to English, his model challenges the hegemony of British and American English as yardstick varieties and gives credit to non-native speakers of English. His model distinguishes between independent national varieties of English along three circles: (1) inner circle Englishes, such as British or American English, which function as the primary language and are learned as a native language by the majority of the population; (2) outer circle Englishes, such as Nigerian or Philippine English, which serve official functions, are often used as an inter-ethnic lingua franca, and are mostly learned as a second/subsequent language in postcolonial countries; and (3) Englishes of the expanding circle, such as German or Chinese English, where English is learned as a foreign language and is mostly used as a medium for international communication. Although Kachru's model has helped to decolonize the English language by advancing research on postcolonial Englishes, the distinction along national lines reproduces methodological nationalism. With the focus on institutionalized/standardized varieties and thus elite speakers and writers, the model "runs the danger of rendering invisible the sociolinguistic hierarchies and linguistic diversities that are internal to nations" (B. Schneider 9). The model ignores language varieties that have no official status (and their speakers), which are often subject to linguistic discrimination, such as pidgins and creoles, non-standard varieties, and hybrid Englishes. Although Kachru's model stresses the global heterogeneity of English, there is an underlying assumption of homogenous national standard varieties of English, i.e. 'one nation, one English.'

In his Dynamic Model of Postcolonial Englishes, E. Schneider does not describe the relationship between different Englishes, but he depicts a shared process in which all postcolonial Englishes evolve. According to this framework, the evolution of English in (post)colonial speech communities is at the core a "sequence of characteristic stages of identity rewritings and associated linguistic changes affecting the parties involved in a colonial-contact setting" (E. Schneider 29). E. Schneider establishes a close link between changing language use and shifting identities: "Speakers keep redefining and expressing their linguistic and social identities, constantly aligning themselves with other individuals and thereby accommodating their speech behavior to those they wish to associate and be associated with" (21). The two groups (called strands) whose identities change in his model are the colonizers (called settlers) and the indigenous population. In the beginning, these two strands are clearly distinct: they view themselves as the other, and for the settlers 'us' is still their 'mother-country.' This relationship changes over time as the settler and indigenous strands merge gradually and become 'us,' while the mother country turns into the other: the two groups become a unified new postcolonial nation with a coherent identity and a new homogenous postcolonial national variety of English. Thus, the model draws on a strong link between nation-building, identity, and language. National linguistic homogeneity is at the core of the evolution process of postcolonial Englishes: "to a considerable extent the emergence of PCEs [postcolonial Englishes] is an identity driven process of linguistic convergence" (30).

E. Schneider describes the evolution of national postcolonial Englishes in five phases. (1) Foundation: English is transplanted to a new territory through colonial expansion. (2) Exonormative stabilization: English expands in its functions, but the mother country determines the linguistic norms. (3) Nativization: as the colony goes through a phase of sociolinguistic and political turmoil, the sociopolitical ties between the colony and the mother country weaken, identity reorientation is intensified, and linguistically a new local variety evolves. Phase (4), i.e. endonormative stabilization, is central to nation-building and the assertion of the new variety and a new national identity as the norm: after political independence, the new nation stabilizes and there are major nation-building efforts and all groups (or ethnicities) are included in this new coherent nation. On a sociolinguistic level, the local variety stabilizes, is codified, and eventually is accepted as the new norm. Homogeneity is a key characteristic of the new postcolonial variety in this fourth phase. (5) Differentiation: the homogenous postcolonial variety diversifies as new group-specific (e.g. regional, social, or ethnic) varieties emerge. E. Schneider illustrates this general sociolinguistic process for sixteen different nation-states. The application of the model works very well for 'monolingual' speech communities, such as the USA (his prime example) or Australia, which have all reached phase five. However, the model struggles to describe the evolution of English in more complex (multilingual or -dialectal) linguistic ecologies where English is learned as a second language or dialect, such as Jamaica, Kenya, or Singapore (Westphal 221–4), of which no speech community has reached the last phase. Thus, it seems that the model is built on Western speech communities and is then applied to non-Western cases.

E. Schneider's and Kachru's models have pushed the decolonization of English giving legitimacy to non-native varieties and their speakers, counteracting 'native-speakerism' in sociolinguistics. However, methodological nationalism is pervasive in both approaches as the nation functions as the 'natural' social and political form of organization. Linguistic national homogeneity is a key characteristic for both models: the ideology of 'one nation, one language' is transformed into 'one nation, one English.' With the focus on institutionalized national Englishes and their elite or "educated speakers" (Kachru 248), the models marginalize non-standardized Englishes as well as their speakers. The models thus follow an official narrative of national linguistic homogeneity that ignores the linguistic realities of speakers who live in multilingual and -dialectal contexts.

3 Multilingual Kenya

Kenya, a former British colony until 1963, is a pervasively multiethnic and multilingual country with more than forty-two indigenous languages, which are primarily used by the respective ethnic groups. The actual number of languages spoken is a controversial issue as it is difficult to distinguish between languages and dialects (Barasa 41). English and Swahili are the two official languages and both function as linguae francae among ethnic groups. The two languages have distinct functions: English dominates in politics, higher education, business, and law. It is also the main language used in everyday conversations of educated Kenyans and professionals. Thus, English indicates prestige and power (Githiora 241–2). In contrast, Swahili is the more widely used pan-ethnic lingua franca signaling solidarity and an anti-colonial stance. Chege Githiora states that Swahili "is widely accepted as the 'national' language, the language of communication among Kenyans of all regional and social backgrounds" (236). Language use is socially stratified: speakers of a higher social class are more proficient in English, while lower status groups rather use Swahili in addition to indigenous languages. There is also an urban-rural divide as indigenous languages are more prevalent in rural areas.

In order to navigate through such a multilingual society, Kenyans need to use different languages in different contexts with different people.[1] Leonard Muaka states that an average Kenyan speaks at least three languages (218).

---

1   For a detailed discussion of language uses in the 2013 Kenyan Presidential Election Campaign, which sheds light on citizens' and politicians' language attitudes, see Natascha Bing's chapter "Talking Kenya*n: Dynamic Practices for a Heterogeneous Nation" in this volume.

This societal and individual multilingualism leads to a situation where (bi- and trilingual) codeswitching is the norm for most Kenyans. Sandra N. Barasa describes codeswitching in East Africa as so pervasive that it is difficult to apply common Western-based theories on codeswitching, which clearly distinguish between the different codes (46). This linguistic diversity culminates in the major metropolitan areas, above all in Kenya's capital Nairobi. In these highly complex multilingual urban spaces, a new hybrid language has emerged which is commonly known as Sheng. Its grammar is mostly based on Swahili, while the lexicon is drawn from Swahili, English, and Kenya's indigenous languages. Sheng is mostly spoken by young Kenyans in urban areas but through travelling back and forth between rural and urban areas as well as *Ghetto Radio*, Kenya's most popular radio station which broadcasts exclusively in Sheng, the variety has spread to the entire country and beyond. Sheng has been a stigmatized variety associated with crime and poverty but has transcended social boundaries and is even used as a linguistic resource to attract young people in advertisements and by politicians (Muaka 220).

Advertisements are a salient domain where different languages are combined at a high density. Annah Kariuki et al. show how Kenyan companies combine Swahili, English, and Sheng in their advertisement slogans (232–4). However, the linguistic choices depend on the type of product. English in combination with Swahili is used for luxury items, such as natural fruit juices and bank accounts. For example, the slogan *na-manage account yangu* ('I manage my account') of the Equity Bank for students' bank accounts combines the Swahili first-person singular pronouns *na* (subject) and (possessive) *yangu* with English *manage* and *account*. In contrast, advertisements for everyday items, such as airtime (i.e. prepaid telephone service), include more Sheng and Swahili. For instance, the Yu Mobile Company tries to convince consumers to switch to their prepaid service with the slogan *je call rate inakatsia maisha* ('does a call rate disrupt life?'), which combines English *call rate* with the Sheng verb *katsia* ('disrupt') and the Swahili interrogative word *je* ('how') and noun *maisha* ('life').

This linguistic diversity is accompanied by a laissez-faire language policy of the Kenyan government. In contrast to Tanzania, where Swahili was developed and pushed as a national language with much effort, Kenya's language policies were rather faltering: although Swahili was established as the national language, English still dominates in many spheres and Kenyan Swahili remains highly variable (Githiora 245–8).

In Kachru's framework, Kenya is classified as an outer circle country as English has an official status and is mainly learned as a second/subsequent language. According to E. Schneider's description, Kenya is currently in the third phase of the Dynamic Model (i.e. nativization), which has begun in the late 1940s (189–97). He states that English is spreading in Kenya and is part of nation-building efforts. Kenyan English as a distinct variety is evolving but its acceptance is lagging behind and there is no codification in sight. He cautions that the potential scope of English is confined by Swahili as the regional lingua franca and by the indigenous languages as primary tools for group solidarity. Thus, E. Schneider describes English as a distinct rival to the other local languages.

Several studies have investigated Kenyans' attitudes toward the country's linguistic diversity. One of the earliest studies by Kembo Sure from 1991 investigates Kenyan pupils' language attitudes toward the two official languages, Swahili and English. The study is based on survey data from 763 school pupils from fourteen schools in rural and urban districts. The results show that the pupils have positive attitudes toward both English and Swahili, but the attitudinal status of the two languages differs. The vast majority of pupils agree that Swahili (1) should be maintained as a tool of development in Kenya, (2) has value in the modern world, (3) is essential to take part fully in national life in Kenya, (4) should be maintained because it is a symbol of Kenyan nationhood, and (5) should be kept for the sake of nationalism. However, they do not agree uniformly that knowing Swahili is an advantage on the job market and that Swahili is bound up with Kenya's national culture. With regard to English, the pupils almost unanimously agree that English is necessary for higher education and international communication. They have mixed opinions on which language should be more important but agree that Kenyans should speak English as well as Swahili and that English is not working against Swahili. Thus, they associate English more with social mobility and view Swahili more as a symbol of nationhood. From the perspective of the Kenyan pupils, there is no conflict between the two languages but rather a "happy coexistence" which resembles a "balanced diglossic situation whereby each language is given fair official and public support in its domain(s)" (Sure 258).

Muaka's study from 2011 also examines the perceptions of Kenyan pupils in urban and rural settings but combines attitudes and speech behavior (i.e. when do young Kenyans use which language with whom and why) including a wider range of languages: English, Swahili, Sheng, and indigenous languages. The study joins answers from 273 questionnaires with qualitative participant observations and interviews. Muaka shows that the young Kenyans use diverse languages and live with two coexisting language ideologies: in institutional contexts, they use and value English and Swahili, thus following the official language policies. In informal settings, they express their identities with Sheng and indigenous languages. The use of Sheng and indigenous languages is stratified along a rural-urban distinction: whereas Sheng dominates in informal situations in urban areas, young Kenyans in rural areas rely more on indigenous languages but "wish to identify with their urban counterparts in speaking Sheng" (Muaka 228). The urban informants' language behavior is also constrained by the type of addressee: they use Sheng with in-group members while they use English and Swahili for the out-group (i.e. adults and authorities). All young Kenyans need and value English and Swahili, which enable them to project an identity of a proficient user of the official languages. Muaka concludes that all of the languages combined are part of the young Kenyans' lives and thus "Kenyan language policies fail to reflect what Kenyans project as their language identities" (229). The results of these two attitude studies paint a picture of coexistence and interaction of English with Swahili, Sheng, and local languages that is neither captured by Kachru's nor by E. Schneider's models. The two empirical studies instead corroborate Barasa's theoretical reflections that render codeswitching between several languages as the *de facto* national language in East African contexts (46–9).

4   Creole and English in Jamaica

Jamaica is the most populous anglophone Caribbean island and was a British colony from 1866 until 1962. English (meaning Standard English) is the sole official language of the country but the majority of the population grow up with Jamaican Creole as their first dialect. The English-based Creole has developed out of intense language contact between British dialects and African languages in a colonial plantation setting. English and Jamaican Creole are closely related and the two mostly blend into a seamless continuum in everyday language use. The question whether Jamaican Creole is a dialect of English or a distinct language is more a political than a linguistic matter. Jamaican linguists support the view of Jamaican Creole as a distinct language and campaign that it gains official status (Christie 61–4). However, Jamaican Creole is often treated as a variety of English: for example, it is included as a variety of English in reference descriptions (e.g. Patrick 609–44) and in E. Schneider's discussion of postcolonial Englishes. Traditionally, there is a clear functional distinction between the two varieties: English is used in official domains, such as law, school, or parliament, while Jamaican Creole dominates in informal conversations. English signals prestige and power while Jamaican Creole is a sign of solidarity (Christie 1–5). This clear diglossic distinction changed in the course of the second half of the twentieth century as Jamaican Creole lost some of its colonial stigma pushing into domains formerly reserved for English, with mass media leading the way (Westphal 26–30). Kathryn Shields-Brodber describes this sociolinguistic change as an erosion of the diglossia of the past (57). In addition to the shifting relationship between the two varieties, a local standard variety of English has been emerging. Standard Jamaican English has gained some official recognition in school curricula as the target of teaching. However, the Jamaican standard variety of English is still highly variable in its form and continues to evolve in a tripartite norm competition between local, (colonial) British, and (newly influential) American norms (Westphal 218–21).

Due to the coexistence of the two closely related varieties, language use in Jamaica is best modeled as a linguistic continuum from Standard (Jamaican) English to Jamaican Creole. These two (idealized) extremes of the continuum are labeled acrolect (i.e. the most standard speech) and basilect (i.e. the most conservative Creole). However, everyday language use is dominated by mesolectal speech (i.e. all intermediate varieties) (Patrick 610–3). Every Jamaican commands a certain span of this continuum (depending on their socioeconomic background) and shift in their language use depending on the addressee, the setting, and the topic, but also for metaphorical purposes; for example, humor and emotions are often expressed in Jamaican Creole (Christie 2).

A telling example illustrating the linguistic tensions, coexistence, and blurriness of English and Creole in Jamaica is Marlon James's award-winning 2014 novel *A Brief History of Seven Killings,* which tells the story of the attempted assassination of Bob Marley in 1976 from the perspective of different Jamaicans and non-Jamaicans from all walks of life. In contrast to most previous Jamaican literature (Lalla 56–71), James does not separate Standard English and Jamaican Creole in his work but combines them and reflects the social stratification of language use. Chapters from the perspective of middle-class Jamaicans are dominated by Standard English but also include Jamaican Creole for various metaphorical purposes. The perspectives of urban working-class Jamaicans, such as the gang members Demus or Bam Bam, are predominantly expressed in Jamaican Creole. Gang leader Josey Wales consistently combines Standard English and Jamaican Creole in his inner monologues. Creole and English are inseparable, often blending to a seamless mix but also have their distinct roles and the exact mix is socially stratified.

Due to this linguistic multifacetedness, Jamaica is difficult to classify in Kachru's model: Jamaica belongs neither to the inner nor to the outer circle, as English is learned neither as a first nor as a second language but rather as a second dialect. In E. Schneider's description (227–38), Jamaica is in phase four (i.e. endonormative stabilization), which has started with Jamaica's independencein 1962. He describes nation-building efforts, which include remembering Jamaica's African heritage and its local manifestations, such as reggae music. For E. Schneider, Jamaican Creole has increasingly become part of this process as it takes on more and more functions in society and thereby threatens the prestige position of English. His discussion solely focuses on Jamaican Creole as a national language, while he ignores Jamaican English. He supports this view by citing Pauline Christie who establishes a distinction between Jamaican Creole as a "symbol of national identity" and Jamaican English as a mere "sign" (63) of it.

Despite the mostly seamless variation between Jamaican Creole and English, Jamaicans mostly perceive linguistic variation in a dichotomous way. Several attitude studies have analyzed Jamaicans' perception of the sociolinguistic situation. For example, Alicia Beckford Wassink carried out a language attitude survey in the semi-rural community of Gordon Town. Her fifty-one informants view both varieties positively but attach different values to them: Jamaican Creole is perceived as suitable for informal settings and in-group members but not for formal settings and an out-group, where English is preferred. Wassink clusters the different evaluative items from her questionnaires into 'feel,' 'hear,' and 'use.' Jamaican Creole is rated most positively on 'feel' items, while English is valued more with regard to 'hear' and 'use.' This means that the Jamaican informants have positive but distinct attitudes toward both varieties and a strong awareness of when which variety is appropriate. The island-wide *Language Attitude Survey of Jamaica* shows similar results: the 1,000 informants generally view Jamaican Creole positively and mainly support that it should become the second official language (Jamaican Language Unit 37). The vast majority of the informants state that they speak both English and Jamaican Creole but prefer to use Creole with friends and family and English with strangers and co-workers. A colonial ideological distinction between English and Creole is shown to linger on: the informants tend to associate English with a higher education and intelligence, while friendliness is associated more with Jamaican Creole. More recently, I carried out an attitude study mainly among Jamaican university students on their perception of linguistic variation on Jamaican radio, which includes Jamaican Creole and different Englishes (i.e. Jamaican, British, and American English). The study results (Westphal 167–99) are based on 187 completed questionnaires and thirty-two group interviews (150–3). The informants value Jamaican Creole for its solidarity quality and for its expressive power. Generally, they prefer Creole in informal radio programs, such as talk shows, but not in formal contexts, especially news, where they prefer Standard English, which they associate with prestige (216–7). However, they are very open with regard to what counts as the standard: Standard English is defined by distance to Creole, which leaves room for variation in the standard (218–21). Particularly in the news context, British- and American-influenced

English used by Jamaican newscasters is highly valued (201–5). The informants agree that the most effective communication to all Jamaicans is achieved through a combination of English and Creole on the radio. However, the adequate mix of the two varieties has to be adapted to the specific context (216).

These three studies show that Jamaicans perceive both English and Creole as integral parts of their daily lives. They view both varieties positively but attach different values to them and have a strong awareness when and with whom the use of which variety is appropriate. Due to their monolingual bias, both theoretical models discussed above do not capture the Jamaicans' linguistic reality and their perception of it: Kachru's model cannot account for creoles and E. Schneider's discussion of Jamaica ignores Jamaican English. Both English and Creole are crucial to the Jamaican nation: the ideology of 'one nation, one language/English' stands in contrast to this linguistic reality.

5   *Decolonizing the Mind* Revisited

The two exemplary discussions of Kenya and Jamaica with respect to language use and particularly the speakers' attitudes have shown that (Standard) English does not exist in isolation from other languages or varieties. Speakers in postcolonial speech communities consistently combine English with other languages/varieties, know when and with whom to use which language or variety, and attach different values to them. Such multilingual or -dialectal practices ensure effective communication in sociolinguistically diverse nations. The different languages or varieties can even be intertwined to such an extent that it is close to impossible to clearly distinguish between the individual components. However, the concepts of languages and varieties, such as English and Jamaican Creole, still exist in the minds of people. The coexistence of different languages and varieties also leads to the emergence of new hybrid forms, such as Sheng. Such hybrid languages and their speakers are often stigmatized and excluded from a national narrative as well as from the prevalent theories on postcolonial Englishes. However, the practice of combining different languages/varieties (with stabilized hybrids as a special case) is essential for successful communication among a diverse population in multilingual/-dialectal (and often multiethnic) nation-states. Individuals need to possess a highly context-sensitive "sociolinguistic competence" (Bourdieu 37) to navigate their linguistically diverse daily routines, cooperate with others, and express their multifaceted identities. They require competences in the individual languages/varieties and need to be able to use the 'socially correct' language/variety or a blend of them in a specific situation.

Such a linguistically integrative view is supported by the results of the language attitude studies. The ideological dispositions of the speakers are very complex and contrast a (European) nationalist ideology of 'one (coherent) nation, one (coherent) language.' The informants value the different languages/varieties on different levels and make a clear distinction between formal and informal situations and between in- and out-group. Thus, different languages/varieties carry different levels of prestige and solidarity depending on the context. This language ideological complexity reflects the multifacetedness of the linguistic situation and the identities of speakers who live with different languages and varieties. The European nationalist ideology of 'one nation, one language' runs counter to the speakers' perspective and does not help to achieve a peaceful and fruitful coexistence in a nation-state as it excludes languages/varieties and their speakers. Similarly, the two theories discussed in detail in this chapter fail to acknowledge the sociolinguistic (i.e. language use and perceptions) complexities in Kenya and Jamaica due to an underlying ideology of 'one nation, one English' which neglects the multilingual or -dialectal ecologies in which postcolonial Englishes mostly exist.

In order to give credit to the complexities of multilingualism/-dialectalism and multilingual/-dialectal speakers in postcolonial speech communities, theory-making needs to critically examine and move away from methodological nationalism, Western-centrism, and a European nationalist ideology of monolingualism. Thus, future theory-making on postcolonial Englishes needs to be based on multilingual/-dialectal speech communities and to take into account the actual users' perspectives. In other words, it is necessary to decolonize theory-making on postcolonial Englishes. For this purpose, I want to revisit Ngũgĩ's *Decolonising the Mind* program briefly. In order to overcome the postcolonial linguistic hegemony of European languages in many African countries, which reinforces global and local inequalities, Ngũgĩ advocates the promotion of indigenous African languages primarily through their use in literature, theater, and fiction. This anti-colonial stance is necessary to preserve local identities, which are tied to indigenous languages and are under threat from the hegemony of English. This promotion and safeguarding of local languages and cultures is in line with the Ecology-of-Language paradigm (Skutnabb-Kangas and Phillipson 441–5), which equates linguistic diversity with biodiversity. Thus, linguistic diversity is seen as essential for the survival of humankind. In contrast to Kachru's and E. Schneider's models, Ngũgĩ's approach highlights that the English language is not apolitical but part of a continuation of cultural imperialism. However, a close reading of Ngũgĩ's arguments reveals that he establishes a close link between one African language, referring to the 'mother tongue,' literature, the soul/culture/nature, and the nation – reminiscent of Humboldt: "I would like to see Kenya peoples' mother tongues (our national languages!) carry a literature reflecting not only the rhythms of a child's spoken expression, but also his struggle with nature and its social nature" (28). Thus, he uses a European ideology of 'one nation, one language' for an anti-colonial nation-building program. Along this line of argumentation, he ignores that English in combination with other languages has become a part of the identity of many Africans. Just like Kachru's and E. Schneider's models, Ngũgĩ's argument does not capture the multi-layered language practices, ideologies, and identities of many language users in postcolonial speech communities. Future theory-making needs to build on Ngũgĩ's *Decolonising the Mind* program, which has an African point of origin, and extend it in a way that acknowledges linguistic diversity. Thus, future theory-making on postcolonial Englishes (and World Englishes) should be based on postcolonial multilingualism/-dialectalism with its accompanying complexities and inequalities.

Works Cited

Anderson, Benedict. *Imagined Communities: Reflection in the Origin and Spread of Nationalism*. Verso, 1983.

Barasa, Sandra N. "Ala! Kumbe? 'Oh my! Is it so?': Multilingualism Controversies in East Africa." *Globalising Sociolinguistics: Challenging and Expanding Theory*, edited by Dick Smakman and Patrick Heinrich, Routledge, 2015, pp. 39–53.

Bourdieu, Pierre. *Language and Symbolic Power*. Polity P, 1991.

Bunting, Ikaweba. "The Heart of Africa." *New Internationalist*, 1 Jan. 1999, www.newint.org/features/1999/01/01/anticolonialism. Accessed 8 Nov. 2018.

Christie, Pauline. *Language in Jamaica*. Arawak, 2003.

CSU. *Chancen für alle: In Freiheit und Verantwortung gemeinsam Zukunft gestalten*, 28 Sept. 2007, www.hss.de/fileadmin/user_upload/HSS/Dokumente/ACSP/Grundsatzprogramme/Grundsatzprogramm_2007.pdf. Accessed 1 July 2021.

Edwards, John. *Language and Identity*. Cambridge UP, 2009. doi: 10.1017/CBO9780511809842.

Fichte, Johann G. *Reden an die deutsche Nation*. Realschulbuchhandlung, 1808.

Githiora, Chege. "Kenya: Language and the Search for a Coherent National Identity." *Language and National Identity in Africa*, edited by Andrew Simpson, Oxford UP, 2008, pp. 235–51.

Haugen, Einar. "Dialect, Language, Nation." *American Anthropologist*, vol. 68, no. 6, 1966, pp. 922–35.

Herder, Johann G. *Abhandlung über den Ursprung der Sprache*. Voss, 1772.

Humboldt, Wilhelm von. *Bildung und Sprache*. 1797. Schöningh, 1997.
Jamaican Language Unit. "The Language Attitude Survey of Jamaica." *The University of the West Indies*. Nov. 2005. www.mona.uwi.edu/dllp/jlu/projects/Report%20for%20 Language%20Attitude%20Survey%20of%20Jamaica.pdf. Accessed 8 Nov. 2018.
James, Marlon. *A Brief History of Seven Killings*. Oneworld, 2014.
Joseph, John E. *Language and Identity: National, Ethnic, Religious*. Palgrave Macmillan, 2004. doi: 10.1057/9780230503427.
Kachru, Braij. "Standards, Codification and Sociolinguistic Realism: The English Language in the Outer Circle." *English in the World: Teaching and Learning the Language and Literatures*, edited by Randolph Quirk and H. G. Widdowson, Cambridge UP, 1985, pp. 11–30.
Kariuki, Annah, et al. "The Growth and Use of Sheng in Advertisements in Selected Businesses in Kenya." *Journal of African Cultural Studies*, vol. 27, no. 2, 2015, pp. 229–46. doi: 10.1080/13696815.2015.1029879.
Lalla, Barbara. "Creole and Respec' in the Development of Jamaican Literary Discourse." *Journal of Pidgin and Creole Languages*, vol. 20, no. 1, 2005, pp. 53–84. doi: 10.1075/jpcl.20.1.05lal.
Milroy, James. "Language Ideologies and the Consequences of Standardization." *Journal of Sociolinguistics*, vol. 5, no. 4, 2001, pp. 530–55. doi: 10.1111/1467-9481.00163.
Muaka, Leonard. "Language Perceptions and Identity among Kenyan Speakers." *Selected Proceedings of the 40th Annual Conference on African Linguistics*, edited by Eyamba G. Bokamba et al., Cascadilla, 2011, pp. 217–30.
Ngũgĩ wa Thiong'o. *Decolonising the Mind: The Politics of Language in African Literature*. James Curry, 1986.
Özoğuz, Aydan. "Leitkultur verkommt zum Klischee des Deutschseins." *Tagesspiegel Causa*, 14 May 2017, causa.tagesspiegel.de/gesellschaft/wie-nuetzlich-ist-eine -leitkultur-debatte/leitkultur-verkommt-zum-klischee-des-deutschseins.html. Accessed 8 Nov. 2018.
Patrick, Peter. "Jamaican Creole: Morphology and Syntax." *Varieties of English 2: The Americas and the Caribbean*, edited by Bernd Kortmann and Edgar Schneider, Benjamins, 2008, pp. 609–44.
Schneider, Britta. "Methodological Nationalism in Linguistics." *Language Sciences*, vol. 76, 2019. doi: 10.1016/j.langsci.2018.05.006.
Schneider, Edgar. *Postcolonial English: Varieties around the World*. Cambridge UP, 2007. doi: 10.1017/CBO9780511618901.
Shields-Brodber, Kathryn. "Requiem for English in an 'English-speaking' Community." *Englishes around the World*, edited by Edgar Schneider, Benjamins, 1997, pp. 57–67. doi: 10.1075/veaw.g19.07shi.

Skutnabb-Kangas, Tove, and Robert Phillipson. "Language Ecology." *Handbook of Pragmatics*, edited by Jef Verschueren et al., Benjamins, 2001, pp. 1–18. doi: 10.1075/hop.11.lan1.

Smakman, Dick, and Patrick Heinrich, editors. *Globalising Sociolinguistics: Challenging and Expanding Theory*. Routledge, 2015. doi: 10.4324/9781315697826.

Sure, Kembo. "Language Functions and Language Attitudes in Kenya." *English World-Wide*, vol. 12, no. 2, 1991, pp. 245–60. doi: 10.1075/eww.12.2.05sur.

Wassink, Alicia Beckford. "Historic Low Prestige and Seeds of Change: Attitudes toward Jamaican Creole." *Language in Society*, vol. 28, no. 1, 1999, pp. 57–92. doi: 10.1017/S0047404599001037.

Westphal, Michael. *Language Variation on Jamaican Radio*. Benjamins, 2017. doi: 10.1075/veaw.g60.

Wimmer, Andreas, and Nina Glick-Schiller. "Methodological Nationalism and Beyond: Nation-state Building, Migration and the Social Sciences." *Global Networks*, vol. 2, no. 4, 2002, pp. 301–34. doi: 10.1111/1471-0374.00043.

Wright, Sue. *Language Policy and Language Planning: From Nationalism to Globalisation*. 2nd ed., Palgrave Macmillan, 2015. doi: 10.1007/978-1-137-57647-7.

CHAPTER 2

Talking Kenya*n: Dynamic Practices for a Heterogeneous Nation

Natascha Bing

1   Introduction

Research in the field of postcolonial linguistics has emphasised the complex interplay of missionary, scientific, and colonial practices in the creation and "artefactualisation" (Blommaert 291) of African languages. In the nineteenth century, language became a key means of identity politics; it remains highly productive in the construction of nationalism and ethnicity today. While the idea of a monolingual nation proved to work as a hegemonic discourse both in Europe and in Africa ('one nation, one language'), the analysis of sociolinguistic practices in postcolonial Africa can open new perspectives into the interplay of national and linguistic (identity) trajectories beyond ideologies of national purity (Beck, "Apparatus" 1–3).[1] Most African states are characterised by high linguistic diversity. This diversity manifests itself not merely in the co-existence of different languages in one nation-state, but also in advanced individual and societal polylingualism.[2] Language use is characterised by dynamic and "turbulent" (Stroud 206) practices. Christopher Stroud understands turbulence as "a source of production in the achievement of transitory orderings" (207). Building on Tim Cresswell and Craig Martin's work (517), he emphasises the productivity of everyday disorderliness while thinking beyond "structural transparency and stasis" (Kroon et al. 2) of linguistic practices.

Taking Kenya's polylingual context as my starting point, I will describe linguistic practices in a pronouncedly diverse postcolonial space in order to scrutinise essentialist concepts of the monolingual nation. Based on the findings of my fieldwork conducted in the run-up to the 2013 Kenyan general

---

1   For a discussion of monolingual bias in theories on postcolonial Englishes and case studies on Kenyan and Jamaican language attitudes, see Michael Westphal's chapter "The Nationalist Ideology of Monolingualism in Postcolonial Theory" in this volume.
2   I use the term polylingualism/polylingual to emphasise not only the command or use of several languages (multilingual) but the combination and simultaneous use of linguistic features that are ascribed to various languages (Jørgensen and Varga 59–60).

elections, I will provide insights into local understandings of language and politics, putting assumptions about the homogeneity of nations, languages, and their interrelation to a test. While Kenyan politicians enforce exclusive (sub-)national identity politics, I argue that they also operate through polylingual inclusive practices, articulating their belonging to a united, yet heterogeneous nation. They appeal to the electorate by using the 'language(s) of the people.' These turbulent practices, I suggest, evolve as a symbol and medium of a distinctive Kenyan way of life, which I label as Kenya*n. The star serves as a placeholder for a broad spectrum of the nation's meanings, irritating the hegemonic idea of the nation and a standardised, stable national language attached to it (Otsuji and Pennycook 240). In this chapter, I show that the construction of 'the' nation – as the potential electorate – is diverse, just like its linguistic practices are dynamic and unstable.[3]

2   Talking Kenya*n: A Fluid Nation and Turbulent Languages

Kenya is a society that is linguistically extremely diverse and heterogeneous. Its population of 49.7 million inhabitants speaks more than sixty-seven languages from at least four different language families (Bantu, Cushitic, Nilotic, Indo-European). This complexity is particularly evident in Nairobi, the largest and capital city with 3.9 million inhabitants. While English and Kiswahili are granted an official status in the constitution,[4] they are not the only languages used in everyday public communication. Depending on the context and participants of a communicative event, further languages may be used, often in innovative strategies of polylingual practices (Nassenstein and Hollington 12–5).

In this dynamic setting of Nairobi, I conducted my research in the run-up to the Kenyan general presidential and parliamentary elections from January to March 2013. During that time, I was able to take advantage of a politicised environment, not only visiting a variety of political events but also following the vivid and omnipresent discussions of the politically interested and engaged Kenyan public. The voters decided for six offices, some of them newly created with the constitution of 2010: the presidency, members of the National Assembly, senators, women representatives, county representatives,

---

3   I sincerely thank Stephanie Rudwick and Susanne Ludwig for their discussion of and comments on this chapter.
4   Kiswahili is given the status of a national language in the constitution: "§ 7 (1) The national language of the Republic is Kiswahili. (2) The official languages of the Republic are Kiswahili and English" (Constitution of Kenya n. pag.).

and governors. The main competitors were Uhuru Kenyatta of The National Alliance (TNA), vying for presidency within the Jubilee Coalition, and Raila Odinga of the Orange Democratic Movement (ODM), the candidate for the Coalition for Reforms and Democracy (CORD). This election was interesting for several reasons: it was not only the first election under the new constitution, but it was also the first nationwide poll after the post-election violence of 2007–08, resulting both in a plethora of reports and scholarly publications on 'hate speech.' These publications all argued that the use of vernaculars, being the main medium of 'hate speech,' enforces 'tribalism,' ethnic voting, and cleansing (Deane and Abdi Ismail; Njoroge et al.; Odera; Somerville). I want to suggest the opposite: I argue that the Kenyan public makes extensive use of turbulent inclusive linguistic practices to create a unified, yet heterogeneous nation. Kenyan politics also work (linguistically) in inclusive ways. Politicians depend on attracting support from multiple ethnic groups beyond their core voting group to be competitive in national elections (Horowitz 917).

In response to the reintroduction of the multi-party system in 1992 and to the violence following the 2007 elections, a broad societal debate on national identity emerged in Kenya in which ideas about nationhood and processes of identification were expressed in new discursive formats. The overall result has been that discussions of and on the nation have become more diverse in content and form. While academic studies and the speeches of the presidential candidates are likewise centred on the traditional ideal of a culturally essentialist, monolingual community on a national and/or sub-national level (ethnicity), the people who are usually referred to as the *common mwananchi* (ordinary/common citizen)[5] increasingly endorse narratives of diversity by employing linguistically fluid and unstable repertoires. These narratives contest a single, stable, and unifying definition of the Kenyan nation (Branch and Cheeseman, "Our Turn" 5). Using the term Kenya*n is my attempt to accommodate this diversity and instability, questioning the hegemonic ideal of the nation and a standardised stable language attached to it. In the interviews and the political speeches I examine, the meaning making of 'the Kenyan nation' goes far beyond a stable monolithic idea. The construction is diverse and consequently its practices are dynamic and unstable, dependent on agents, contexts, and the contents of communication. My analysis of the corpus shows

---

5 *Common mwananchi* is an often-used term in Kenya. It represents an internal and external ascription that becomes constitutive in the construction of a Kenyan citizenry as part of which the speaker articulates him- or herself. By using this widespread label, the speaker describes him- or herself as an ordinary citizen, a normal or everyday representative of Kenyan society (Bing 79).

various interpretations of the nation that merge in a consistent diversity and multidimensionality unfolding an integrative power. As a symbol and medium of this distinctive Kenya*n way of life a linguistic practice I call 'Vi-Swahili' evolves in everyday practices. The replacement of the singular prefix [ki-] of Kiswahili by the plural marker [vi-] serves as an index of the multiplicity of Swahilis being used. The grammatical plural denotes the idea of a variability and flexibility of different Swahilis as opposed to the standardised national language Kiswahili.

To make this complexity clear, I would like to draw attention to three different, yet complementary trajectories in the run-up to Kenya's 2013 election, focussing on diverse political strategies in language use: (i.) the presidential candidates' emphasis on unity, (ii.) the variability and turbulence in the citizens' discourse, and (iii.) incipient changes of the hegemonic discourses of 'one nation, one language.'

My analysis builds on the discourse-analytical findings of Ruth Wodak (2011; 2015), Wodak et al. (2009), Anton Pelinka and Wodak (2002), and Norman Fairclough (2005) on language and national identity. I mainly collected the corpus for this analysis in direct exploration through participatory observation and qualitative interviews. At the same time, I followed the presidential candidates' speeches and the discussion of the *common mwananchi*. The events, such as campaign speeches, open forums, discussion evenings, political education, and meetings of civil society groups, included speech acts in Kiswahili, Sheng, Gĩkũyũ, and/or English. The conversations that I recorded were mostly conducted in more than one language. If not indicated otherwise, the translations into English are mine.

3   Candidates' Focus on National and Subnational Unity

Most of the following examples I took from campaign speeches given by Uhuru Kenyatta, one of the eight candidates vying for presidency in Kenya's 2013 general election. His speeches stand out as prime examples of a rhetorical strategy to construct national unity, which enables him to present his coalition as the unique and only representative of a united Kenya:

> [T]he jubilee coalition is … actually a national movement for peace unity development and transformative leadership for the people of kenya/ kenya has arrived at a turning point in our history/ and it is time to fully embrace our destiny/ it is time to rededicate ourselves to the task of nation building … a renewed kenya where we celebrate our diverse

cultures and history ... a renewed kenya where we share our history of ethnic tension and social divisions/ a renewed kenya where all of us irrespective of who you are ... we all live as one people/ in one nation ... (Kenyatta qtd. in Bing 205)[6]

Kenyatta's statement, made at the launch of the electoral blueprint of his Jubilee Coalition one month ahead of the election, neatly summarises the foci of the eight competitors' speeches which I assign under the political slogan or category of 'Kenya has come of age' (Bing 211). Like his political rivals, Kenyatta constructs the election as a nationwide decision to choose the right path for the future, discursively building on a national community of destiny. At the same time, his statements refer to a shared history and a united bright future that will bring all Kenyans together despite their differences in religion, ethnicity, social class, and gender. The very name Jubilee Coalition and the fact that it is composed of former political rivals enforce the idea of a 'community of destiny.'[7] This is quite surprising, considering the context of an election, which normally relies on the open expression of dissenting views among competing candidates. By contrast, Kenyan politicians emphasise the idea of 'unity despite diversity' even while competing for the presidency.

The rhetorical construction of national unity gains importance especially in front of a heterogeneous audience in Nairobi. The candidates build their speeches around a pronounced affinity and deep allegiance with Kenya. The call for unity is underlined by the use of Kiswahili, the national language enshrined in the constitution: "nawaomba wakenya wote tu kujikujue kama ndugu na dada/ tuwaache ubaguzi wa kikabila wa kirangi wa kidini/ mwishoni mwaka huu wa jubilee mungu atupatie mwanzo mpya/ tujiwe kama wakenya" (Kenyatta qtd. in Bing 203).[8] Kenyatta's appeal not only illustrates the motto 'unity *despite* diversity' in its content, but gives it a formal realisation. By using

---

6   All quotations presented here are transcripts of spoken language, which in its transcription depicts the realisations of actual speech and its peculiarities. The transcript is done according to the GAT2, a system to transcribe talk-in-interaction. An explanation of the transcription conventions can be found at the end of this chapter.
7   In the 2013 elections, Uhuru Kenyatta and William Ruto formed a political alliance despite having been political rivals in the 2007 elections. Both were charged with crimes against humanity at the International Criminal Court (ICC) in The Hague following the Kenyan general election in December 2007. The charges in both cases were dropped in December 2014 (Kenyatta) and April 2016 (Ruto).
8   "I am asking all kenyans to understand/(feel/see) themselves as brothers and sisters/ to leave behind discrimination of ethnicity colour or religion/ finally this year of jubilee god bring us a new beginning/ let us raise (become) as kenyans."

Kiswahili, he offers a shared medium for all Kenyans beyond their diverse 'mother tongues,' while at the same time avoiding 'elitist' English, a language acquired primarily via formal schooling that is hence socially divisive.

The campaign material specifically produced for the election also highlights the emphasis on national unity in content and form. The political messages are transferred with a nationwide reference and an inclusive use of Kiswahili. Independent of the political parties and languages being used, Kenya is described as a "24/7 working nation," characterised by transparency and unity in its industriousness. The TNA/Jubilee, for instance, used slogans like "I believe – tunaweza," "tunaamini kusema na kutenda," and "Uwazi, Umoja, Uchumi." The ODM/CORD, in turn, used messages like "Pamoja tuko tayari" and "tuko tayari makabila yote kenya tuko tayari" (qtd. in Bing 214).[9]

In their campaigns, the presidential candidates express their belief in the enduring strength of a homogeneous united Kenyan nation, mostly in a normative sense, asking for the banishment of 'ethnic tension.' The politicians are keen to construct a united, reconciled community, being collectively responsible for Kenya's future. Irrespective of the unity-building focus of the recorded speeches, the medium chosen by the speakers is mainly determined by the performances' contexts. Even though none of the speech acts I analysed were delivered in one language only, it must not be overlooked that Kiswahili dominates and is generally used as a frame in the introductory and concluding statements, including the calls for creating unity among their followers. When talking about sensitive issues such as corruption, 'internally displaced persons,' or tangible campaign promises a switch to long passages in English can be observed, as well when the performance is broadcast on (national) TV. Speeches are only rarely interrupted when given in English. A switch to Kiswahili or other languages, by contrast, may initiate vivid interaction with the audience, creating a community of action.

Next to English and Kiswahili, politicians also make use of the so-called 'mother tongues' assigned to the respective regions in which they speak. They shift the idea of a homogeneous community from a national to a subnational (ethnic) level. In assuring the support of their constituency, they ask for unconditional solidarity within the respective groups in explicit demarcation from other 'communities' mostly by using the locally dominant language:

---

9 TNA: "I believe – we can/we are able," "we believe to say and to act," and "openness, unity and economy/progress." ODM: "together we are ready" and "we are ready all kenyan tribes are ready."

AUDIENCE:	umwe
UHURU KENYATTA:	nĩguo andũtũrute wĩira tũrĩkĩndũkĩmwe?
AUDIENCE:	ĩĩĩĩ
UHURU KENYATTA:	people of murang'a today and our leaders here to agree that as we shall all unite and work as a team and we as central province shall become one_ya kwamba sisi sote tutasimama pamoja
AUDIENCE:	king of the gĩkũyũ community. (Kenyatta qtd. in Bing 189)[10]

Outside of Kenyatta's electoral district Gatundu South Constituency, the call for unity among 'the Gĩkũyũ' is not as productive. It is only this specific rural Gĩkũyũ setting that calls for unity at a subnational level, thus performing a national divide. Kenyatta thus changes to Kiswahili and English when he emphasises internal homogeneity by external demarcation. When talking about or addressing his political opponent Raila Odinga, he switches to Kiswahili:

UHURU KENYATTA:	na ndio mimi nasema hata kwa watu wa nyanza/ sisi hatuna shida/ tuko tayari kuungana pamoja na wao/ shida yetu ni mtu mmoja tu peke yake/ province mzima ni mtu mmoja tu peke yake/ tuko na shida/ na huyo mtu anaitwa nani
AUDIENCE:	raila ...
UHURU KENYATTA:	amen/hiyo tu/ hakuna shida zingine sisi tuko nayo/ kwa sababu huyu ndiye ametuletea vurugu/ ambazo tumeona katika taifa letu la kenya. (Kenyatta qtd. in Bing 190)[11]

---

10 AUDIENCE:	one
UHURU KENYATTA:	so that people we work as one
AUDIENCE:	yes
UHURU KENYATTA:	people of murang'a today and our leaders here to agree that as we shall all unite and work as a team and we as central province shall become one_that is to say we'll all stand up together
AUDIENCE:	king of the gĩkũyũ community
11 UHURU KENYATTA:	and yes i am saying even to the people of nyanza/ we do not have problems/ we are ready to join together with them/ our problem is only one person alone/ a whole province is one person alone/ we have problems and what is that person's name
AUDIENCE:	raila ...
UHURU KENYATTA:	amen/ only this/ there are no other problems with us/ because he is indeed the one who has brought us the riots/ which we have seen in our kenyan nation

Raila Odinga becomes the personified instigator of the 2007 violence. In constructing a common enemy, Kenyatta enforces the internal homogenisation of the Gĩkũyũ community. At the same time, he creates a homogeneous community of the "people of Nyanza"[12] in direct opposition to a Gĩkũyũ community.

To sum up, not only do the politicians adapt the content of their speeches and the construction of the community to their contexts and audiences, but also their language(s). Competing for the presidency, the candidates are keen to form a unified national community while not negating internal differences. Their discourses can be summarised under the label 'unity *despite* diversity.' Against the background of the 2007 elections, references to any ethnic conflict and the related questions of land and 'internally displaced people' are rare.[13] Even the new electoral system introduced with the constitutional referendum in 2010 plays into the hands of the unity-focused campaign speeches: the candidate is only declared president if he receives more than half of all the votes cast in the election and at least twenty-five per cent of the votes cast in each of more than half of the counties (Constitution of Kenya § 138 (4) n. pag.). Kenyan politicians cannot only appeal to their 'core' voting group but depend on attracting support from other (co-)ethnic groups to be successful (Horowitz 901).

4   Variability in the Citizens' Discourses

The *common wananchi* challenge the presidential candidates' ideas by questioning the image of a homogenous nation of equal citizens. They understand Kenya as an entirely diverse and heterogeneous nation: only the existence and combination of various ethnic groups, different languages, and habits make Kenya meaningful for them. I summarise the discourses of the *common wananchi* under the category of 'diversity *in* unity' (Bing 101, 144), which is among other speech acts expressed in the statement "we are a mix." In a conversation about Kenyan national identity, two interviewees, for example, stated:

---

12   "People of Nyanza" refers to Raila Odinga's birthplace Maseno in the Kisumu District of Nyanza Province.
13   In the 2007 Kenyan elections, the competition for land became a key feature of the conflict between various 'ethnic' groups. As a result of the violence triggered by the elections' outcome, more than 300,000 Kenyans were displaced (Branch and Cheeseman, "Democratization" 14).

> because we are already a mix/ we were mixed when it started/ and there is nothing wrong with the mix/ the mix works.
>
> kenya it's a combination of all people here/ from different mhm/ from different mhm/ even from different citizens/ from *kalenjin luo*/ we are all kenyans/ that is. (*Common mwananchi* qtd. in Bing 101)

In the examples above, heterogeneity is described as unproblematic. By using the negated form "nothing wrong," the speaker implicitly refers to the idea of a homogeneous community as the ideal, while at the same time rejecting it in confrontation with a lasting mixture that works for Kenyan society. S/he articulates national unity only in prior reference to an omnipresent diversity. Moreover, diversity is essential in the citizens' statements about language and in the linguistic practices themselves.

The variability in my interviews with and group discussion of the *common wananchi* reflects a consistent heterogeneity of linguistic practices in Nairobi's ordinary life. The speakers make Kenya meaningful only in the commonplace merging of several languages. As a manifestation of the heterogeneity, they make use of varieties of Kiswahili that bridge differences and bring diverse speakers together. Their dynamic practices are consistent with the common means of everyday communication in Nairobi. They show agreement with a variety called Sheng, Nairobi's urban vernacular based on a highly non-standard use of Kiswahili (Beck, "Sheng" 51; Githiora 160; Mazrui 169). However, I prefer to label them as Vi-Swahili instead of naming them Sheng. In my analysis, I use Vi-Swahili as a descriptive category to formally represent linguistically heterogeneous phenomena and to distinguish its actual use from increasingly stabilised practices labelled as Sheng. There is no uniform, standardised form of Vi-Swahili but several variations, such as a 'real/full,' an actual, 'total/perfect Sheng' ('sheng kiasi') or a 'Kikwetu-Sheng,' as one of my interviewees makes clear:

> sheng hihi pia wengi wao siku hizi/ sheng/ tunatumia sheng/ lakini sidhani kama sheng yetu_yenu tumianga [sic]/ ni sawa na real sheng yetu/ tumechanganya fanyefanye [sic]/ hapo so tumeshachanganya [sic]/ but mwenyewe ninongea sheng/ lakini siyo real sheng/ siyo sheng kamili/ so tunatumianga [sic] sheng huko mtaani/ but ile sheng ya kikwetu yaani siyo sheng sawa/ lakini si tunaita sheng/ but siyo real sheng ... mtaani kwenda ndani ndani/ yah/ kuna waviijana [sic] wanajua sheng kiasi. (*Common mwananchi* qtd. in Bing 108)[14]

---

14   sheng hihi/ as well these days many of them/ sheng/ we use sheng/ but i don't think sheng as ours_their use/ is like our real sheng/ we have mixed like 'fanyefanye'/ so there/ so we

In the interviews, the speaker describes Sheng as the medium of urban communication that establishes proximity between those interacting. Differences in 'native language' or 'mother tongues' are overcome. My interviewee conceives of it as a dynamic form which brings together a broad range of speakers. According to her view, Sheng is anything but a stable, standardised national language controlled by state institutions. By making use of this new variety, language and social differences are blurred. The interviewee suggests:

> we have also a patois of swahili which is called sheng which we use a lot ... and the moment you switch to say for example sheng it's probably even closer so there is something i just noticed in the last few years that's it's there it's like a major it's something that brings people together (*Common mwananchi* qtd. in Bing 107)

When using Vi-Swahili the speakers primarily refer to their urban affiliation rather than to their ethnicity, which is overshadowed by a (sub-)urban affiliation. Ethnic associations lose their significance:¹⁵ "sheng is a mixture of so many languages/ in kenya we can talk gĩkũyũ, luyha, jaluo/ iko poa/ and those they have meanings of different tribes/ but you pull them together/ they make sheng." (*Common mwananchi* qtd. in Bing 108). As this speaker indicates, using Vi-Swahili unites the interlocutors beyond their diverse 'mother tongues'. In this sense, the standardised national language Kiswahili loses its power as an integrative symbol whereas Vi-Swahili becomes the unifying medium in everyday practices. The interviewer's argument is in accordance with daily talk in the urban context of Nairobi: instead of a stabilised variety of English or Kiswahili, innovative, unstable, and dynamic forms are used, fulfilling an integrative function with a national reference.

Kenyans make extensive use of dynamic language practices to enact the nation. Everyday communication in Nairobi becomes a trans-lingual, trans-ethnic, and trans-class activity and can be understood as a metrolingual practice questioning the norm of a standardised national language (Otsuji and Pennycook 246). Language use formally reflects fluid constructs of the nation that are shaped by ethnic and linguistic tolerance and enable a community of

---

have already mixed/ but i myself i speak sheng/ but not real sheng/ not full sheng/ so we use sheng with each other there in the suburb/ but that sheng of ours that is not the same/ but we call it sheng/ but it's not real sheng/ the inner suburbs the inner ones/ yah/ there are the youth who know the real sheng.

15   For a post-ethnic interpretation, see Beck ("Apparatus" 9) and Laughlin (13).

interaction beyond colonial national-linguofied demarcations.[16] The dynamic practices of the *common mwananchi* are an accomplishment of a polylingual, urban lifestyle I label as Talking Kenya*n.

My analysis of citizens' everyday practices and discourses in Kenya make explicit that the metadiscourse of 'one nation, one language' remains successful in the understanding of Kiswahili as a national language, establishing Kiswahili as the one and only national language. My interviewees define the nation by making language a feature of it. In their understanding, the only language imaginable as the symbol of a unified independent Kenya is Kiswahili. In addition, the interviewees evaluate the characteristics of Kiswahili positively. For them, it is a very expressive language, full of metaphors and comparisons, which, unlike English, does not allow any ambiguities. They describe Kiswahili as their most natural and comfortable means of communication, the default language choice. It is the language that everyone in Kenya understands and through which the nation comes together, whether young or old, educated or without any degree. According to their understanding, Kiswahili is a local language and, unlike English, evokes intimacy. In contrast to their 'mother tongues,' my interview partners describe Kiswahili as an ethnically neutral language. Furthermore, they recognise it as a characteristic of and requirement for Kenyan citizenship. Kiswahili is also the only language that the speakers combine with the adjective "national." By this, the interviewees unite the national community linguistically. In subscribing to the official narrative of Kiswahili as the sole national language written into the Kenyan constitution, the speakers in the interviews and group discussions create a sense of community and mutual belonging.

Even though many Kenyans and official documents uphold the nexus of Kiswahili and Kenya, it finds little correspondence in its practical implementation. Ideally, to be Kenyan means to speak a stable, standardised Kiswahili. In practice, however, dynamic, and innovative forms of Vi-Swahili are used. Officials, politicians, language experts and citizens may advocate standardisation and homogeneity, but fluid and dynamic practices of Vi-Swahili in daily language use dismantle these very concepts. What is expressed in these practices is a redefinition and re-articulation of national identity which is characterised by inclusive diversity, not exclusive homogeneity. Analogous to the nation, language itself becomes an unstable concept. In the previous examples, I have shown that the Kenyan community is constructed through porous,

---

16   The term national-linguofied is deduced from Rose Marie Beck's discussion of "linguo-ethnified" concerns ("Apparatus" 9).

fluid practices that make it difficult to keep languages and communities clearly apart. My analysis indicates that the nexus between language and nation as a form of heritage of colonial domination becomes fragile. In the daily practices of the *common mwananchi,* language loses its function as a marker of difference, exclusive identity, and inequality. Linguistic practices in Kenya are characterised by a pronounced creativity that overcomes the boundaries of languages and communities. The language use resolves supposedly insurmountable boundaries.

But even these dynamic forms are subject to processes of standardisation. The exclusive label Sheng, regularly used by my interview partners, marks and enforces the difference to other languages. Users of Sheng express a demand for stabilising the dynamic forms by referencing authoritative or authentic 'native' speakers of Sheng. The interviewees point towards these speakers as role models of a correct or right use of Sheng, suggesting that one would find the best speakers in the 'slums' of Nairobi. The youth of the 'slums' thus become the primary and authoritative reference group. In this context, I recognise early tendencies of an unofficial user-oriented standardisation process. Speakers and linguists alike turn a dynamic practice into a static and codified variety which can be taken out of its context and supposedly be described by listing its formal features, much in the way that other national languages have been abstracted from their sociohistorical origins. This codification creates a unit that linguists can identify, work with, and publish a grammatical sketch on (Blommaert 292).

5 Change of Hegemonic Practices

For the politicians, it becomes necessary to address their potential electorate in a language they can understand and identify with. They appeal to them best in using the 'language(s) of the people.' The fluent linguistic practices described in this chapter are gradually being adopted in official domains, e.g. in campaign speeches or political advertisements. Politicians make use of mixed linguistic forms in their political messages, as Peter Kenneth's slogan "*tunawesmake*" (we can make it), Raphael Tuju and his "*Poa Campaign,*" as well as Musalia Mudavadi's slogan "*Niko Freshi*" illustrate.

Especially Kenneth, one of the eight candidates vying for presidency, tried to appeal to the youth – the bulk of Kenyan voters – not only by the way he dressed but also by coining his slogan "*Tunawesmake.*"[17] However, using a linguistic practice which is common among Nairobi youth did not win him the

---

17   Kenneth's slogan is aligned to Barack Obama's campaign slogan "Yes we can" in the 2008 United States presidential elections.

vote. Mike Mbuvi Sonko and Rachel Shebesh were more successful in appealing to Nairobi's young voters. Mike Mbuvi, popularly known as *Sonko*,[18] saw the advantage of running with a Sheng name. Vying under his legalised name Mike Mbuvi Sonko, he won the Nairobi County Senate seat in the 2013 elections. In a similar way, Shebesh appealed to the youth, obtaining the Nairobi County Women's Representative seat in 2013. She also branded herself with a Sheng slogan, *"Manzi wa Nai"* (Young girl from Nairobi). Kelvin Okoth, executive officer at Go Sheng – a Kenyan radio station promoting the urban variety – understands Sheng not just as a language, but as "an identity for youths, and politicians know that it is the easiest and quickest way to connect with them" (qtd. in Gathigah 24). Kenyan politicians thus increasingly see the advantage of using Sheng in connecting with young voters. In their speeches they express a new understanding of a heterogeneous nation in fluid linguistic practices as fulfilling the aspirations to a unified nation.

6 Conclusion

In this chapter, I have examined how languages function as unifying and differentiating symbols in the construction of a national, subnational, or urban community. Based on my findings, I argue that the understanding of a stable national language needs to be broadened, especially in a polylingual postcolonial context. In the previous analysis, I have made clear that in terms of creating a sense of unity and belonging, it is not the standardised medium only that guarantees solidarity among the citizens, but that there are fluid and turbulent linguistic practices at work in the construction of the Kenyan nation.

In Kenyan politics, the potential of a 'one nation, one language' nexus (as it informed European processes of nation-building) must be re-evaluated. Whereas the political elite is eager to maintain the ideal of a homogeneous monolingual nation in order to secure its powers, the 'common citizen' makes sense of a diverse national community. The citizens' discourses have revealed a broad range of meanings and strategies, such as fluid language usage and non-standard forms which can be labelled as Vi-Swahili.

However, ideas of one national language still prevail when it comes to the language attitudes of Kenyan speakers. For my interview partners, Kiswahili is the only language linked with the Kenyan nation. Kiswahili therefore

---

18 *'Sonko'* is a Sheng word designating a rich or wealthy person.

retains an integrative power in the interlocutor's statements while losing the very same in its formal realisation. Although they understand Kiswahili as the only medium that guarantees national unity and inclusion, it is not the medium of Kenyan speakers' talk. Daily language use in the urban context of Nairobi displays a variety of linguistic practices in various forms of Vi-Swahili. Therefore, I see a rift between the unconditional nexus of one language and nation and everyday heterogeneous practices. The heterogeneous and dynamic practices of the interviews, group discussion, and political speeches I analysed question the metanarrative of a sociolinguistically homogeneous nation.

In their turbulent linguistic practices, the *common wananchi* express very different, sometimes opposing meanings of the nation, thus challenging prevailing language ideologies of 'one nation, one language.' Just as they shake off the ideological burdens of (post-)colonial language politics, they also question the discursive orders of linguistic nationalism. The speakers do not only challenge the ideal of a monolingual homogenous nation, but also the notion of clearly distinct linguistic entities.

Against this background, I see a need to re-assess concepts of language. While building on everyday practices in a postcolonial and polylingual setting, I question colonial hegemonies of the discourse of 'one nation, one language.' In accordance with the concept of the nation, I also understand the notion of language as a social construct. I use nation as well as language and their nexus as descriptive categories, which are socially and historically contingent and thus subject and object of constant processes of negotiation and reconstruction. Not so much their stability, but their variety, dynamics, and variability became relevant in my analysis. My approach challenges the ideological framework of a stable (sub-)national identification closely bound to a language, which has been overlooked in many publications on Kenyan politics and language thus far.

In understanding linguistic and political practices and their interrelation in Kenya, new approaches which consider the dynamicsof everyday life beyond clear demarcations of linguo-ethnified identity politics are necessary. The struggle of Kenyan voters goes together with new social dynamics, not only affecting linguistic practices and codifications, but equally political ones.

TABLE 2.1 Transcription Conventions (GAT 2)

Pausing	Micro (up to 0.2 sec.)	(.)
	Short (0.2–0.5 sec.)	(-)
	Intermediate (0.5–0.8 sec.)	(--)
Word/sense boundaries	Two words = one expression	_
	Boundary sense-unit	/
Turns	Merging turns	=
Other segmental transcription	Characterisation of a non-linguistic event	(sigh)
	Interpretive comment	<<laughing>> texttext>.
	Focus accent	TEXT
Intelligibility	Unintelligible passage	()
	Assumed wording/difficult to understand	(possible text)

Works Cited

Beck, Rose Marie. "Language as Apparatus: Entanglements of Language, Culture and Territory and the Invention of Nation and Ethnicity." *Postcolonial Studies*, vol. 21, no. 2, 2018, pp. 1–24. doi: 10.1080/13688790.2018.1462085.

Beck, Rose Marie. "Sheng: An Urban Variety of Swahili in Kenya." *Youth Languages and Urban Languages in Africa*, edited by Nico Nassenstein and Andrea Hollington, de Gruyter, 2015, pp. 51–79. doi: 10.1515/9781614518525-005.

Bing, Natascha. *Talking Kenya*n. Sprache, Nation und Politik: Die diskursive Konstruktion von Nation in Kenia*. 2017. U Leipzig, PhD dissertation.

Blommaert, Jan. "Artefactual Ideologies and the Textual Production of African Languages." *Language & Communication*, vol. 28, 2008, pp. 291–307. doi: 10.1016/j.langcom.2008.02.003.

Branch, Daniel, and Nicholas Cheeseman. "Democratization, Sequencing, and State Failure in Africa: Lessons from Kenya." *African Affairs*, vol. 108, no. 430, 2009, pp. 1–26. doi: 10.1093/afraf/adn065.

Branch, Daniel, and Nicholas Cheeseman. Introduction. *Our Turn to Eat: Politics in Kenya Since 1950*, edited by Branch, Cheeseman, and Leigh Gardner, Lit, 2010, pp. 1–21. Afrikanische Studien/African Studies 34.

Constitution of Kenya. 2010. *Kenya Law*, www.kenyalaw.org:8181/exist/kenyalex/act-view.xql?actid=Const2010. Accessed 10 Aug. 2020.

Cresswell, Tim, and Craig Martin. "On Turbulence: Entanglement of Disorder and Order on a Devon Beach." *Tijdkrift voor Economische en Sociale Geografie*, vol. 103, no. 5, 2012, pp. 516–29. doi: 10.1111/j.1467-9663.2012.00734.x.

Deane, James, and Jamal Abdi Ismail. "The 2007 General Election in Kenya and Its Aftermath: The Role of Local Language Media." *The International Journal of Press/Politics*, vol. 13, no. 3, 2008, pp. 319–27. doi: 10.1177/1940161208319510.

Fairclough, Norman. "Critical Discourse Analysis in Transdisciplinary Research." *A New Agenda in (Critical) Discourse Analysis. Theory, Methodology and Interdisciplinarity*, edited by Ruth Wodak and Paul Chilton, John Benjamins, 2005, pp. 53–70.

Gathigah, Miriam. "Politicians Went Sheng to Woo Kenyan Youths." *Perspectives: Political Analysis and Commentary from Africa*, no. 1, 2013, pp. 24–5.

Githiora, Chege. "Sheng: Peer Language, Swahili Dialect or Emerging Creole?" *Journal of African Cultural Studies*, vol. 15, no. 2, 2002, pp. 159–81. doi: 10.1080/1369681022000042637.

Horowitz, Jeremy. "Ethnicity and the Swing Vote in Africa's Emerging Democracies: Evidence from Kenya." *British Journal of Political Science*, vol. 49, no. 3, 2017, pp. 901–21. doi: 10.1017/S0007123417000011.

Jørgensen, Jens Normann, and Somogy Varga. "Norms and Practices of Polylingual Behaviour: A Sociolinguistic Model." *Journal of Estonian and Finno-Ugric Linguistics*, vol. 2, no. 2, 2011, pp. 49–68. doi: 10.12697/jeful.2011.2.2.03.

Kroon, Sjaak, et al. "Truly Moving Texts." *Language, Literacy and Diversity: Moving Words*, edited by Christopher Stroud and Martin Prinsloo, Routledge, 2015, pp. 1–15.

Laughlin, Fiona Mc. "Introduction to the Languages of Urban Africa." *The Languages of Urban Africa*, edited by Fiona Mac Laughlin, Continuum, 2009, pp. 1–18.

Mazrui, Alamin. "Slang and Code-switching: The Case of Sheng in Kenya." *Afrikanistische Arbeitspapiere: Schriftenreihe des Kölner Instituts für Afrikanistik*, vol. 42, 1995, pp. 168–79.

Nassenstein, Nico, and Andrea Hollington. "Youth Language Practices in Africa as Creative Manifestations of Fluid Repertoires and Markers of Speakers' Social Identity." *Youth Language Practices in Africa and Beyond*, edited by Nassenstein and Hollington, de Gruyter 2015, pp. 1–22. doi: 10.1515/9781614518525-003.

Njoroge, Martin C., et al. "New Media in Kenya: Putting Ethnicity in Perspective." *Cultural Identity and New Communication Technologies: Political, Ethnic and Ideological Implications*, edited by D. Ndirangu Wachanga, IGI Global, 2011, pp. 40–65.

Odera, Edna Ipalei. *Radio and Hate Speech: A Comparative Study of Kenya (2007) and the 1994 Rwanda Genocide*. 2015. U Nairobi, Master's thesis.

Otsuji, Emi, and Alastair Pennycook. "Metrolingualism: Fixity, Fluidity and Language in Flux." *International Journal of Polylingualism*, vol. 7, no. 3, 2010, pp. 240–54. doi: 10.1080/14790710903414331.

Pelinka, Anton, and Ruth Wodak. *'Dreck am Stecken:' Politik der Ausgrenzung*. Czernin Verlag, 2002.

Somerville, Keith. "Violence, Hate Speech and Inflammatory Broadcasting in Kenya: The Problems of Definition and Identification." *Ecquid Novi: African Journalism Studies*, vol. 32, no. 1, 2011, pp. 82–101. doi: 10.1080/02560054.2011.545568.

Stroud, Christopher. "Afterword. Turbulent Deflections." *Language, Literacy and Diversity: Moving Words*, edited by Stroud and Mastin Prinsloo, Routledge, 2015, pp. 206–16.

Wodak, Ruth. *Discourse of Politics in Action: Politics as Usual*. Palgrave Macmillan, 2011.

Wodak, Ruth. *The Politics of Fear: What Right-Wing Populist Discourses Mean*. SAGE, 2015.

Wodak, Ruth, et al. *The Discursive Construction of National Identity*. Edinburgh UP, 2009.

CHAPTER 3

The Hindi Language and the Imagination of the Indian Nation: Ramchandra Shukla's Construction of Indian Civilization

Prachi Gupta

1   Introduction

Language, next to religion, has played an important role in shaping the national identities in South Asian countries. According to the census of 2011, there are 122 languages in India spoken by more than ten thousand people. The constitution of India accommodates this diversity through provisions for the official recognition of languages and institutions for education in minority languages. Twenty-two languages are recognized as scheduled languages and efforts are made for their development and promotion by the state. Despite the acknowledgement of the gigantic diversity of languages, it is interesting to fathom that there is yet one language that enjoys privileges unmatched by any other language in the country. In India, especially in the Northern region, Hindi has emerged as an important instrument in shaping nationalist politics.

This chapter looks into the indomitable stature the Hindi language enjoys in Indian politics and the nationalism that emanates from it. During the independence movement in the twentieth century, several languages contested for the status of the national language and attempted to define the upcoming Indian nation in their respective ways. By the 1940s, Hindi had emerged dominant in this project. Its major contender Urdu moved out of the competition with the formation of Pakistan. Support for Hindustani, a mix of both Hindi and Urdu words written in Persian or Nagari script and formerly promoted by important leaders such as Mahatma Gandhi, Vinoba Bhave, and the novelist Munshi Premchand, waned (Dasgupta 139).

Hindi came to prevail over the imagination of nationalism that was to take root in post-independence India. This chapter investigates the ideological link between Hindi and the Indian nation that dominates Indian politics by moving beyond the chronological assessments of political developments and the role of leadership to analyzing the arguments that strengthened the claim for Hindi as the language of the nation.

To understand the link between the Hindi language and nationalism in India, it is important to take into account the role of the English language in the independence movement. The colonial rule introduced English as the language of liberal ideas and progress especially for the Western-educated urban professionals in India. These people were able to utilize their access to ideas of democracy and liberalism in their critique of colonial rule. As the language of the conqueror, English was associated with privilege and higher status in the colony (Raina 281). In the anti-colonial movement, this valorized position of English was criticized by representatives of different ideologies who promoted the use of vernacular and indigenous languages (Sonntag 136).[1] The growth of nationalist sentiments led to a search for affinity which many felt could be expressed only in native languages. Even though English continued to dominate in elite and official circles, native languages such as Hindi began to enjoy a special bond to the ideas of nation and nationalism in India.

Several theorists have discussed the role of language in the process of nation-building. Ernest Gellner argues that nationalism is the cultural requirement of industrial societies which demand a culturally interchangeable, mobile, and literate working-class population. The use of a common national language is crucial to impart cultural homogeneity to the population (Gellner 35–6). Historian Etienne Balibar notes the importance of language in constituting a "fictive ethnicity" which supports the perception of a nation as "natural" and "immanent" rather than imagined. "A people" can recognize the "ideal nation" through a common language that becomes the fundamental element of their lives (Balibar 138–42). Apart from these functional roles accorded to language in the rise of the nation, Benedict Anderson offers another theory of the origin and expansion of nationalism in which language plays a constitutive role. In Anderson's account, language imparts to the nation a "sense of fatality" embedded in history, while it also provides for the imagination of the nation as a contemporaneous community. Anderson emphasizes that the conception of a nation is always based in language (134).

The imagined community as a nation made possible by a language and through print capitalism is not an empty whole. What is more, language provides a constitutive character to the idea of the nation. A language is able to define the 'nature' of the nation. As I shall demonstrate, Hindi provided the key source of inspiration to at least one of the dominant imaginations of the

---

1   Gandhi strongly voiced his opinion against the hegemony of English which he thought had created the rift between the masses and the elites (Raina 284). The novelist and writer Premchand echoed Gandhi's concerns, believing that the English language had enslaved the will and intelligence of the educated classes (285).

Indian nation. To illustrate this point, this chapter analyzes the writings and texts of Ramchandra Shukla (1884–1941) who was a prominent literary critic and political thinker. He is best known for his seminal work on the history of Hindi literature which has continued to shape the Hindi language until today. Laying out the history of the language and its literature, Shukla defined the then present and future of the nation. He offers an emphatic understanding of the nation as imagined from the vantage point of the Hindi language. The relation between Hindi and the community of its speakers, and the speakers with the nation comes out centrally in his account of the history of Hindi literature.

Born in a Brahmin family in the district of Basti in the North Indian state of Uttar Pradesh, Shukla grew up with Hindi and Urdu. His education commenced in Urdu. At home, his grandmother introduced him to reading Hindu scriptures like *Ramayana* and *Mahabharata*. After the family shifted to Mirzapur in 1893, Shukla spent much of his time reading works in English and Hindi at the Mayo Memorial Library in the city. This was the period that witnessed the rise of the literary works in the Khari Boli dialect of Hindi spearheaded by the nineteenth-century literary giant and thinker Bharatendu Harishchandra (1850–1885). Shukla was introduced to the Hindi literary circle through writers who were associates of Harishchandra. He became the editor of the literary journal *Anandkadambini* in 1903.

In 1908, he joined Nagari Pracharini Sabha (the Society for the Promotion of Nagari) in Benares as the assistant editor of a Hindi dictionary.[2] It was a society founded in 1893 by a group of Hindi enthusiasts with the motive of expanding and popularizing the Nagari script. His association with the society was a major milestone in his political career. He organized several lectures, meetings, and conferences for the cause of the Nagari script and the Hindi language. The proceedings of these meetings were published in the Sabha's periodical. By 1910, he was executing several responsibilities in the society as editor of the Hindi dictionary and the Sabha periodical and as a jury member in various committees. This is the time when he wrote extensively, publishing poems, articles, stories, and essays. His seminal work, *Hindi Sahitya ka Itihaas (The History of Hindi Literature)*, was published in 1940, although parts of it had already appeared in journals from 1919 onwards. Through his writings and ideas, Shukla cemented the nascent field of literary criticism in the Hindi language and literature. He is credited with the authority of foregrounding

---

2   This was a major project of collecting words which concluded in 1929 with an astonishing eleven volumes, *Hindi Shabd Sagar*. It contained a total of 93,155 words.

the self-consciousness of the Hindi language by standardizing and defining sharply the boundaries and nature of the language (Kumar 180).

In *The Nationalization of Hindu Traditions,* Vasudha Dalmia looks at Harishchandra's authority to establish the beginnings of the standardization of the Hindi language for a national stature. Dalmia rightfully sees Harishchandra as the progenitor of the idea of 'one's own language' (*nij bhasha*), a concept which he linked to the notions of respect and progress of the people. Harishchandra proposed that it was the language spoken in households that had to be the national language (Dalmia 203). However, he also recognized that there is no uniform language of the household even within the small territory of a village (Harishchandra 1055).[3] I argue that this conundrum remained unresolved with Harishchandra as the gap between the need for a standard language for the national status and the diversity of dialects at the household level could not be bridged.

This chapter suggests that it is in the works of Shukla that one can uncover the convolution of household dialects and languages spoken at home and the standardized language for official use into one grand construction of Hindi. Through this language, Shukla constructs a homogeneous and exclusionary imagination of Indian civilization that operates a dominant idea of the Indian nation.

In a period marked by rigorous debates on the multiple imaginations of the upcoming nation, the overlap between the literary and political sphere in nationalist discourse is an important arena of research. Shukla provides a junction where language politics intersects with nationalist discourse. His construction and standardization of the Hindi language explain the unassailable symbolic role the Hindi language came to assume in the debate on nationalism in Indian politics. In critically reading Shukla's works, this chapter offers an analysis of the reasons for the dominance of the North Indian Hindi speaking belt in Indian politics and the continued cultural importance attached to Hindi. In the first section of this chapter, I discuss the crucial link Shukla establishes between Hindi and Indian civilization to offer a uniform image of the latter. In the second section, I analyze Shukla's ideas of the community and nation as they occur in his account of the history of Hindi literature. Before concluding, I argue that the post-independence language politics in the Hindi

---

3 In response to the question posed by the Hunter Commission in 1882 regarding the vernacular language of the area, for instance, Harishchandra answered that several dialects exist in the North Western Provinces alone. He also recognized that language changes vis-à-vis the occupation and caste location of the person (Harishchandra 1055–6).

speaking belt can be seen as the outcomes of, or at least inspired by, the arguments found in Shukla's writings.

2   Language as the Anchor of Indian Civilization

Religion is the key variable employed by orientalist scholars and indigenous intellectuals to make sense of the Indian civilization (Mahajan 70).[4] Shukla offers an alternative in which language is the major category to gauge all the facets of Indian civilization. For Shukla, language is important because it brings the speakers together and connects them with their physical environment ("Apni Bhasha" 14). He holds that the cultural, social, and natural experiences of the community of speakers are exhibited in the words and meanings in their language (15).

There are two central arguments that Shukla puts forth in support of using the lens of language for tracing the past of Indian civilization. Firstly, language is crucial as the source of affinity for its speakers. Shukla writes, "One's own language is central to the very existence of the community so much so that if a language ceases to continue or is overridden by a foreign language, the civilization is rendered into deformity" (16).[5] He emphasizes that it is the speaker's own language that defines his or her social and cultural roots and constitutes a community. Secondly, shifts in language depict the historical trajectory of the shared meanings and sentiments of the speakers over time. Shukla argues that when there is congruence between the experiences of the speakers and the language used for expression, one can understand the 'true nature' of the community of speakers and the civilization they are a part of ("Hindi aur" 71).

Shukla shifts the emphasis from religion to language as the central category to understand Indian civilization. Instead of religious texts (mainly Hindu),[6] the onus is moved to the study of literature. What is crucial to note here is

---

4   Vivekananda believed that the spiritual aspects reflected the true quality of Indian civilization. In Sri Aurobindo's view, it was the unity of the spirit with the supreme consciousness which defined the core conception of Indian civilization. In Gandhi, one finds that it is in the ideals of duty and morality that one can locate the key aspects of Indian civilization. For Rabindranath Tagore, Indian civilization could be seen as syncretic and reminiscent of *dharma* (Gupta 26).
5   This quotation, as well as all other references to Shukla's works in English in this chapter, were translated by me.
6   Orientalist scholarship focussed on the Sanskrit religious texts as valued by the Brahmins, the highest rank holders in the caste hierarchy, to be the source of understanding the mind of Indian civilization (Inden 85).

that religion as a category is not ignored entirely in Shukla's writing. It emerges when Shukla discusses literary religious texts and attaches more importance to one category over the other. Nevertheless, the vantage point for Shukla's imagination of Indian civilization is language through the study of literature. He asserts that the literature of a nation is the reflection of collective sentiments and the expression (*chitvriti*) of the people (*Hindi Sahitya* 1).

When Shukla was writing, literature was perceived as a major realm of asserting protest against British colonialism and the oppressive social order (Orsini 123). The eminent Hindi novelist Premchand (1880–1936), for example, claimed that the role of literature was to bring to the forefront the fissures in society under colonial rule (*Kuch Vichar* 16). On the contrary, Shukla argues that literature exhibited the unity and collectivity of society. In so doing, he puts forward a specific conception of Indian civilization in which the community of speakers transforms into a united body against intruders such as the British. In my view, the idea of the unity of expression is the essential element in Shukla's linkage of literature and civilization because it establishes popular support as the foundation of his idea of Indian nationhood. Through this strategy, Shukla is able to portray his ideas of the nation as not that of an elite class but of the masses.

After establishing the link between language, literature, and civilization, Shukla makes the case for Hindi language and literature as the representatives of Indian civilization. He suggests that an unhindered tradition of Hindi literature running for a thousand years is indicative of Indian civilization and its central essence ("Hindi aur" 63). He elaborates on the idea of a Hindi language which might swallow in its ambit the massive diversity of languages that the physical landscape of the country encompasses. Unlike the Hindi we know today, the Hindi language that Shukla writes about appropriates regional languages like Bengali, Marathi, and Gujarati, for in his view, these languages share vocabulary and meanings with Hindi. His idea of Hindi literature subsumes literature of regional languages and dialects. In this homogenizing idea of Hindi, Shukla deprives regional languages of their distinctive characters in favor of the creation of a uniform language. The diverse speaker community is in turn represented as speaking a language broadly called Hindi and sharing uniform interests.

There is a simultaneous process of homogenization and exclusion at work in the grand language that Shukla constructs. Owing to his emphasis on the link between language and physical environments, centuries of an intermingling of Persian and Arabic influences are discredited because these languages originated outside the territory of India. Despite prominent voices contradicting his ideological rigor such as Premchand's,[7] Shukla excludes the contribution of an entire community of people who wrote in Urdu and Persian from participating in Indian civilization. This filtration of the tradition of Hindi and Indian civilization denies equal participatory rights to other languages, religions, and cultures and had implications for the idea of the nation that so emerged.

3   Hindi and the National Community

Shukla's history of the Hindi language and literature provides a continued trajectory of Indian civilization, according it a distinct essence. To understand Shukla's imagination of Indian civilization, it is helpful to discuss his conception of the history of Hindi literature. He arranged his canon under four major epochs from the preceding 900 years. In each of these four moments in history, an intrusion from the outside of the country's territory had impacted the literature of the period. Shukla identifies themes or sentiments that became dominant in the major literary works of particular periods and which then provided the nomenclature for that era (*Hindi Sahitya* 14). He refers only to those literary texts in his canon that were in line with the dominant theme of a period. Other literary writings that depicted varying themes are treated as sectarian. That Shukla's canonization exhibits an ideological agenda is later highlighted by other literary critics who present more diverse themes and multiple influences on literary writings for the periods Shukla marks out.[8]

In the first period, 993–1318, Shukla maintains, Hindi literary works seem to be predominantly occupied with writing tracts of valor and bravery of the respective kings and rulers in the period. Shukla argues that in retaliation of the Muslim invasion, the literature in this period expresses the sentiments of the people in extolling the chivalry of their native rulers (18). He refers to this period as *Veer-gatha kaal* (sagas of bravery period). Shukla argues that most of the literature during this period seems to be united in support of the native rulers, in the protection of their homeland.[9]

---

7   For detailed arguments, consult *Kuch Vichar* by Premchand.
8   See, for example, Dwivedi 34.
9   The two eminent writers of the period who did not subscribe to the theme of valor and chivalry were the Sufi poet Amir Khusro (1253–1325) and the Maithili poet Vidyapati. Even though both poets wrote in the popular vernaculars of their respective regions, Shukla argues that they wrote poetry with the themes of beauty and devotion and are therefore put in the sectarian column.

In the second period of Shukla's history, Hindi literature turns towards devotion and faith. Shukla calls this period *Bhakti kaal* (period of devotion, 1318–1633), seeing its main motivation in resistance to the expansion of Islam. He asserts that people turn to a form of devotion that strengthens their sense of community and enables them to resist the intrusion from Islamic forces (40). Most of the literature that emerges in this period consists of devotional poetry and songs of faith for their gods (35). Shukla also proposes that the metaphysical musings of Natha and Siddha sects[10] disenchant people from their religion.

Shukla lists various literary texts within this period mainly under the religious sub-categories of *sagun* (determinate/with form) and *nirgun* (indeterminate/formless). He prioritizes the determinate form of devotion over the indeterminate one. He argues that the *sagun* form of devotion allows people to come together in collective worship of popular symbols from their everyday life and experiences. Within the *sagun* tradition, it is the worship of *Rama* as exemplified in Tulsidas's *Ramacharitmanas* that is presented as the ideal religion (*Goswami Tulsidas* 36). According to Shukla, *Ramcharitmanas* values familial, caste- and kinship-based responsibilities for maintaining harmony in society and, as such, is worthy of worship through its revered characters.

After these two crucial periods, the third and fourth epochs are relatively modern. The third era, which Shukla refers to as *Ritikaal* (period of procedure),[11] is the period when Hindi literature gains stability and delves into an elaboration of courtly aesthetics in poetry. This period sees the erotic aspect of poetry taking prominence. In the fourth period, *Gadyakaal* (period of prose), which is the modern period, prose emerges as a new genre where writers experiment. Shukla hails the rise of Bharatendu Harishchandra in this period for identifying what he sees as the nerve of his time: the need for love and esteem for one's nation and community (*Hindi Sahitya* 246). Amidst dependence under colonial rule, people express a sense of pride in their nation and love for their community as reflected in the works of Harishchandra. This is the culmination of the tradition of Hindi literature that, in Shukla's view, has flowed continuously across centuries and presents a glorious picture of India's civilization.

Shukla insists that the history of Hindi literature is not just a series of literary works arranged chronologically but an unobstructed tradition where, while the themes may change in different periods, the essence remains the

---

10 Natha and Siddha sects are the sub-sects of Shaivism combined with Tantric practices of Buddhism. The followers were known as Yogis/Jogis who mastered *hathyoga*, a strict form of yoga.

11 In this period, the figures and theory in poetry took priority over the content.

same ("Hindi ki Purv" 39). In each of the discussed eras, Shukla highlights the enduring tendency of the people to act as a community whose expression appears united in defending their society and country. In the *Veer-gatha kaal*, the fear and anger against Muslim invasions unite the voice of the people as a community, which is reflected in the songs of valor. In the medieval period, the *Bhakti kaal*, this community rises to the defense of its religious faiths. This unity of the people against an attack on their territory and community continues in the nineteenth century in the modern period. Hindi literature still expresses sentiments of nationalism and self-respect, this time against the oppressive colonial rule.

The idea of a community uniting under adverse circumstances and working for the *lok-sangrih* (preservation and sustenance of the community) is the essence of Indian civilization that Shukla constructs in his canon of Hindi literature. The sharing of experiences through a common language is what gives rise to a commonality of interests among the people. This community now shares interests in preserving its culture, territory, and religion. Shukla thus elevates a long-standing community of language speakers to the status of a modern national community that can overcome the immediate considerations of caste and kinship ties for an abstract ideal based in linguistic and territorial (i.e. national) identities. For Shukla, this community is based on a common Hindi identity capable of trumping all other interests for a united national cause.

The idea that there had always existed a community of people represented through Hindi literature is the key intervention made by Shukla. In the early part of the twentieth century when Shukla was writing, most of the prominent thinkers and leaders addressed the prevalence of differences in terms of language, caste, region, and religion in Indian society.[12] Some leaders thought this diversity acted as a hindrance in national development and in posing a united attack against colonial rule.[13] Others believed that

---

12   Leaders such as Gandhi, Bal Gangadhar Tilak, and Jawaharlal Nehru constantly attempted to resolve the question of lack of unity in Indian society. As mentioned earlier, Gandhi felt that masses like industrial workers, farmers, and women were disconnected from the independence movement as it was led by the elites. He also struggled with disenchantment among Muslims and lower castes. Nehru struggled with questions of the diversity of languages even in the post-independence period.

13   Most of the important leaders of the nationalist movement recognized the wide diversity of the country. But they also felt that this diversity posed concerns regarding unity, progress, and development. Lala Lajpat Rai called it "The Indian Problem" where the variety and diversity of interests produced complexities for the country (229).

these factions raised questions about an unequal and oppressive social order.[14] The discussion about the historical trajectory of these heterogeneities and schisms was important for most of these thinkers. For Shukla, the view of Indian civilization from a history of Hindi literature resolved this issue as national interest became the uniting concern for all factions.

By using an assimilatory concept of the Hindi language as his primary indicator, Shukla envisages the national community as a homogeneous group of speakers who share uniform interests. The streamlining of the history of Hindi literature allows Shukla to delineate a continuity of the national community that foreshadows their respective interests for a united cause. He ignores the multiplicity of influences limiting his focus principally to external intervention. Shukla also creates outsiders within Indian society by excluding the diversity of themes in literature, other languages, and their speakers from the history of Indian civilization. The national community that he constructs is an exclusionary group constituted of people who speak Hindi and protect the boundaries not just from external forces but also threatening voices within the community. Instead of highlighting the mutual learning that has been crucial in Indian civilizational past, the important aspect for Shukla is the maintenance of the status quo as he interprets it from the theme of *lok-sangrih*.

In my understanding, Shukla presents a metonymic idea of the nation through the prism of the Hindi language in which one part defines the whole of the nation. This form of nationalism values uniformity over diversity. The latter requires deliberation and conciliation among participants in a democratic setup. But once an overarching tradition of the Hindi language and the national community that this metonymy creates becomes the guiding framework for the nation, it dismisses the need for debate and discussion. Alternative articulations of sentiments as expressed in literary themes and cultures represented in languages and the values connected to them are denied recognition. The regional and minority voices are confined as sectarian, outside the definitional framework of the nation. Such a conception of the nation may seem to speak for all but is essentially predisposed to the interests of hegemonic political forces.

---

14 B. R. Ambedkar was one such voice who addressed the question of the caste system in India and the inhuman conditions it created for the lower castes.

4 The Hindi Language and Post-Independence Politics

The idea of the nation that emerges in Shukla's ideas of the Hindi language and Indian civilization gained popularity among many leaders of the independence movement. These ideas were circulated in the literary and political sphere through journals and meetings. Prominent politicians such as Mahatma Gandhi, Madan Mohan Malaviya, and Purushottam Das Tandon headed literary organizations (e.g. Hindi Sahitya Sammelan and Nagari Pracharini Sabha) which allowed a free flow of ideas from literary to the political sphere (Orsini 342). The propaganda for elevating the Hindi language to national status heightened as the voices for independent nationhood for India grew.

In the aftermath of the partition of India in 1947, the demand for Hindi in Nagari characters as the official language of the nation became more assertive since Urdu was now considered the language of Muslim secessionism. Alongside Malaviya, Tandon, Sampuranand, and Acharya Narender Dev, Govind Ballabh Pant, and Mahadevi Verma condemned efforts to support Urdu in the state assembly; in the independent nation no concession was to be made for Urdu or any variant of it while Hindi stood for the unity of the nation (Kudaisya 378–89).

Malaviya emphasized the role of Hindi for establishing self-rule and for the development of a national literature. For Tandon, Hindi was the prime identity of an ancient Indian civilization; it was the vehicle driving the social harmony and unity of its culture. For Sampuranand and Dev, politicians as well as editors and teachers with literary associations, Hindi was the only Indian language that could take over the dominance enjoyed by English. Francesca Orsini writes that despite their ideological differences, these "Hindi politicians" (331) held similar beliefs. They envisioned a homogeneous ancient India and trusted its traditions would unify and harmonize the newly independent Indian nation (273). Arguably, the ideas expressed by these prominent politicians can be traced to Shukla's works.

Further, these arguments also influenced the way different states came to view their status in the new nation in the post-independence polity. The Hindi-speaking state of Uttar Pradesh, then United Provinces, assumed a hegemonic role in Indian politics presiding over other, non-Hindi speaking regions. In 1947, a motion was brought in the United Provinces legislative assembly to change the name of the state. A committee was constituted by the state government to consider the various proposals and to suggest appropriate names. Among these proposals were the names Aryavarta, Aryavarta Pradesh, Hindustan, Bharat Khand, Ram Krishna Pradesh, and Uttara Khand. In 1949, the Cabinet and the Provincial Congress Committee approved the name Aryavarta (abode of the Aryas) with an overwhelming majority. However, once the decision was conveyed to the Constituent Assembly, it was shot down by the Central leadership (Kudaisya 356). It was found unacceptable to other provinces because it "signified not merely [United Provinces] but the whole of India" and it asserted unduly the United Provinces' claim to be "the super-most province" (R. K. Sidhwa qtd. in Kudaisya 355).

The names that were proposed by the United Provinces state legislators suggest that in their imagination, they were the inheritors of ancient Indian civilization. They belonged to the province where Aryans originally settled and wrote the Vedas (Kudaisya 354). In other words, the legislators assumed that the symbolic meaning of the name of the nation and the United Provinces could be the same. For them, the people of the United Provinces inherited and represented the national culture. It did not occur to them that the national culture had multiple contributors from states in the North other than the United Provinces (Punjab, Kashmir), Southern, Northeastern, and Western regions.

I see the continued pre-eminence of these ideas in the present scenario in Indian politics. In April 2017, the then President of India, Pranab Mukherjee, approved 117 recommendations made by the Committee of Parliament on Official Language (Sharma n. pag.). These recommendations aim to promote and spread the use of Hindi across the nation through steps like setting a compulsory minimum knowledge of Hindi for all government services at the central and the state levels, compulsory Hindi education in all educational institutions, compulsory communication in Hindi only for legislators from Hindi speaking states, and to derecognize schools that do not impart education in Hindi (*President's Order*). There is a symbolic value attached to Hindi as the foundation of national identity which, I propose, can only be fully understood through Shukla's concept of the language and the civilization as portrayed in its literary canon.

Orsini traces the beginning of the nationalist discourse of language to the authority of Mahavir Prasad Dwivedi, who, in the first decade of the twentieth century, forged the ideological link from *nij bhasha* (one's own language) to the *rashtra bhasha* (language of the nation). She argues that the metaphor of the mother employed by Dwivedi for Hindi encouraged a connection between mother tongue and motherland. This metaphor of mother tongue then became the basis for arguing that "Hindi was the real language of the province; that despite regional variants, it was one language, i.e. the mother tongue of all Hindus who lived in the United and Central Provinces, Bihar, Rajputana, Punjab, and the various states in central India" (Orsini 128). However, this rhetoric does not satisfactorily explain how the Hindi language came to symbolize ancient Indian civilization, a concept which can be found in Hindi politicians' statements until 1950.

In my understanding, it is in an elaborate construction of the idea of the Hindi language and the subsequent imagination of Indian civilization through literature that the common ground for Hindi as the national language for the entire nation emerges. In linking the Hindi language and Indian civilization, Shukla accords to Hindi the exalted status of the repository of Indian culture and tradition while the community of speakers is envisaged as the national community.

5   Conclusion

Shukla's idea of Hindi attempts to carve 'historical' and 'popular' reinforcement for his idea of nationalism in India. Through his discussion of Hindi literature, Shukla espouses a lived community involved in an everyday exchange of experiences and sentiments which permits a deep-seated affinity among its members. He envisages a version of Hindi in which any regional language that shares words and meanings with it comes within its ambit. Shukla provides a picture of the ideal religion in the form of determinate worship of Lord Rama as depicted in Tulsidas's *Ramcharitmanas* for the upcoming national community. His notion and canon of literature in Hindi create a strong compound currency of language and religion with an emphasis on uniformity.

Shukla's conception of the Hindi language implies that language has been employed to fill the contents and characteristics of the imagination of the collective called 'nation.' His idea of the Hindi language becomes a potent foundation for subsequent nationalisms. One reason behind this popularity is the unambiguous and homogenizing picture of the nation that this idea draws. This idea of Hindi and nationalism, however, was duly contested not just in Shukla's period but even later. Hazari Prasad Dwivedi, another prominent literary critic, did not dismiss the question of a united national sentiment or expression. But for him, unlike for Shukla, unity evolved; it had to be cultivated and negotiated. Despite these criticisms, Shukla's construction of the Hindi language and the idea of the nation rooted in it still holds relevance in the contemporary period as successive governments continue to emphasize Hindi for a uniform nationalism in the country.

Works Cited

Anderson, Benedict. *Imagined Communities: Reflections on the Origin and Spread of Nationalism*. Verso, 2006.

Balibar, Etienne. "The Nation Form: History and Ideology." *Becoming National*, edited by Geoff Eley and Ronald Grigor Suny, Oxford UP, 1996, pp. 132–50.

Dalmia, Vasudha. *The Nationalization of Hindu Traditions: Bharatendu Harishchandra and Nineteenth-Century Banaras*. Orient Blackswan, 2010.

Dasgupta, Jyotirindira. *Language Conflict and National Development: Group Politics and National Language Policy in India*. U of California P, 1970.

Dwivedi, Hazari Prasad. "Hindi Sahitya ki Bhumika." *Hazariprasad Dwivedi Granthawali*, edited by Mukund Dwivedi, Volume 3, Rajkamal Publishers, 2013, pp. 33–59.

Gellner, Ernest. *Nations and Nationalism: New Perspectives on the Past*. Cornell UP, 1983.

Gupta, Prachi. *Hindi Language and the Imagination of the Indian Nation: An Analysis of Ramchandra Shukla's Idea of Indian Civilization*. 2017. Jawaharlal Nehru U, Mphil Dissertation.

Harishchandra, Bharatendu. "Education Commission Evidence of Babu Harishchandra." *Bharatendu Harishchandra Granthawali*, edited by Hemant Sharma, Hindi Pracharak Sansthan, 1989, pp. 1056–60.

Inden, Ronald B. *Imagining India*. Indiana UP, 1990.

Kudaisya, Gyanesh. *Region, Nation, 'Heartland:' Uttar Pradesh in India's Body-Politic*. SAGE, 2006.

Kumar, Krishna. "Quest for Self-identity: Cultural Consciousness and Education in Hindi Region, 1880–1950." *Economic and Political Weekly*, vol. 25, no. 23, 1990, pp. 1247–55.

Mahajan, Gurpreet. *India: Political Ideas and the Making of a Democratic Discourse*. Zed, 2013.

Orsini, Francesca. *The Hindi Public Sphere 1920–1940. Language and Literature in the Age of Nationalism*. Oxford UP, 2002.

Premchand, Munshi. *Kuch Vichaar*. Saraswati P, 1945.

"President's Orders on the Recommendations of the Committee of Parliament on Official Language." *Committee of Parliament on Official Language*, 2011, www.rajbhasha.gov.in/sites/default/files/cpolreport9-chapter11eng.pdf. Accessed 9 Nov. 2018.

Rai, Lala Lajpat. "The Indian Problem: A Few Stray Thoughts." *Political Thinkers of Modern India*, edited by Verinder Grover, Volume 15, Deep and Deep Publishers, 1993, pp. 229–41.

Raina, Badri. "A Note on Language, and the Politics of English in India." *Rethinking English: Essays in Literature, Language and History*, edited by Svati Joshi, Oxford up Delhi, 1994, pp. 264–97.

Sonntag, Selma K. "The Nation Form: History and Ideology." *Ideology, Politics and Language Policies,* edited by Thomas Ricento, John Benjamins Publishing, 2000, pp. 133–50.

Sharma, Aman. "President Pranab Mukherjee Okays Call for All Speeches to be in Hindi." *Economic Times*, 17 Apr 2017, www.economictimes.indiatimes.com/news/politics-and-nation/president-pranab-mukherjee-okays-call-for-all-speeches-to-be-in-hindi/articleshow/58213420.cms. Accessed 9 Nov. 2018.

Shukla, Ramchandra. "Apni Bhasha par Vichar." *Ramchandra Shukla Granthavali*, edited by Omprakash Singh, Volume 4, Prakshan Publishers, 2007, pp. 14–22.

Shukla, Ramchandra. *Goswami Tulsidas*. Kranti Publications, 2007, pp. 26-36.

Shukla, Ramchandra. "Hindi aur Hindustani." *Ramchandra Shukla Granthavali*, edited by Omprakash Singh, Volume 4, Prakshan Publishers, 2007, pp. 62–75.

Shukla, Ramchandra. "Hindi ki Purv aur Vartman Sthiti." *Ramchandra Shukla Granthavali*, edited by Omprakash Singh, Volume 4, Prakshan Publishers, 2007, pp. 38–40.

Shukla, Ramchandra. *Hindi Sahitya ka Itihaas*. Nagari Pracharini Sabha, 1993.

Shukla, Ramchandra. "Urdu Rashtrabhasha." *Ramchandra Shukla Granthavali*, edited by Omprakash Singh, Volume 4, Prakshan Publishers, 2007, pp. 23–28.

PART 2

The Songs and Sounds of Nationalism

CHAPTER 4

Singing the Postcolonial Independent in Trinbagonian Calypso

Arhea Marshall

1   Introduction

On August 31, 1962, Trinidad and Tobago[1] celebrated Independence[2] from British colonial rule. The now twin-island republic was the second island nation in the Caribbean Sea to gain political sovereignty. It has been more than fifty years since this momentous event, with the effects thereof rippling through the Caribbean region, and furthermore setting the tone for the field of Caribbean postcolonial studies. What has changed since then remains to be addressed less from a political but more so from a cultural perspective. Independence as a political event has, of course, heralded real changes in the island state's internal governance and its relations to other nations. Yet independence also needs to be considered as a cultural turning point not only in the country's history but in the lives of its nationals. This chapter focuses on mapping out the crossroads of independence, the postcolonial, and nationalism in Trinbago. I will explore how nationalism developed and how it continues to operate in the Caribbean through the sung national narrative of Independence. Selected entries from the Trinbagonian Independence Calypso Contest of 1962 serve as concrete examples of how the national narrative is constituted by cultural practice. I argue that through calypso the postcolonial nation began singing itself independent over half a century ago and is still singing today. I will examine what was sung about the pre-Independence period, what came thereafter, and record the processes involved in singing the postcolonial independent.

---

1   In this essay, Trinidad and Tobago is used interchangeably with the term 'Trinbago.' Following suite with other scholars (e.g. Jocelyne Guilbault and E. M. Phillips), I will at times use Trinbago as a shortened version of Trinidad and Tobago.
2   I use Independence with a capital letter 'I' to refer to the political moment in which the nation acquired the status of self-governance similar to Ray Funk's usage of the term, and independence with the lower-case 'i' to refer to the ongoing process of cultural independence with its lasting impacts on national identity through the (re-)creation of national symbols and signs.

This chapter begins with a brief overview of calypso as a national art form, then it delineates the entangled development of calypso with Independence narratives. This is followed by a discussion of independence terminology, the cofounding presumptions, and the inconsistencies of *being* and *becoming* an independent nation. Then, the chapter shifts to the instrumentalisation of calypso and calypsonians and their perception as free social figures in the 1962 Independence Calypso Contest. I read their calypsos as a multistrand cord that sings independence from the colonial into postcolonial ranges of the nation. Considering the perspectives presented in the calypsos composed for the competition, I scrutinise who became independent from colonial rule. I then focus on the emergence of a symbolic 'home' in these texts that moves from the private into the public realm as the place of independence. I suggest how the calypsos construct images of home that contribute substantially to the goals of nation-building for Trinidad and Tobago. Finally, the chapter concludes by connecting these constructs of home with power relations in calypso and by looking toward the future of independence in the postcolonial Caribbean.

2   Calypso

The current literature on calypso spans comparisons to Shakespearean sonnets (Rampaul) and calypso's roots in the national identity of Trinbago through the history of emancipation, indentured labour, and nation-building (Dean; Dudley; Lashley; Liverpool). However, few scholars have focused on the intersections of calypso and independence, with the well-noted exceptions of Ray Funk and Hollis Liverpool. Calypso and its link with the carnival tradition, as it is celebrated in Trinidad and Tobago, show connections to West African griot culture and Catholic practices.[3] Ethnomusicologist Shannon Dudley highlights the hybrid nature and origins of calypso when he locates its roots in African song and European folk traditions (23). The relation to griot culture is established by the political role calypsos play in reflecting the higher classes and as a performance and communication practice involving not only the calypsonian and the subject of the song but also the audience. The subthemes that fall under the overarching category of calypso include political and social

---

3   Griots sang praises, celebrated and documented the lives and accomplishments of their hiring, typically African nobles. There are visible similarities to this tradition in Calypso, particularly during the reign of the British Crown in the Caribbean islands (Funk 1). Calypso is typically associated with carnival festivities, which have their roots in Catholic lenten traditions.

commentary, boasting, humour, smut (obscenity), nation-building, and road march (24–5).

The traditional Trinbagonian calypso can be traced back to the early twentieth century.[4] Under British colonial rule, broadcast calypsos were censored and amended until they corresponded to preset standards and the political agenda of the Crown to maintain the fortress of one-sided power relations (Guilbault 44). In the era of autonomous governance in Trinidad and Tobago, similar attempts have been made to "muzzle the calypsonian" (Lashley 5). As early as 1958, there were reports of calypsos of a "patriotic nature ... [in which] calypsonians were singing praises to [Trinidad and Tobago]" (Blood n. pag.). These tunes of praise have not necessarily entailed an acceptance of the reigning party nor the politicians in power, which distinguishes calypsonians from griots. This form of cultural censorship is reminiscent of the more well-known Caribbean music style reggae, which also thematises independence. In *Time and Memory in Reggae Music,* a study on temporality and remembrance in reggae, Sarah Daynes contends that Independence in Jamaica was an "event that provoked a social and political explosion that resulted in a phase of intense cultural creativity together with the idea of freedom and the affirmation of Jamaican identity" (28).

I claim that Independence challenged social and political norms, resulting simultaneously in an eruption of old ideological landscapes and a bloom of cultural practice in Trinidad and Tobago. In Jamaica's instance, reggae was born out of the Independence period; calypso, on the other hand, was born long before Independence.[5] However, the so-called Independence calypsos did indeed become for Trinbago what reggae was for Jamaican identity – they expressed freedoms, affirmed and celebrated national existence. As the national music and a sung archive of collective memory of Trinbago, calypso lends itself well to analysis.[6] Additionally, calypso plays a significant role in modelling how the nation and its citizens communicate about themselves and

---

4   The term 'calypso' is thought to be the anglicised version of the Hausa word 'kaiso,' which happens to be another form of Trinbagonian music. Trinbagonian calypso had its debut as popular music beyond the Caribbean region through the recording industry. The 1930s to 1950s were its heyday in the United States. As a seasonal performance art, it is also practiced in the Bahamas as part of Junkanoo and in Barbados as part of Crop Over (Dudley 23).

5   Another productive scope of comparison could be calypso and mento, a music form seen as a precursor to reggae with a similar musical formation to calypso.

6   Calypso is also referred to as "one of the indigenous music forms of Trinidad and Tobago" (Lashley 2). This is an assertion which again depicts unfortunate attempts at re-writing history with the initiation of a culture, in which 'indigeneity' becomes interchangeable with Independence and its practices.

their context, as noted by E. M. Phillips: "the calypso functions as a facilitator in a dialectic that is attempting to resolve contradictions or oppositions in either the socio-political or economic domains of Trinbago" (55). Despite its varying thematic categories, it can be said that calypso highlights inconsistencies. This characteristic makes it especially useful for the study of the differences between cultural practices of remembering becoming independent and the political status of being independent. These active and deeply rooted communicative modes which relate singers and listeners through the singing voice distinguishes calypso from most high-brow art. Calypso acoustically addresses the masses locally and internationally.

Beyond serving as a category of song, Independence became the social context shaping numerous calypsos, which spotlighted aspects of national life and pre-nationhood. In order to understand Independence in the current axiomatic postcolonial period, it is fundamental to identify the ways in which independence as an ideology of autonomy, liberty, self-sufficiency, and practice has always contributed to the process of becoming independent and vice versa.[7] Through the lyrics sung by the calypsonian, as a free person, a historian keeping record, and a voice of the masses, one can hear how postcolonialism is viewed, adapted, and interacts with political Independence.

3   Independent at Last

The transience of the moment of Independence fades in comparison to its ability to delineate effectively a redefinition of history. In the case of Trinbago, the date 31 August 1962 belongs to a chronology leading up to this moment of defining a shift in power relations from colonial politics.[8] This chronology includes the military service of Trinbagonians as well as other West Indians serving in British military regiments, the workers' movement during the world wars, the establishment of a labour party and nationalist movements. The outcome of Independence in Trinbago was a switch from crown colony rule to a parliamentary democratic republic, bearing in mind that Trinbago first became a republic in 1976. Independence then served as the music notes

---

7   Judith Shklar emphasises the interchangeability of the concepts of autonomy, independence, liberty, and self-sufficiency as they can carry the same meaning (xv). I, however, attempt to point out some of the differences in the affects of these terms in discourses about political Independence.
8   Colonial society in Trinidad and Tobago has been analysed extensively by sociologists. For an account of a politics of revolution and a politics of security, see Millette.

for the symphony of nation-building. Mighty Dougla sings in his entry to the inaugural Independence Calypso Contest in 1962: "To write out a new page in history / Independence at last we free / What a glorious moment in history / Independence at last we free" ("At Last We Are Free" 00:12–00:24, my transcription).[9] This verse exemplifies what Funk observes as a shift from "a respectful deference to colonial rule to a new postcolonial consciousness" (1). Dougla declares that, in the postcolonial moment of Independence, the long-sought freedom has been obtained. He refers to Independence as a "new page" and "a glorious moment" which he connects to the freedom of the "we." This freedom does not only reference a political change of guard but a transformation in the narrative of people's histories. Dougla orchestrates the sound of a divine moment that had been yearned for and was, as he sings, "at last" there. The fact that Dougla as well as other calypsonians such as Chiang Kai Shek, Lord Pretender, and The Hawk observe that Independence was received expectantly and even anxiously rebukes the view that it came as the natural progression to colonialism.[10] Not only calypsonians saw independence as a page-turner. The first national party of Trinbago, People's National Movement (PNM), attempted to "confirm its independence from the colonial powers not only politically but also culturally" through the establishment of a national culture, using state institutions which sponsored nationwide events to increase national pride in local cultural heritage (Guilbault 50).[11]

Independence did not come as time would have had it and it was not the original seed that planted a unified vision of continued progress in the

---

9   A note on the citation of lyrics in this essay: I received most of the recordings of the calypsos from private sources in digital form, many of them recorded from radio renditions. The songs by Lord Brynner and Mighty Sparrow can be found on *YouTube*. In both cases, I transcribed the lyrics myself. The songs are referenced by their titles here and in the Works Cited list which also states the calypsonian and not necessarily the lyricist/calypso writer. The timestamp (where available) identifies the location in the recording or *YouTube* video when the lyrics are sung.

10   In their 1962 Independence Calypso Contest renditions, Chiang Kai Shek sings repeatedly the refrain "Independence has come / I am sure you are glad / Tobago and Trinidad" (00:52–00:59, my transcription). Lord Pretender sings "Yes at last, at last / All our dreams are coming to pass" (01:26–01:32, my transcription), and The Hawk echoes these sentiments with "At last the dream of many years has finally come true / on the 31st August (of) 1962" (00:22–00:34, my transcription).

11   This was also the period when the national archives of Trinbago were created "to document the cultural practices of the nation" (Guilbault 50). The link between independence and documentation and thus accepting cultural practices as a part of the nation's identity is an enlightening topic, which I only touch upon with the example of calypso. Unfortunately, it is beyond the scope of this chapter to go into the role of the archive as a form of nationalism.

proceeding sovereign nations. In the case of Trinidad and Tobago and other Caribbean isles, Independence was a long fought for break from the colonial system of the British Crown. The postcolonial period was welcomed and embraced with hopes, joys, and expectations – particularly accompanying the announced freedom. This promise of freedom suggested a genesis moment, the start of something new. However, it was neither a beginning nor an end. Nationalist movements had already been active during the colonial period (Duke 80), envisioning former subjects who had been divided along lines of race and heritage as a united collective with equal rights. Likewise, in the postcolonial Anglophone Caribbean today, freedom is still in the process of being achieved.

4 Independence Calypso Contest 1962: Calypsonians and Calypsos

> I could write a song to make government strong
> I could write a song to bring government down. (Gypsy qtd. in Regis x)

Although 31 August marks the date on which the citizens of Trinbago officially gained and celebrated their Independence in 1962, the commemoration of the official proclamation had been prepared weeks earlier. As part of these preparatory procedures, on 9 August 1962, twelve calypsonians (see Table 4.1) vied for the title of inaugural Independence Calypso King and the accompanying prize money. In the ranks were known calypsonians, such as Mighty Sparrow and Lord Pretender, as well as outsiders and up-and-coming calypsonians, such as the unexpected first-place winner Kade Simon as Lord Brynner. Louis Regis, in his study of calypsos and their function in political opposition, reiterates the implications of the 1962 contest as he reports on the eight restagings of the 1962 Independence Calypso Competition in the decades following Independence, only a few of which took place in years of large-scale commemoration (19–20). The calypsonian has been widely studied as "a man of words" and the mouthpiece of the masses (Abrahams qtd. in Dudley 23; Lashley 2). The relationship between calypsonians was shaped by the various calypso competitions hosted before and after Independence in the private and public sectors, respectively (Guilbault 50). As early as the 1930s, there was already a proto-nationalist movement tightly knit within the Calypso community (Regis 198).

We see thus that the calypsonian is not a passive peripheral figure displaced in Trinbago's postcolonial history; the calypsonian and his calypso exist in the country's political and cultural centre. Funk states that "the calypsonian's conscience is clearly postcolonial and his Independence from the Mother Country ... [through] calypso seems to be complete" (11). Moreover, he suggests that "the calypsonian is not finished with wrestling to achieve a sense of self, personal independence and nation-building as the disengagement from colonialism continues" (12). Using the calypsonian as a proxy for national independence, it can be said that the nation is not finished striving. In fact, we may ask what it should strive after. Independence was not a milestone that represented an arrival, but rather a marker along the voyage of creation. Calypsonians accomplish this perspective through frames and masks. One of the tools calypsonians use as a mask is their sobriquet (Phillips 57). The calypsonians who performed in the 1962 Independence Contest sported sobriquets, which evoked images of animalism, strength, nobility, and figures known through the various heritages of the Trinbagonian people and international pop culture stars. Aldric Farrell performed under the sobriquet (Lord) Pretender, Clifton Ryan as The Mighty Bomber, Nathaniel Randolph as Nap Hepburn, Valentine Winston as Chiang Kai Shek,[12] Ken Hayword as The Hawk, Percy Obington as Mighty Stryker, Christopher Laidlow as Lord Cristo, Claytis Ali as Mighty Dougla, Sonny Francois as Mighty Power, Kade Simon as Lord Brynner, and last but not least, Slinger Francisco as Mighty Sparrow,[13] as can be seen in Table 4.1.

The fact that there have been few new competitions and more re-enactments of the original contest testify to calypso's role not just as a stable but also a generational archive which passes through the mouths of the people. It does so not as an artefact but as a vibrant and enduringly current comment on the experiences of past, present, and future generations. In the following section, I will analyse a selection of calypsonians, Lord Brynner, Mighty Sparrow, Nap Hepburn, Chiang Kai Shek, and The Hawk, and their entries in the 1962 Independence Calypso Contest in order to develop an understanding of what Independence meant to Trinbagonians at the time.

---

12 He is also known with orthographic variations of his sobriquet.
13 My research on the background biographies of the competing calypsonians reveals that some sobriquets have multiple carriers (Mighty Bomber also refers to Kenny Cooper, Hawk also refers to Keith Barrow, and Mighty Stryker/Striker also refers to Dennis Alleyne), and some calypsonians have altered their sobriquets throughout their careers (e.g. Nathaniel Randolph, Slinger Francisco).

TABLE 4.1 The Independence Calypso Contest 1962 – calypsonians, their entries, and the 2012 re-enactment calypsonians[a]

1962 Calypsonian	Calypso entry	2012 Re-enactment calypsonian
(Lord) Pretender	"Praise to Dr Willie"	Regeneration
The Mighty Bomber	"The Meaning of Independence"	Luta
Nap Hepburn	"This Is My Flag"	Versatille
The Mighty Sparrow	"A Model Nation"	Deavon Seales
Chiang Kai Shek	"Independence (for Trinidad)"	Crazy
Lord Brynner	"Independence 1962"	Bally
The Hawk	"Build Our Nation"	Raskommanda
(Mighty) Stryker	"We Could Make It"	Regeneration
(Lord) Cristo	"Ah Glad for Independence"	Michelle Henry
(Mighty) Dougla	"At Last We Are Free"	Krisson Joseph
(Mighty) Power	"Hurrah for Independence"	Chalkdust
Lazy Harrow	-	-

[a] This table was constructed on the basis of a flyer from the 2012 University of Trinidad and Tobago's Academy of Arts, Letters, Cultures and Public Affairs entitled "Re-enactment of The Independence Calypso Contest 1962" (provided via the National Archives of Trinidad and Tobago), in addition to Nasser Khan's 2012 article on the contest. The calypsonians' sobriquets or official names used at the time they performed are given. In parentheses, I have included the sobriquet modifiers, where they were listed.

5 Independent from Colonial Rule? The Postcolonial Sings Forth

The winning calypso in the 1962 contest, Lord Brynner's "Independence 1962," merges the historical highlights leading up to Independence with future expectations towards independence beyond it occurring "democratically" and "constitutionally" to "educationally" and "conscientiously" ("Independence 1962" 02:13–2:30, my transcription). In the fourth stanza of the calypso, Lord Brynner hesitantly declares the beginning of the postcolonial era by announcing that colonial rule has come to an end: "Whether your status is high or low, / The time has come to pass when there is no more / Colonial rule I believe / So together we will aspire, together we will achieve" (03:32–03:43, my transcription). This excerpt presents the chequered history of colonial rule as the antithesis of a collective nationalism in which the people strive and succeed together. The indirectness of Lord Brynner's statement – he does not refer to British rule but instead claims that there is no colonial rule of any imperial power over the islands – highlights the subversive nature of calypso. The opening lines of this stanza address the audience, "whether your status is high or low." Lord Brynner directs this statement to everyone residing on the islands regardless of their economic and social status. His inclusive announcement to them all suggests that "no more colonial rule" should be felt throughout any ranks of society. Furthermore, he refers vaguely to "the time" when colonial rule no longer is the form of governance on the islands, avoiding a specific unit of time such as "day," "year," or "decade." As a result, Lord Brynner appears to assert that all nationals, his referenced "we," can initiate collective progress.

In Trinbago's case, the process of becoming a unified 'we' entailed a revolution of identity for its diverse population. There were at least three incorrect assumptions which were rarely challenged in European colonial philosophies of the nineteenth century and which actively divided the population. These assumptions were:

a) [t]hat non-white people were incapable of governing themselves and therefore needed the constant guidance of Europeans.
b) [t]hat systems of governance brought to this region by Africans and Asians (who formed the majority of the population) had to be quickly discarded and replaced by Western, Christian-derived norms. What was British was best and those who could not conform were effectively shut out of the process.
c) [t]hat in order to ensure European dominance every effort was made to implement the policy of *Divide Et Impera* (Divide and Rule). This caused each ethnic or religious group to see each other as the enemy and not the manipulative colonial overlords. (The Parliament of Trinidad and Tobago 6, emphasis in original)

The postcolonial population needed to redefine itself through an advancement away from these conventions. Ella Shohat echoes what Lord Brynner communicates in his calypso; she explains that, aligned with their shared prefix, 'postcolonial' and 'post-independence' imply a progression (104). Nonetheless, both terms relate to a previous system or moment – colonialism and Independence.

Shohat thus urges us to consider the precise reference points of independence: from what and to what is Trinbago supposed to become independent? One answer is independent *from* colonial rule both politically and culturally. Shohat's terms emphasise a distinct break with colonialism (111); yet the prefix also connotes a "movement beyond," "a passage into a new period and a closure of a certain historical event or ages, officially stamped with dates" (101). This historical closure did not end the desire of calypsonians to continue singing about independence beyond Trinbago's Independence. Calypsonians continued to sing of moments – acoustic glimpses of independence in African nations and even in other Caribbean islands (Funk 10). This reveals another aspect of Lord Brynner's verse. Although his calypso is set in the context of Trinbago's declaration and celebration of Independence, he prophesies as well that other nations will also be free of colonial rule. The 'post-colonial' in calypso then becomes not a static period of linear time but rather a set of dynamic reference points, correlated with the dates and moments when various nation-states attained their respective Independences. Colonial rule did not only have effects on the political system of Trinbago, it influenced the everyday lives of the islands' residents just as Independence had to extend to independence in the societal realms beyond politics.

Calypso contributed to the decolonisation process in Trinbago as it propagated independence and deconstructed the assumptions concerning British rule and the division of Caribbean peoples in the pre-Independence period as I cited above. Funk points out that the first- and second-place calypsos from Lord Brynner and Mighty Sparrow look "to past leaders and [are] a celebration, a griot's homage to a remarkable achievement, but [that they] celebrate the achievement of becoming free and independent of the kingly rule by a foreign power that had preceded" (10). This celebration carries on throughout the generations with two of the calypsos from the 1962 Independence Calypso Contest even remaining on the "25 Top Patriotic Calypsoes (1962–2012)" list, as published on the website of the Trinidad and Tobago Guardian, one of the nation's daily newspapers (Blood n. pag.).

The relationship between colonialism and independence lingers and connects their subsequent forms: post-Independence "invokes an achieved history of resistance, shifting the analytical focus to the emergent nation-state ... it implies a nation-state telos ... Whereas 'post-colonial' suggests a distance from colonialism, 'post-independence' celebrates the nation-state" (Shohat 107). The attempts to distance the Independent nation from colonialism and to celebrate the nation simultaneously can become precarious, especially when an absolute distancing cannot be achieved in a globalised world. A discrepancy in these two goals is visible in the process of legal appeals in Trinbago, where the final appeals, as of 2005, were still being dealt with by the British Privy Council (Funk 11). In a personal interview I conducted with Trinidadian writer Earl Lovelace, we discussed the Independence Movement and the state of culture in Trinbago. He asked, "What is independence doing?", to which I responded by reframing his question to incorporate the cultural dimension of independence. I asked, "What is calypso, what is Independence calypso still doing?" Building on thoughts from Lars Eckstein and Jocelyne Guilbault, I conceive of calypso as still amplifying the "production of the nation" (Guilbault 40), as well as the diaspora outwards. Independence calypso is still performing in ways which have not been previously considered, such as creating images of Trinbago as a primeval home, which, I argue, accounts for its "intricate medial and material realities," that even in the twenty-first century aid in theoretical and staged engagements "with the world as it is today" (Eckstein 454).

6   Independent to Be at Home

"Model Nation," performed by Mighty Sparrow, combines a reflection on the plenteous national resources of Trinbago and portrays a nation that even in the weeks before its momentous Independence was worthy of being called a model nation. Calypsos depicting and building the model nation did not stop in 1962; in the following years and decades, more calypsonians began to lend their voices to the creation and strengthening of the national narrative. The image of the model nation has taken on a new shape for postcolonials: it represents the space where they are a family and no longer colonial children and celebrate in diverse ways. The nation, as the product of Independence, identifies its people as the "most precious resource," even in the national constitution (Hamel-Smith 41); in short, the nation offers a space, a home, to be independent.

Returning to "Independence 1962," Lord Brynner sings in the chorus that this space belongs to everyone referring to the new nationals, a synthesis of "your" and "my" proprietorship. Trinbago belongs to the national postcolonial collective – as "one happy family," it no longer belongs solely to colonial authorities: "Because this is your land, just as well as my land / This is your place and also it is my place / So let us put our heads together / And join like one happy family / Democratically, educationally, / We'll be independently [sic]". ("Independence 1962" 02:13–2:30, my transcription). The physical land is given the spotlight in the chorus, which is repeated unmodified four times throughout the song. The political transition from the Crown Colony of Trinidad and Tobago to the state of Trinidad and Tobago had not transformed the materiality of the country. Yet it was already in the thoughts of those who saw themselves as connected to the land through vocation and heritage that the ownership of the national terrain was changing hands. The immediate period of independence as sung in Lord Brynner's calypso had the effect of allowing Trinidadians and Tobagonians to envision their diverse population as a singular unit, "one happy family" with a common home. Everything that had meaning for the people of the country in their daily lives before and after becoming Independent happened in this home and made up its cultural practice (Grossberg 98). Fortunately, Independence does not stop at the door. Brynner welcomes independence into the democratic and educational rooms in the house of the new nation, to which calypsonian The Hawk intoned a foundation.

The Hawk's calypso, as its title "Build Our Nation" implies, is a model nation-building calypso: his text streamlines the new nation with little reference to its past and focuses firmly on the tasks ahead. He produces a textbook example of what Guilbault describes as the outcome of calypso competitions; they "render audible and visible ... imaginations of longing, belonging, and exclusion" (40). He sings repeatedly in the chorus: "No more shall we the children be of Mother England / Thanks to Dr Eric Williams independent we now stand / The fight for freedom is over / But our task has just begun / So with the help of God let's join together / And build our new nation" (00:47–1:12, my transcription). The Hawk alludes to Great Britain's political role as the mother of the colonies. His passage references the monarchical familial rule (the Queen as the mother in the royal family, the subjects as children). It is a striking allusion to the hierarchy of coloniser and colonised as a relation of kinship, in which the islands are defined to be in a subordinate position relative to the colonising power. The familial bond between mother and child is one of co-dependence in which the children are unable to outgrow their inferior status. The Hawk's metaphorical use of maternity in "Build Our Nation" also signals the emotions of leaving behind a former home, gaining a new identity, and having the authority to define this home on new terms. The Hawk refers to the process of gaining Independence as "the fight for freedom," by which he could mean emancipation, liberation from indentureship, freedom to rule the nation from the inside, and to be a sovereign land with cultural claims (a flag, a history, and practices like dance, music, traditions); however, it neglects the fight for legislative sovereignty in Tobago, which is still ongoing. The Hawk marks this battle as finished. He deems Dr Eric Williams, the first Prime Minister of Trinidad and Tobago, with his patriarchal icon-like status as centrally responsible for this feat. Simultaneously, Hawk acknowledges that "our task" commences, which I read as an invocation of the advancement of cultural independence and nation-building. Hawk's suggestion that this endeavour needs to be completed "with the help of God" points to the mammoth task of building a new nation not on a blank canvas but out of a patchwork of ethnic heritages and varied social and political experiences on the island.

Nap Hepburn, in his "This Is My Flag," encourages the listener to celebrate in multiple ways:

> For independence and for freedom for one and all
> Let us sing, let us dance and let us all pray
> To celebrate Trinidad and Tobago's Independence day
> So regardless of your race, your colour or class
> Let we love one another, drink up and play we mas. (0:54–1:17, my transcription)

Nap Hepburn here seems to spur on celebration and the acknowledgement of independence and freedom. He is the only one of the competitors who explicitly separates Independence from freedom. He further highlights aspects of Trinidad and Tobago's culture through which he constructs the image of a postcolonial nation-home as a place to sing, dance, pray, celebrate, love, drink, and be merry. Like Lord Brynner, he also urges his audience to celebrate irrespective of their race, colour, or class, whereby he provides an inclusive vision of the new nation.

In the Independence calypsos, home is presented as a weapon, a place of ownership which formerly had been violently suppressed and in independence home symbolises an attack on the former possibilities offered to colonial subjects. Home is sung as a place of rights, belonging, and thus full identity. Calypso serves as an arena for participatory culture, including defence, privileges, celebration, and lineage. Concurrently, home, that is, the new nation-state, emerges as a postcolonial space of transition moving from identifying with Great Britain as the central reference point and home to identifying with building the new nation worthy of equal, if not greater, acceptance.

7 "Trinidad, if Not also Tobago"

In the foreword to his study on the colonial society in Trinidad, James Millette notes that his arguments are valid for "Trinidad, if not also Tobago" (vii). This phrase sums up the imbalance in Independence literature concerning Trinidad and Tobago. The scarce references to Tobago can be traced back to the colonial history of the islands (Matthews n. pag.). Their joint history began when Tobago was made a dependent of the Crown Colony of Trinidad. This perspective falls flat when Tobago's role as a leader in New World political development is considered, namely as the first system to have a bicameral legislature as early as 1768. This fact has been overshadowed by its later status as a ward of Trinidad beginning in 1898. From this point until Independence a new singular colony was born out of two: the Crown Colony of Trinidad and Tobago (The Parliament of Trinidad and Tobago, 13–4). This status carried the connotation of Tobago being 'dependent on Trinidad' politically and economically. Eric Williams alleged in a session of the Legislative Council in 1956 that "Tobago had exchanged the neglect of United Kingdom imperialism for the neglect of Trinidad imperialism" (qtd. in Dumas 16). Before and after national Independence motions were brought forth to establish an internal self-government on Tobago, none of which have accomplished it.[14] Although there was a tendency to sing about Trinidad independent of Tobago in the 1962 Independence Calypso Competition, there are a few calypsos which bring the discontinuity of the joint Independence to light.

Lord Pretender sings in the first stanza of his entry "Praise to Dr Willie" of the change in the demonym used to identify him: "Long time they used to call me Tobagonian / But I am now a full-fledged Trinidadian" (0:35–0:42, my transcription). In the first stanza of his calypso, Chiang Kai Shek sings "Independence (for Trinidad)" and motions to Tobago in the refrain: "independence has come/ I am sure you are glad/ Tobago and Trinidad" (0:52–0:57, my transcription). Dougla sings repeatedly in his refrain both "Trinidadians and Tobagonians [to] lift your voice[s] loud and clear"[15] ("At Last We Are Free" 0:35–0:40, my transcription), which again shows a marked distinction in the identity of residents of the two islands. Interestingly, the demonym 'Trinbagonian' has been most likely used since political Independence. Additionally, we see a hope for a shared future in Sparrow's refrain: "Trinidad and Tobago will always go on" ("A Model Nation" 1:00–1:06, my transcription). The singular time Trinidad and also Tobago is mentioned in Lord Brynner's winning calypso is in the form of a question: "What's the proper meaning (Independence) for Trinidad and Tobago (Independence)"? ("Independence 1962" 0:47–0:51, my transcription).[16] This question encompasses the scope of my investigation from seeing

---

14   During his terms in the Trinidad and Tobago Legislative Council from 1946–1960, A.P.T. James fought continuously for Tobago to return to internal self-government. Then, in 1971, A.N.R. Robinson called for internal self-government for Tobago as a platform for his Democratic Action Congress. For a list of reasons debated as to Tobago's right to self-government, see Dumas 17.

15   I see Mighty Dougla's use of "voice" (singular) as an attempt to foreshadow the two islands as constructing a unified voice through Independence, while his explicit referencing of "Trinidadians" and "Tobagonians" expresses the reality of identities perceived as separate.

16   The text in parentheses indicates backing vocals sung intermediately in the calypso.

Independence as a political event but moreover an everyday experience transforming the nation from becoming to being independent, which is recorded as such by the calypsos.

8 Coda: The Postcolonial Independent

The lyrics of the 1962 Independence Calypso Contest entries show that independence aimed to change systems of land ownership, belonging (citizenship), family ties and generational knowledge, democracy, and education. It also released the power in celebration and communal identity across the islands. The calypsos remind us of the overarching task with which independence rings forth: to continue building into the postcolonial. This is the timely and timeless aspect of the musical archive; it narrates to each generation and their specific contexts anew. The calypsos written for and performed on the occasion of Trinbagonian Independence speak to the power held in non-systematic archives such as oral tradition. Calypso is a record keeper of historic events occurring in the present. These archived experiences capture moments of expectancy, relationships between places, people, and political power. These experiences are celebrations and informal gatherings to establish and boast the agency of having a and being at home, the future of freedom, even the different forms independence takes. Investigating moments of concrete change and ideological turns reveal that although the nation is postcolonial, it is still gaining independence, a process in which the calypso is still playing its part. This is the case for Trinidad and Tobago and assuredly numerous other postcolonial nations. Non-systematic archives such as national songs shed a new light on the significance of the independence melody in the moment as well as into the present and future.

Works Cited

"A Model Nation." 1962. Mighty Sparrow. *YouTube*, uploaded by cool4rocknroll, 18 July 2011, www.youtube.com/watch?v=_VL3p_9e4QY&feature=youtu.be.

"At Last We Are Free." 1962. Mighty Douglas. Personal recording.

Blood, Peter Ray. "Patriotism through Calypso." *Trinidad and Tobago Guardian Online*, 31 Aug. 2012, www.guardian.co.tt/article-6.2.429921.47e04b1fea. Accessed 20 Oct. 2020.

"Build Our Nation." 1962. The Hawk. Personal recording.

Daynes, Sarah. *Time and Memory in Reggae Music: The Politics of Hope*. Manchester UP, 2010.

Dean, Darryl. *Calypso as a Vehicle for Political Commentary: An Endangered Musical Species.* 2015. Carleton U, Master's thesis.

Dudley, Shannon. *Carnival Music in Trinidad: Experiencing Music, Expressing Culture.* Oxford UP, 2004.

Duke, Eric. "A Beacon for a Unified and Independent West Indian Nation: Charles Petioni, Black Diaspora Politics and Transnational Nation-Building." *In the Fires of Hope: Trinidad & Tobago at 50,* vol. 2, edited by Debbie McCollin, U of the West Indies, 2016, pp. 78–101.

Dumas, Reginald. "Tobago and Constitutional Development in the Context of the Parliamentary Process." *Evolution of a Nation: Trinidad and Tobago at Fifty.* Hansib, 2012, pp. 13–24.

Eckstein, Lars. "Sound Matters: Postcolonial Critique for a Viral Age." *Atlantic Studies,* vol. 13, no. 4, 2016, pp. 445–56. doi: 10.1080/14788810.2016.1216222.

Funk, Ray. "In the Battle for Emergent Independence: Calypsos of Decolonization". *Anthurium: A Caribbean Studies Journal,* vol. 3, no. 2, 2005, n. pag. doi: 10.33596/anth.48.

Grossberg, Lawrence. *We Gotta Get out of This Place: Popular Conservativism and Postmodern Culture.* Routledge, 1992.

Guilbault, Jocelyne. "Audible Entanglements: Nation and Diasporas in Trinidad's Calypso Music Scene." *Small Axe,* vol. 17, no. 9.1, 2005, pp. 40–63. doi: 10.1215/-9-1-40.

Hamel-Smith, Timothy. "Re-Engineering the Constitution of Trinidad and Tobago for Participation and Performance." *In the Fires of Hope: Trinidad & Tobago at 50,* vol. 1, edited by Patrick Kent Watson, U of the West Indies, 2015, pp. 41–9.

"Independence." 1962. Chiang Kai Shek. Personal recording.

"Independence 1962." Lord Brynner. *YouTube,* uploaded by mightysparrowaz, 23 June 2012, www.youtube.com/watch?v=K_ItBb6GqNI&feature=youtu.be.

Khan, Nasser. "Lord Brynner, 1962 Independence Calypso King." *Trinidad and Tobago Guardian,* 1 September 2013. www.guardian.co.tt/entertainment/lord-brynner-1962-independence-calypso-king-6.2.407014.fea8fe3331. Accessed 20 Oct. 2020.

Lashley, Lynette M. "The Calypso as 'Political Football' in Trinidad and Tobago: The Status of Contemporary Political Commentary (a Work in Progress)." The 26th Annual Caribbean Studies Association Conference, 27 May–2 June 2001, pp. 1–23. *University of Florida,* ufdcimages.uflib.ufl.edu/CA/00/40/02/59/00001/PDF.pdf.

Liverpool, Hollis. "Calypso: Speaking Truth to Power, 1962–2012." *First Magazine,* 2012, pp. 90–5.

Lovelace, Earl. Personal interview. 6 Feb. 2018.

Matthews, Gelien. "Tobago – In and Out of Colonial Empires." *Caribbean Atlas,* edited by Romain Cruse and Kevon Rhiney, 2013, www.caribbean-atlas.com/en/themes/waves-of-colonization-and-control-in-the-caribbean/waves-of-colonization/tobago-in-and-out-of-colonial-empires.html. Accessed 29 Nov. 2020.

Millette, James. *Society and Politics in Colonial Trinidad*. Zed Books, 1985.

Phillips, E. M. "Recognising the Language of Calypso as 'Symbolic Action' in Resolving Conflict in the Republic of Trinidad and Tobago." *Caribbean Quarterly*, vol. 52, no. 1, 2006, pp. 53–73, doi: 10.1080/00086495.2006.11672287.

"Praise to Dr Willie." 1962. Lord Pretender. Personal recording.

Rampaul, Giselle. "Shakespeare, Empire, and the Trinidad Calypso." *Borrower and Lenders*, vol. 9, no. 2, 2015, pp. 1–25.

"Re-enactment of The Independence Calypso Contest 1962." *Academy of Arts, Letters, Cultures, and Public Affairs, University of Trinidad and Tobago*. 2012. Flyer provided by the National Archives of Trinidad and Tobago.

Regis, Louis. "The State and the Song: Our Anniversary of Independence Calypso Competitions." *In the Fires of Hope: Trinidad & Tobago at 50*, vol. 2, edited by Debbie McCollin, U of the West Indies, 2016, pp. 198–212.

Shklar, Judith N. *Freedom and Independence*. Cambridge UP, 1976.

Shohat, Ella. "Notes on the 'Post-Colonial'." *Social Text: Third World and Post-Colonial Issues*, vol. 31/32, 1992, pp. 99–113. doi: 10.2307/466220.

The Parliament of Trinidad and Tobago. *Evolution of a Nation: Trinidad and Tobago at Fifty*, Hansib Publications, 2012.

"This Is My Flag." 1962. Nap Hepburn. Personal recording.

CHAPTER 5

Singing the Nation: The Condition of Englishness in the Lyrics of PJ Harvey and Kate Tempest

Sina Schuhmaier

1   Introduction: The 'Condition of England,' Empire, and the 'Crisis of Englishness'

The 'crisis' of English national identity is ubiquitous. While the rhetoric of crisis has accompanied most discussions of Englishness, the definite article commonly used in these contexts is not only misleading given the persistence of a crisis that has been conjured up since World War II; it furthermore presupposes a tacit agreement on the existence of this crisis whose nature is all but lucid but then deemed unnecessary to define. More crucially still, the talk of crisis implies that English national identity was once unspoilt, and it complies with a discontent with modernity and its narratives of lost community and identity (Chase and Shaw 6–8). Thus, the construction of a 'lost identity' serves the myth-making of nationalism, more precisely a nationalism in the Romantic tradition, which presents itself as an antidote to modernity and claims continuity with a 'national' past. This past, when Englishness was supposedly still intact, then becomes a site of nostalgic longing which provides a fragile, if not polluted ground upon which to imagine contemporary identity. Essentialising national identity, the phantom of loss resurrects a fictitious homogeneity that nurtures nationalism and its myth of purity and is unable to accommodate Britain's postcolonial present. In this chapter, I will redefine the notion of Englishness in crisis and analyse conceptions of Englishness that come to the fore in the song lyrics of PJ Harvey, a singer-songwriter who has crossed the genres of punk, blues, alternative, indie, and folk rock, and in the work of the spoken word and hip-hop artist Kate Tempest. Both artists sense a crisis of national identity within the generic framework of writing the 'Condition of England.' I will argue that PJ Harvey's account simultaneously deconstructs and bemoans a 'lost England' and thus articulates a national identity that is bound up with the past and the pastoral, while Kate Tempest confronts the 'postcolonial melancholia' that informs Harvey's unwitting nostalgia. In order to fully comprehend both artists' takes on Englishness, the context of British popular music briefly sketched below will be vital.

In the field of literary production, the 'Condition of England' genre emerged in the first half of the nineteenth century in response to the 'social problems' industrial capitalism brought about. Since then "it has been produced at various subsequent moments when novelists have felt compelled to reflect on a state of perceived national crisis" (Perkin 101). Thus, the genre not only illuminates conceptions of national identity; it also opens up a space where said identity can be interrogated. It is then all the more significant that writing the 'Condition of England' has systematically excluded the very same England's imperialist undertakings. Elizabeth Gaskell's *North and South* (1854), for instance, stages a "binary conflict" between factory owners and workers that enables social criticism but simultaneously conceals the third party involved in the cotton industry, slaves on US-American plantations (Parry 40).[1] Simon Gikandi introduces his *Maps of Englishness* with some reflections on the 'Condition of England' as diagnosed by literature to detect a tendency in collective consciousness and literary studies to dissociate imagined Englishness from colonialism. Gikandi recounts his discovery that "the versions of Englishness that I had inherited as a child of colonialism, the Englishness of F. R. Leavis, an Englishness in which the national culture found its untroubled refuge in the works of its great writers ..., were the result of a *false totality*" (xvii, emphasis added).[2] For Gikandi, "Englishness, far from emerging from a body of stable value and shared experiences, had been produced by a continuous conflict between the center and its Celtic and colonial peripheries" (xvii). The state of postimperial Britain further obscures its entanglements with colonialism. If the mutual production of identity of colonies and the imperial centre was ever acknowledged, it surely ended with decolonisation. Britain after the empire then either declares a thorough cut, a 'zero hour' and locates its 'rediscovered' identity in a domestic past that evades the period of imperialism,[3] or, and both mechanisms are not mutually exclusive, it dwells in "imperial nostalgia" (21), which similarly distorts the past, preventing it from becoming meaningful for the present.

---

1 In line with Edward Said's findings on the English novel in *Culture and Imperialism* (Parry 47), the empire provides a decorative backdrop of Indian shawls and the like in Gaskell's novel, but it is by no means conceived of as integral to the condition of England.
2 In light of the prevalence of this "false totality" in the discipline of history, scholars such as Antoinette Burton have advanced the 'new imperial history,' "which has sought to write the history of the British Empire as a whole, by placing metropole and periphery within the same analytical frame" (Thompson 455).
3 A process analogous to the nationalist movements in many former colonies (Gikandi 4, 16).

This perspective wilfully ignores and denies the irony that, according to Gikandi, "the disappearance of empire has made what used to be purely colonial issues ... a domestic affair and thus turned the colonial event into probably the most cogent force driving the demand for new histories and narratives of identity in the metropolitan space" (24). In other words,

> [t]he age of decolonization has not marked the radical dissociation between England and its colonies, as nationalists on both sides of the divide had expected; on the contrary, the large migration of formerly colonized subjects into the metropolitan center itself has created temporal conjunctures and disjunctures in areas previously marked by the mythology of the island nation. (49)

Gikandi's work thus allows me to rethink the 'crisis' of Englishness as follows: while I do not aim to downplay the disruptive impact developments like deindustrialisation have had on (working-class) identities, or the fact that Britain has seen crises after World War II, I want to stress that 'the crisis of *Englishness*' does not result from Britain's demise as a world power or the immigration to Britain from its former colonies, but from a specific conception of national identity. I locate this crisis in the very fact that national identity has been conceived without understanding (former) colonies as part of the (post) imperial self, that is, in the failure or refusal to reflect the constitutive roles of imperialism, colonialism, and the postcolonial in imaginations of Englishness.

The psychological dimensions of this cognitive elision have been analysed by Paul Gilroy, who discovers Britain in the grip of a postcolonial melancholia that rests on a pathological inability to process the loss of the empire. Britain finds itself in a state of collective paralysis that precludes the full history of its imperialism from becoming a means of self-understanding: "Once the history of the empire became a source of discomfort, shame, and perplexity, its complexities and ambiguities were readily set aside. Rather than work through those feelings, that unsettling history was diminished, denied, and then, if possible, actively forgotten" (Gilroy 90). This absencing of empire cultivates a nationalist soil where xenophobia may spread, for Englishness turned tabula rasa is cleansed and purified to such a degree that it cannot but be contaminated. In other words, the *crisis of Englishness that postcolonial melancholia is* is covered up by 'crises' of immigration and national decline. Gilroy illustrates how the "silence" cast over Britain's (post)imperial responsibilities "feeds an additional catastrophe: the error of imagining that postcolonial people are only unwanted alien intruders without any substantive historical, political, or cultural connections to the collective life of their fellow subjects" (90). With the notion of a "convivial culture" that draws attention to "multiculture [being] an ordinary feature of social life in Britain's urban areas" (xv), Gilroy identifies a powerful alternative to postcolonial melancholia, but neither of the two dominant modes of thinking Englishness after the British empire, imperial nostalgia and the recourse to an insular past, seek to overcome postcolonial melancholia by confronting

> the painful obligations to work through the grim details of imperial and colonial history and to transform paralyzing guilt into a more productive shame that would be conducive to the building of a multicultural nationality that is no longer phobic about the prospect of exposure to either strangers or otherness. (99)

2   'Pop Englishness' between Subversion and Affirmation

The persistent neurosis of postcolonial melancholia manifests itself in troubled images of past glory that haunt the collective consciousness in unexpected places. In Salman Rushdie's 1994 short story "The Courter," set in the early 1960s, the adolescent narrator's family has moved from India to London, where his mother and nanny are racially insulted in public. While this incident is deplorable but not surprising (the story mentions Enoch Powell's infamous 1968 "Rivers of Blood" speech in passing),[4] it is striking that the two offenders are described as physical doubles of The Beatles, and similarly, that some thugs who beat up the porter of the family's residence earlier in the story bear resemblance to Mick Jagger. What is the connection between 60s popular music, idolised by the narrator, racism, and the postcolonial? Rushdie's story highlights that the link between ideas of Englishness (as epitomised by the music of The Beatles and Stones) and the postcolonial is severed. Not only does this severance engender xenophobia; British popular music furthermore perpetuates the exclusion. This omission disregards the fact that British music has emerged as the synthesis of diverse styles from all over the world, notably from the African diaspora, and that artists with diverse backgrounds make up the canon of British popular music. When it comes to performing Englishness,

---

4   This somewhat confuses the chronology of the story, which supposedly unfolds from 1962–64, but so does the reference to The Beatles and The Rolling Stones as national icons. Rushdie perhaps favours his point on the omnipresence of racism in British culture over the reliability of his narrator's memory, or he might toy with the boundaries between fact and fiction as in other works.

British music has again and again silenced the stories set in contact zones such as those told by dub music; stories of resistance, transformation, and hybridity. Musical confrontations with traces of the empire have therefore been explosive. As much becomes evident from Britain's conflicted skinhead scene, where an affinity with ska-music has concurred with the rise of a fascist subculture.

Ironically enough, British popular music from the 'British invasion' in the 1960s to 1990s Britpop has meanwhile celebrated a *triumph* of Englishness considered even to outweigh its 'crisis.' This music – mostly falling into rock-related genres – has been eager to attack the nation, its symbols, and institutions and yet, within these acts of subversion, fundamentally relied on its own 'Englishness.' A vast strand of British popular music has not only been successful *as British music*, it has also built this success on its elaborate *performance of Englishness*, its "pop Englishness" (Cloonan 47), and its attendant exclusion of the postcolonial. The obsession of this share of British popular music with national identity[5] is indeed symptomatic of postcolonial melancholia, which here reveals its full scope: this music is stuck in a recurring pattern of actively attempting to escape the cognitive structures of postcolonial melancholia while falling back on its very categories at the same time. Thus, a curious double dynamics of attacking the nation(alist) and thereby affirming it holds sway over many artists. This oscillation does not affect all but a considerable branch of British popular music from the 1960s onwards, and though it may swing more decidedly towards one pole (transgression, subversion, ironisation) or the other (anachronism, nostalgia, mourning), it remains caught in-between.

The 'triumph' of Englishness is thus overtaken by its crisis; it is haunted by an uneasy ambivalence of simultaneous rejection and longing. Martin Cloonan, too, observes how "ambiguity and ambivalence often accompanies pop's Englishness" (48). The past that is left unprocessed by postcolonial melancholia returns as a continual point of reference, so that the gaze backwards, even if it is demystified, becomes the defining motif of much of British music – but it is a gaze directed towards a projected past. Hence, The Kinks ridicule the delusion of a bygone "land of hope and the gloria" (01:40–3) and yearn for "Victoria" at the same time, and The Smiths declare that "The Queen Is Dead" in a song that "alternately attacks the old order and mourns it" (Brooker 31).[6] The Libertines, an indie-rock band founded in 1997, similarly debunk the chimera of "The Good Old Days" in their eponymous song only to conjure them

---

5 Laid bare, for instance, in its practices of rendering the Union Jack a cultural icon (Groom 276–88).
6 Former front man and singer Morrissey's more recent pronouncements, meanwhile, manifest an outright postcolonial melancholia (Eckstein 216).

up in the end: "these are the good old days" (01:06–8). The profitability of a seemingly reinvigorated but not reformed Englishness, of 'Cool Britannia' (the echo of 'rule Britannia' is indeed instructive) has had its share in cementing the dynamics of postcolonial melancholia. This commercialisation reached its peak with Britpop, which constitutes such a worrying cultural and medial phenomenon because it no longer ambiguously oscillates. Rather than struggling with the state of the nation, traditionalism, and the national past and history, Britpop straightforwardly indulges in postcolonial melancholia.[7] This is matched, in Simon Reynolds's words, by Britpop's "symbolic erasure of Black Britain … Even more than the insularity of Britpop's quintessentially English canon …, it's the sheer whiteness of its sound that is staggering" (n. pag.).

The marketable liaison of Englishness and British song re-established after the 1960s in Britpop has since then survived – The Libertines provide a prominent example, and titles such as Elton John's 1997 version of "Candle in the Wind" thrive on this trend – but it has also been challenged by artists diagnosing the state of the nation in more reflective terms. These artists acknowledge and negotiate the empire and its consequences and may thus design a still difficult but less pathological 'national' identity that always already transcends the national. Primarily voices from backgrounds of migration and diaspora have formulated forceful alternatives to the tropes of postcolonial melancholia.[8] Asian Dub Foundation's "Real Great Britain," analysed in detail by Lars Eckstein, dismantles New Labour's 'Cool Britannia' campaign as complicit in a self-serving neoliberal politics whilst critically examining Britpop's morbid celebration of Englishness, thus providing one example of how "alongside and against the melancholic pedagogy of Britpop, alternative visions of Englishness have emerged from within the Asian British music scene" (218). Artists such as M.I.A. or the grime scene similarly recast notions of Britishness, articulating in particular a London identity based on the multiple, fluid identifications the city's pluralistic makeup and convivial culture offer.

In what follows, I will read two contemporary song lyrics – PJ Harvey's "The Last Living Rose" and Kate Tempest's "Europe Is Lost" – that in raising the 'Condition of England' question exemplify some of the tendencies of British popular music after the cultural turning point of Britpop and therefore also illustrate the pitfalls as well as the possibilities of the genre in the twenty-first

---

7 Lars Eckstein is more tentative, but he also "read[s] the success of the *media-phenomenon* 'Britpop' as another belated symptom of postcolonial melancholia" (217, emphasis in original).
8 A more conscious reflection of contemporary Britain in British music has also been sought by white artists such as The Clash; Gilroy similarly lists Billy Bragg and The Streets (96).

century. Both songs were written prior to Brexit, but both anticipate this further symptom of postcolonial melancholia. Neither Harvey nor Tempest promote Brexit; in fact, both warn against an isolation from Europe and a nationalist glorification of England. Yet, in doing so, "The Last Living Rose" displays the very oscillation described above that proves structurally akin to and uncannily foreshadows the workings of postcolonial melancholia which have (co-) produced Brexit. In contrast, Kate Tempest forcefully revises the 'Condition of England's' systematic blindness towards the (post)colonial by emphasising the need to process the imperial past. "The Last Living Rose" was released in 2011 on PJ Harvey's *Let England Shake*, and "Europe Is Lost" appeared as a single in 2015 and then on the 2016 album *Let Them Eat Chaos*. With these albums, both songwriters locate themselves in a prophetic tradition of diagnosing and decrying the 'signs of the times' like Thomas Carlyle[9] or William Blake two centuries earlier, as announced by the albums' imperative titles that infuse their work with a momentum of overcoming established structures. PJ Harvey, however, also follows in the footsteps of Blake's "Jerusalem," which marries Englishness with the "green & pleasant Land" (line 16) of the Romantic pastoral idyll[10] and thus excludes from the imagined topography of Englishness those urban, postcolonial spaces that Kate Tempest deliberately attends.

3   "Take Me Back to Beautiful England": PJ Harvey's Pastoral Elegy

Tropes of the pastoral are firmly entrenched in the English literary tradition and have come to visualise a landscape of imagined Englishness. Elton John's aforementioned "Candle in the Wind" is a case in point. When he, or, to be more accurate, his lyricist Bernie Taupin, rewrote the lyrics of "Candle in the Wind" for the deceased Princess Diana in 1997, he rephrased the line "Goodbye Norma Jean" (John and Taupin, "Candle" [1973] 00:07–9) – a reference to Marilyn Monroe – as "Goodbye England's rose" (John and Taupin, "Candle" [1997] 00:07–9). Accordingly, "and I would have liked to know you, but I was just a kid" ("Candle" [1973] 00:53–8) became "and your footsteps will always fall here, along England's greenest hills" ("Candle" [1997] 00:53–9). These lines

---

9   Carlyle's views on slavery, conveniently swept under the carpet in discussions of the 'Condition of England,' provide one example of how questions of race and racism are excluded from English cultural history (Gikandi 57–8).

10   This, of course, is the popular reception of "Jerusalem," which Blake wrote in the preface to *Milton a Poem*, but neither titled nor published as an individual poem. Blake's own cosmology is vaster and more complex.

draw on stock ingredients of Englishness provided by the pastoral: the English rose, this peculiar equation of a woman's natural beauty with England and its landscape, and "England's greenest hills" upon which the feet of its inhabitants tread, a theme promoted by the "feet in ancient time, / Walk[ing] upon Englands [sic] mountains green" (1–2) of Blake's "Jerusalem." The mourning for Diana, then, catalyses the mourning for a national identity as embodied by the princess that is felt to have been lost. The pastoral is most efficient when it denotes a space (and life) lost – it is an idealised projection that comforts because it does not exist, because it is available only in the imagination. Therein, it complies with the workings of nostalgia, which similarly succumbs to "[t]he temptation ... to conjure up a past defined not by the painstaking investigation of the historical record but by positing a series of absences, of negatives" (Chase and Shaw 8); that is, the deficient present is redeemed by an "imagined past" (9) towards which one's yearning may then be directed. PJ Harvey's title, "The Last Living Rose" – that is, England – reflects all this, but the song does not manage to imagine England differently. This limitation is "troubling," Gilroy remarks in another context, "because it excludes all urban and metropolitan spaces from the forms of moral and aesthetic rearmament that are necessary if the country is to be reinvigorated and restored" (115).

The issue at stake is that PJ Harvey deconstructs the topos of pastoral England and at the same time evokes it. In the end, the song mourns the decay of an England whose rottenness it has exposed. Lyrically, "The Last Living Rose," not unlike "Candle in the Wind," is an elegy. In his reflections on postcolonial melancholia, Gilroy discusses Matthew Arnold's "Dover Beach" as a poem that conveys a similar mood in contemplating the speaker's relation with England. Arnold expresses, according to Gilroy, an "imperial melancholy" that preceded melancholia (90–1). Facing the white cliffs of Dover (assumed to have inspired the term 'Albion') "where today's asylum seekers still fear to tread" (90) and the sea below, symbolic reminders of Britain's insularity that might either signify its openness or isolation, the speaker chooses retreat to the private over political engagement as signalled by the near French coast. As the sensed metaphysical void of modernity coincides with an intuition of the failure of the project of modernity in imperialism, it gives way to a "tendency to become sad and pensive in the face of the empire's demanding geopolitical responsibilities" (91). Dover's cliffs then also stand for the British withdrawal into an Albion of beautiful, awe-inspiring landscapes. This is what Martin Aston has in mind when he observes that "[t]he title of Polly Harvey's seventh album, 2007's White Chalk [sic], seemed to address England's psycho-geography by way of Dover's iconic coastline" (n. pag.). On the preceding album, "The Last Living Rose" evokes said "psycho-geography" forcefully, its two first lines exclaiming "Goddam'

Europeans! / Take me back to beautiful England" (00:05–13; lines 1–2).[11] In their almost parodic exaggeration, the lyrics here attack the Brexit-esque rhetoric of scapegoating and isolationism, but what appears to be subversive mimicry shifts to straightforward yearning with the invocation of "beautiful England," a phrase that reverberates powerfully through Harvey's intonation.

Her lyrics, then, stage a retreat – in the words of Matthew Arnold, "on the French coast the light / Gleams and is gone" (lines 3–4), replaced by the much more comforting "beautiful" English landscape – although the following lines in the same verse challenge precisely this flight into an 'untroubled' England by unveiling its ugly downside: "& the grey, damp filthiness of ages, / and battered books and fog rolling down behind the mountains, / on the graveyards, and dead sea-captains" (00:14–32; 3–5). England is in decay; it has gathered dust and probably gone mouldy in a "grey, damp" environment. Its antiquatedness also applies to the knowledge it has produced, an outdated, crumbling Western epistemology contained in "battered books." Fog shrouds the situation and makes it hard to see clearly (a metaphor that Kate Tempest will pick up). Furthermore, the "fog *rolling down* behind ... *mountains*" (emphasis added) neither lifts over rolling hills, nor does it paint a sublime Romantic picture; it creates an oppressive scenery stretching to the inevitable destination towards which this England is heading: "graveyards." These cemeteries are populated by "dead sea-captains," once the bearers of empire, now rotting in their graves. This morbid landscape, the English pastoral distorted, does not only declare the old order expired; it deflates the glory attached to it. Most importantly, it links the scenery of domestic, rural England with the nation's global actions and responsibilities and therefore counteracts the amnesia of postcolonial melancholia. With regard to the full album, Abigail Gardner even goes so far as to argue that through sampling diverse materials, Harvey "maps out the differences within Englishness that are a mirror of a contemporary national identity, a patchwork of diasporic and transatlantic conversations, journeys and relationships" (146). Yet what is at work in the above lines is a melancholic mourning that has nothing to do with having processed the empire in its full scope.[12] Burying the empire also covers

---

11 © Hot Head Music Ltd. Kobalt Music Services II Ltd. All Rights Reserved. International Copyright Secured. The lyrics as quoted in this chapter follow the spelling and line organisation provided in the liner notes of *Let England Shake*. Otherwise, my transcription of the lyrics is based on the performed song, whose lyrics differ from the printed text in parts. In case of inconsistencies, the quotes given reference the performance. For each quote, minutes and seconds based on the recording as well as line numbers based on the printed lyrics are provided.

12 The lesson in (new imperial) history precluded here is perhaps redeemed by the album's thematic focus on war and especially the battle of Gallipoli. The music videos for the

up its postcolonial presence. The lyrics thus remain caught up in postcolonial melancholia, unable to escape the attraction of "beautiful England" and its pastoral topography whilst being repulsed by what this England implicates. These are the antipodes between which the song oscillates, and its antithetical structure continues to organise the two succeeding verses.

The speaker's location shifts in the following lines: "Let me walk through the stinking alleys / to the music of drunken beatings, / past the Thames River, glistening like gold / hastily sold for nothing" (00:33–52; 6–9). She now wanders the streets of London, a city that does not provide an alternative to pastoral England but is fathomed in Romantic terms valorising nature *ex negativo*. The parallels to Blake's "London" poem are conspicuous. Reminiscent of Blake's persona, who observes, listens, and laments, PJ Harvey's speaker decries the 'corrupted city,' where she is confronted with stench, alcoholism, and violence. The Thames "glistening like gold" briefly converts the cityscape into a Wordsworthian vision, but the next line returns to Blake and thereby refigures the simile of the previous line: the Thames is "hastily sold," commercialised – "charter'd" in Blake's terms ("London" line 2) – "like gold." At the same time, mention of the Thames, whence many a journey into the 'heart of darkness' was commenced, refers back to the nation's imperial endeavours, characterised here as pointlessly driven by economic greed.

An anaphora links the second to the final verse, which leaves the city by route of the river for a view over the countryside:

> Let me watch night fall on the river,
> the moon rise up and turn to silver,
> the sky move,
> the ocean shimmer,
> the hedge shake,
> the last living rose quiver. (01:15–37; 10–5)

This scene is peaceful only on the surface. Not only does "the moon ... turn[ed] to silver" suggest a profitability like that of the Thames; what is more, nature in these lines is on the move. Active verbs used in conjunction with elements of nature – "night fall[s];" "the moon rise[s];" "the sky move[s]," and so on – forebode a climactic finale to close the song. Similar momentum is built up structurally, as an imperative phrase introduces all three verses. The anaphoric "[l]et me ... "-construction of the second and third verses' first lines in turn

songs on *Let England Shake* were directed by war photographer Seamus Murphy. Again, however, themes of loss and mourning prevail.

echoes the album title *Let England Shake*. England, however, is not shaken to its foundations in "The Last Living Rose:" it "quiver[s]." The momentum evaporates; the three verses push one another but do not culminate in a cathartic chorus; the song stays stuck. The England envisioned as a "last living rose" is outdated and barely alive, as the lyrics emphasise, and yet, the last *living* rose proves resilient. Sung by PJ Harvey, "quiver" acquires a sighing quality; it is accentuated by a preceding pause, stretched in duration, and alternates in pitch, all of which renders the speaker's expression mournful. Her mourning evinces her attachment – she is discernibly unable to let go of "the last living rose" and thus partakes in its preservation. "The Last Living Rose" is a nostalgic elegy for a 'lost England,' yet all the while it sees how faulty this England has always been. It is no coincidence that "quiver" rhymes with (the "sold") "river" as well as "silver" through assonance and consonance. One of the critiques weighed here is that honoured notions of England and national identity are likely to serve as mere facades of capitalist enterprises. The rhyming might also hint beyond the lucrative days of the empire and at England's economic situation in 2011, though. When Harvey's album was released, England, still severely affected by the financial crisis of 2008, found itself in the grip of the austerity measures. Phases of economic depression, David Cannadine argues, have repeatedly led to the emergence of "a recognizable and distinctive public mood …: withdrawn, nostalgic and escapist, disenchanted with the contemporary scene, preferring conservation to development, the country to the town, and the past to the present" (258–9).

The pastoral setting of "The Last Living Rose" reiterates tropes of nostalgia most prominently found in heritage film and television. As Rosalía Baena explains, "the established iconography of heritage production" includes characteristic shots of a "pastoral landscape" (124) and more specifically "exterior long shots of untouched rural landscapes, characterised by rolling hills, hedges, farmland, some trees and an expanse of clear sky" (Cardwell 120 qtd. in Baena 124). Although the first verse of Harvey's song deliberately undermines the pastoral and its use in the creation of "a nostalgic vision of a lost way of life" (Baena 124), an evocative image of the pastoral recurs at the latest with the mention of a "hedge" in verse three. This is reinforced by the music video of "The Last Living Rose," which intercuts PJ Harvey performing the song in what is most probably a living room with a view of the sea through a window (the same point of view is held by Matthew Arnold's persona), implying that the camera follows her gaze. Thereupon, the camera cuts to, amongst others, shots of a framed photograph of cliffs and sea hanging on a wall; lavish, magical trees and bushes covered in fog lit by sunbeams; a cornfield on a hill; a map of England placed on a rose-printed tablecloth; and grassland and a lake with birds and a pony. In the lyrics, though, the "hedge *shake*[s]" (emphasis added), and similarly, upon closer inspection of the music video, there are cracks in the wall with the photograph, and a dark shadow begins to cover the cornfield prompted by the line "fog rolling down behind the mountains." What is more, these shots that equate England with the pastoral (mapping it on rose-print) are juxtaposed with more sinister and unsettling pictures of waste and alienation in contemporary England, such as that of a worn out, naked children's doll placed next to a pan filled with water and leaves, and they are framed by a human skeleton on display in a museum appearing at the beginning and end of the video.

This awareness and criticism of England's desolate condition, however, does not automatically release the speaker from the mechanisms of its pathology. In her monograph on *PJ Harvey and Music Video Performance*, Gardner argues that *Let England Shake* "might be positioned as part of a critical contestation of Englishness" (139) and characterises Harvey as a radical poet given the inclusivity and emotional appeal of her take on national identity. While this certainly describes the attempt the album performs, I would contest Harvey's 'radicalism.' "The Last Living Rose" meets my earlier description of British music that sits uneasily with postcolonial melancholia and nevertheless yields to it, a conflict that produces a constant lyrical ambivalence. In the establishing and closing shots of the video, the camera again views through glass, but this time, it is placed inside the showcase with the exhibit. The speaker who gazes upon decaying England is herself caught within a moribund state of mind (this is where the withdrawal commenced in "Dover Beach" leads). "[T]he last living rose quiver[s]" – England is ailing, but the song really ponders the 'Condition of England' in portraying the *condition of Englishness*. Englishness itself is in poor condition, failing to escape the paralysing dynamics of postcolonial melancholia, instead compulsively "[t]ak[ing] [itself] back to beautiful England."

4   Europe, America, London Lost: Kate Tempest's Indictment of Past and Present Wrongs

Kate Tempest, who locates herself first and foremost in Europe rather than solely in England, reverses the idea of a 'lost England' and 'lost identity' by claiming that "Europe," including Britain, "is lost" (01:05–6; 15);[13] it is doomed.

---

13   The lyrics of "Europe Is Lost" are extensive and will not be reproduced in full. The notation follows the spelling and line breaks provided in Tempest's long poem *Let Them Eat Chaos*, which has been set to music on the eponymous album. Otherwise, my transcription of the lyrics is based on the performed song, whose lyrics depart from the printed

Her album *Let Them Eat Chaos* explores the lives of seven individuals living on the same London street. We encounter them insomniac, worried, and isolated at 4.18 in the morning. These personae allow Tempest to disentangle her structural critique of the capitalist system from the fates of individuals, who, under neoliberal conditions, blame themselves for their failures when blame should be sought within the system. Before shifting into the more manifesto-esque tone of "a state-of-the-world address" (Clark n. pag.), "Europe Is Lost" introduces Esther, an overworked carer who has just returned from work. A "black and white picture / of swallows in flight" (00:26–8; 14) on her wall that could be taken straight out of the music video of "The Last Living Rose"[14] is contextualised differently here,[15] within the dismal existence of Tempest's character who lives in a run-down flat next to "dump[ed] ... mattresses" (00:05; 13), other people's disposed signs of life. While Arnold and Harvey present us with a motion of gazing out (only to return to concerns of the inner mind), Tempest makes the listener look through the walls that encapsulate Esther, adopting a popular device of 'Condition of England' texts[16] that serves their agenda of social documentary.

Seeing is a central motif in Tempest's work – her 2014 poetry collection *Hold Your Own*, for instance, channels the blind prophet Tiresias – and the "mattresses" of the first lines foreshadow the interlinked trope of sleep. In "Europe Is Lost," Tempest draws on the metaphor of sleep (and thus the inability to see) to denote the ideological workings of the capitalist system, which is conceived as "traffic," constantly "moving" (01:18–9; 15) in perpetual stagnation. Individuals are lulled into oblivion: "To sleep, to dream, to keep the dream in reach. / ... *What am I gonna do to wake up?*" (02:03–12; 17, emphasis in original). The drowsy culture unmasked in the song is one of self-absorbed selfie-taking, consumerism, and corporate-controlled hedonism that only on the surface appears as individual self-fulfilment. This 'veil of illusion' or perverted "dream" inhibits one from awakening to and thereby *seeing* the reality of global crises,

---

text in parts. In case of inconsistencies, the quotes given reference the performance. For each quote, minutes and seconds based on the recording as well as page numbers based on the poem are provided.

14 In fact, a black and white photograph of birds in flight covers the DVD of Murphy's music videos for *Let England Shake*.

15 The black and white music video of "Europe Is Lost" faithfully illustrates Tempest's breathless lyrics through an overwhelming plethora of fast cut images from TV and film recordings, amongst them pictures of right-wing politicians, unrest, human suffering, and excessive consumerism.

16 John Lanchester's 2012 novel *Capital*, for instance, also enters the lives of several residents of one London street by zooming in into their houses (Perkin 104, 107).

"massacres" (03:00; 19), environmental concerns, and the ruthless exploitation of the Global South (the continuation of imperial endeavours). Kate Tempest formulates a knowledge that surfaces but is ultimately repressed in PJ Harvey's "The Last Living Rose" much more consequently. What Tempest's speaker does is precisely to wake up and see "[a]ll of the blood that was bled for these cities to grow, / ... I see it tonight / in the stains / on my / hands" (01:35–44; 16). This vision includes an awareness of the colonialist, imperial past and historical responsibility and guilt to which the ignorance of contemporary culture extends. The speaker fashions herself as a biblical prophet of this culture, whose Christ-like stigmata bear evidence of sins. Tempest's stance cannot escape a somewhat elitist degradation of the 'ignorant masses,' just as her critique of capitalism reduces the totality of ideology to the question of partaking or resisting. Nonetheless, her impetus to "wake up" is also a call to arms to overcome the blindness of postcolonial melancholia, "to work through," like she does, "the grim details of imperial and colonial history and to transform paralyzing guilt into a more productive shame," as Gilroy puts it. Looking at the state of the nation, however, "the land / where nobody / gives a fuck" (05:18–21; 24)[17] and postcolonial melancholia sticks firmly, Tempest diagnoses: "Europe is lost / America lost / London lost / still we are clamouring victory. / ... we have learned nothing from history" (01:05–14; 15).

The social malaise Tempest outlines here reveals itself in spontaneous outbursts of violence provoked by the essential meaninglessness of nights out. What is more, the inability to process imperial history finds expression in a xenophobic and nationalist discourse – "England! / England! Patriotism" (03:34–5; 19) – exemplifying postcolonial melancholia par excellence. The figure of the immigrant in particular serves as a scapegoat. Such a discourse is powerfully invoked and dismantled in the context of Tempest's lyrics, illustrating that the whitewashing of national identity may be a comfort once one realises that the neoliberal dream will not lead to fortune, and a source of orientation in times of global "chaos," as Tempest's album title puts it. Gilroy exposes how the guilt felt in relation to the empire is aroused by the appearance of and in a preceding step projected onto immigrants from the former colonies, who "represent all the discomforting ambiguities of the empire's painful and shameful but apparently nonetheless exhilarating history" (100). The pathology, of course, begins with the elision of Britain's imperial history and its postimperial implications, as Tempest's lyrics show.

---

17 A rhyme with "buck" in the preceding lines (05:17; 23) once again invokes PJ Harvey.

5   Conclusion: Chronicling the Condition of Englishness

There is nothing triumphant to Englishness in either PJ Harvey's or Kate Tempest's lyrics. Both chronicle a crisis of national identity that is not a crisis of loss but of oblivion. Thereby, they prove the versatility of the 'Condition of England' genre, adapting it to the twenty-first century by revising its conventionalised blanks. Nevertheless, "The Last Living Rose" is inhibited from tackling the crisis it decries. Following numerous musical predecessors – such as The Kinks, who mock imperial nostalgia in "Victoria" but fall prey to its appeal in the meantime – PJ Harvey's song oscillates not merely paradoxically, but dialectically. It voices an inherent contradiction of rejection and attraction that interlinks with images of pastoral England, while Kate Tempest shifts her setting to the city where Gilroy locates the existence of a convivial culture. "Europe Is Lost" echoes the words of Simon Gikandi:

> And thus one is almost obliged to begin by calling attention to the unstable zones and contested boundaries that conjoin and divide metropolitan cultures and colonial spaces, to the frontiers in which the dialectic of imperialism is played out, and to that ill-defined space in which the experience of empire and its long past seem to cast an aura – which is also an anxiety – over contemporary culture. (2)

Kate Tempest's confrontation is uncomfortable (and it cannot avoid overt didacticism at some points, comparable to its literary ancestors addressing the 'Condition of England'), but it is productive. "Europe Is Lost" undermines the phantasm of purity that prompts the search for identity in a fabricated past and emerges in pastoral landscapes of identity. In other words, "The Last Living Rose" invalidates the pastoral but laments its corruption as a way of life all the same – England shakes – while "Europe Is Lost" hails chaos for an England thus conceived.

Works Cited

Arnold, Matthew. "Dover Beach." *The Poems of Matthew Arnold*, edited by Miriam Allott, 2nd ed., Longman, 1979, pp. 253–7.

Asian Dub Foundation. "Real Great Britain." *Community Music*, FFRR, 2000.

Aston, Martin. "PJ Harvey Let England Shake Review." *BBC*, 2011, www.bbc.co.uk/music/reviews/bgm5/. Accessed 17 Nov. 2018.

Baena, Rosalía. "Performing Englishness: Postnational Nostalgia in *Lark Rise to Candleford* and *Parade's End*." *Emotions in Contemporary TV Series*, edited by Alberto N. García, Palgrave Macmillan, 2016, pp. 118–33. doi: 10.1007/978-1-137-56885-4_8.

Blake, William. "Jerusalem ('And Did Those Feet in Ancient Time')." *Milton a Poem in 2 Books: Preface*, pl. 1. *The Complete Poetry and Prose of William Blake*, edited by David V. Erdman, Anchor Books, 1988, pp. 95–6.

Blake, William. "London." *Songs of Innocence and of Experience*, pl. 46. *The Complete Poetry and Prose of William Blake*, edited by David V. Erdman, Anchor Books, 1988, pp. 26–7.

Brooker, Joseph. "'Has the World Changed or Have I Changed?': The Smiths and the Challenge of Thatcherism." *Why Pamper Life's Complexities? Essays on The Smiths*, edited by Sean Campbell and Colin Coulter, Manchester UP, 2010, pp. 22–42. doi: 10.7765/9780719095023.00006.

Cannadine, David. *The Pleasures of the Past*. Norton, 1991.

Cardwell, Sarah. *Adaptation Revisited: Television and the Classic Novel*. Manchester UP, 2002.

Chase, Malcolm, and Christopher Shaw. "The Dimensions of Nostalgia." *The Imagined Past: History and Nostalgia*, edited by Christopher Shaw and Malcolm Chase, Manchester UP, 1989, pp. 1–17.

Clark, Alex. "Kate Tempest: Let Them Eat Chaos Review – A State-of-the-World Address." *The Guardian*, 9 Oct. 2016, www.theguardian.com/stage/2016/oct/09/kate-tempest-let-them-eat-chaos-review. Accessed 8 May 2018.

Cloonan, Martin. "State of the Nation: 'Englishness,' Pop, and Politics in the Mid-1990s." *Popular Music and Society*, vol. 21, no. 2, 1997, pp. 47–70. doi: 10.1080/03007769708591667.

Eckstein, Lars. *Reading Song Lyrics*. Rodopi, 2010. doi: 10.1163/9789042030367.

Gardner, Abigail. *PJ Harvey and Music Video Performance*. Ashgate, 2015.

Gaskell, Elizabeth. *North and South*. 1854. Edited with an Introduction by Patricia Ingham, Penguin, 1995.

Gikandi, Simon. *Maps of Englishness: Writing Identity in the Culture of Colonialism*. Columbia UP, 1996.

Gilroy, Paul. *Postcolonial Melancholia*. Columbia UP, 2005.

Groom, Nick. *The Union Jack: The Story of the British Flag*. Atlantic Books, 2006.

Harvey, PJ. "The Last Living Rose." *YouTube*, 28 July 2011, www.youtube.com/watch?v=B4gSzkkOZO0. Accessed 17 Nov. 2018.

Harvey, PJ. "The Last Living Rose." *Let England Shake*, Island/Universal, 2011.

John, Elton, and Bernie Taupin. "Candle in the Wind." *Goodbye Yellow Brick Road*, MCA Records, 1973.

John, Elton, and Bernie Taupin. *Something about the Way You Look Tonight / Candle in the Wind*. Rocket, 1997.

Lanchester, John. *Capital*. Faber and Faber, 2013.

Parry, Laura. "Remapping Elizabeth Gaskell's *North and South* within a Global Network." *Oxford Research in English*, no. 2, 2015, pp. 37–52.

Perkin, J. Russell. "John Lanchester's *Capital*: A Dickensian Examination of the Condition of England." *Journal of Modern Literature*, vol. 41, no. 1, 2017, pp. 100–17. doi: 10.2979/jmodelite.41.1.07.

Reynolds, Simon. "Reasons to Be Cheerful: The Case against Britpop." *Frieze*, 11 Sept. 1995, www.frieze.com/article/reasons-be-cheerful-0. Accessed 8 May 2018.

Rushdie, Salman. "The Courter." *East, West*, Vintage, 1995, pp. 143–71.

Tempest, Kate. "Europe Is Lost (Official Video)." *YouTube*, 1 Feb. 2017, www.youtube.com/watch?v=QSVyyykaEO0. Accessed 17 Nov. 2018.

Tempest, Kate. "Europe Is Lost." *Let Them Eat Chaos*, Caroline (Universal Music), 2016.

Tempest, Kate. *Let Them Eat Chaos*. Picador, 2016.

Tempest, Kate. *Hold Your Own*. Picador, 2014.

The Kinks. "Victoria." *Arthur (Or the Decline and Fall of the British Empire)*, Reprise, 1990.

The Libertines. "The Good Old Days." *Up the Bracket*, Rough Trade, 2002.

The Smiths. "The Queen Is Dead." *The Queen Is Dead*, Rough Trade, 1986.

Thompson, James. "Modern Britain and the New Imperial History." *History Compass*, vol. 5, no. 2, 2007, pp. 455–62. doi: 10.1111/j.1478-0542.2007.00391.x.

PART 3

Nationalisms in Postcolonial Popular Culture

CHAPTER 6

Pop Culture: A Vehicle of State Nationalism in India

Idreas Khandy

1   Introduction

This chapter explicates how the realm of popular culture becomes imbricated in the project of making a national culture and what that means for high politics. To that end, the chapter takes a genealogical approach to demonstrate how the postcolonial Indian state has instrumentalised the realm of pop culture to reify the image of an Indian nation that is always facing threats, both internally and externally. The chapter argues that the recent increase of acts such as vigilante violence, the crackdown on dissent, and attacks on the institutions of higher learning in India can only be understood when the role of pop culture in furthering a narrative of the country as a Hindu nation[1] that is perpetually under threat is taken into account. This essay mainly focuses on Hindi cinema such as *Desh Premee* (*The Patriot*, 1982) and soundtracks such as *Ae Watan Ae Watan* (*Oh Nation, Oh Nation*) from the movie *Shaheed* (*The Martyr,* 1965), *Mere Desh Ki Dharti Sona Ugle* (*The Soil of My Nation*) from the movie *Upkar* (*Beneficence,* 1967) that speak of nation, nationalism, or national identity in overt or subtle ways. Using movies and soundtracks from the early 1950s to contemporary times, the chapter focuses on songs from Bollywood that enjoy a central place in the project of Indian state nationalism and its performativity. These songs are analysed through the interdisciplinary lens of discourse analysis.

Theoretically, this chapter aligns with the social constructionist approach to nationalism. As such, it takes nationalism as a discourse,[2] which engenders and reifies the nation[3] and places it at the centre of cultural and political movements and policies. Culture, in the discourse of nationalism, plays the role of a boundary maker and is no longer just a way of life embodied in material things; it becomes the emblem of a political community, the nation-state. Accordingly,

---

1   Such representation erases the heterogeneity of the Hindu community and portrays the upper-caste Hindu codes and beliefs as all pervasive norms.
2   The term discourse is used in the Foucauldian sense, i.e. "practices that systematically form the objects of which they speak" (Foucault, *Archaeology* 49).
3   See Calhoun (4–5) for a discussion of the multiple meanings attached to 'nation.'

culture is represented to a world of nation-states as the national culture, with a political significance, which has become "a permanent feature of political reality" (Greenfeld 136). Nationalism demands that the state derives some, if not all, legitimacy from the existence of a "single national identity" (Guibernau 25–6). The locus of this supposed singular identity is sought in cultural unity, thus making the task of laying the foundations of such a national culture a priority for the state. Culture, therefore, is incorporated into the discourse of nationalism in myriad ways. The impact of such incorporation becomes visible and significant when national culture metonymically substitutes the nation itself.

Each national culture, in turn, can be said to be constituted of state culture and popular culture. By state culture, I mean those cultural markers which are chosen to embody the heritage of the nation, including myths, poetry, symbols, art, and legends that the state promotes and patronises. This repertoire is presented as though it were neutral and representative of all the sections of the population the state asserts authority over. State culture primarily is the culture of the dominant classes. Pop culture, by contrast, is the realm that is accessible to the masses at large, who not only consume it but also are its active producers. Whether the producers of pop culture are aligned with the state and its regimes or not depends on how they position themselves vis-à-vis the state's claim of legitimacy. Stuart Hall sums up popular culture succinctly as "one of the sites where the struggle for and against a culture of the powerful is engaged ... an arena of consent and resistance" (*Deconstructing* 239).

Together state culture and pop culture form the national culture that the government actively strives to form and uphold. It must be noted that national cultures are not monolithic or static; rather, they can vary temporally due to changing ideologies of the state. The realm of pop culture is the site where all classes are engaged in a battle to preserve or to transform the state culture and, subsequently, the national culture itself. Nevertheless, some features and beliefs remain central to the national culture, regardless of the ruling ideology. This contingent nature of the national culture is downplayed as official nationalism (Anderson 83), historicises the nation-state, and reifies its myth of antiquity.[4] To give credence to the claim of antiquity, aspects of pre-national cultures are appropriated, modified, and made to depict the nation-state's journey through history. Once something becomes national equipment, it acquires value as a nationally consumable and appreciable entity. In short, the

---

4 The USA, Australia, and New Zealand are clearly some exceptions to this argument. However, over time the official nationalism in these states too has sought to assimilate the pre-existing native cultures to further reinforce its claim of representing all residents within their territorial limits.

cultivation of national culture involves "inventing traditions" (Hobsbawm and Ranger 1–14), "myth-making" (Smith, *Myths and Memories* 57–9), and the "suppression/co-option of rivals" (Billig 27).

One task that the state faces is how to disseminate and to facilitate its internalisation by its citizens. National myths must be transmitted in ways that are pervasive and easily decipherable. To quote Tom Nairn, "the masses must be invited into history, and the invitation cards must be written in a language they understand" (340), and in the contemporary world, that language is pop culture. Through pop culture, the nation is performed in the language of the masses; it is neatly grafted onto everyday products, making it ubiquitous. Billboards, advertisements, music, and caricatures become the carriers of the national myths. The internet has facilitated this trend. According to Thomas Hylland Eriksen, "the internet is used to strengthen, rather than weaken, national identities" (1). National messages broadcast statist visions of the nation to the masses in a way that the state's ideological, territorial, and cultural claims are naturalised, a phenomenon that Pierre Bourdieu called "the doxa" (164).

The logical end of this process brings us to a moment where being a citizen of a state is not enough; one must also be a national, lest one's loyalties are questioned. To that end, the state, armed with its modern paraphernalia of surveillance, functions as a "total institution" (Goffman 319–39) that exerts "disciplinary power" (Foucault, *Discipline and Punish* 170–7). The exercise of disciplinary power creates nationals who acquiesce with the state's narrative of national culture. The two processes, making a national culture and making nationals, go hand in hand. National culture needs nationals who not only accept its validity but also situate the locus of their identity within this culture. Over time, these nationals become the protectors of the national culture from perceived threats and the enforcers of it for those who show signs of deviance. Such protection and enforcement take visible and invisible forms. Once the citizens internalise this sense of national duty, vigilante justice is normalised as a response to acts which in other circumstances might be treated as innocuous and inconsequential.

So far, I have provided a general illustration of why states seek to possess a singular national culture throughout their territorial domain and what measures they take to achieve the goal of forging a national culture and making it popular. The subsequent sections of this essay address how a national culture was brought about by the Indian state and how the putative Indian nation is portrayed in such state-certified culture as homogenous, monolithic, and under threat.

2   Building the Indian State and Making the Indian Nation

Although India as a state-nation came into existence on 15 August 1947, the processes of state-building and nation-making had already been in motion for many decades before the end of colonial rule. India, as we know it, is a colonial construct. Building on centuries of gradual centralising processes undertaken by the Mughal Empire, the British East India Company was able to lay the foundation of British India (Deol 40). The foundations of many institutions which differentiate feudal governance structures from the modern Weberian state were laid during the colonial era (Goswami 46–59; Robb 252).

According to Manu Goswami, anti-colonial nationalists discursively reconstructed British India, at first solely as *Bharat* and later as *Bharat Mata* (Mother India), through a series of interconnecting mechanisms. The most significant sites of such active reinterpretation of history and its conflation with the prevailing political, social, and economic circumstances were education and pop culture. School and college texts of the mid- and late 1800s on geography, history, and even algebra were written in vernacular languages and actively used to naturalise an upper-caste Hindu vision of the colonial space as *Bharat Mata* which needed to be expropriated from foreign rule (188-94). A gendered vision of the nation, which promoted India as the mother, was thus put in place. Such allusions were and are meant to capitalise on the affective bond between a mother and her children. The shrewd conflation of nation and mother inadvertently meant that the nation (*Bharat Mata*) must be respected and protected. By equating nation with mother, the relationship between nationals and the nation is construed in such a way that state interests become questions of honour. The children must defend her honour from those who intend to desecrate her. The purity of the nation is to be maintained by guarding the mother's womb. According to this logic, malcontents and intruders intent on dishonouring *Bharat Mata* must be punished to keep the nation pure and safe.

Pop culture was also pressed into service to promote the nation as *Bharat Mata*. Works such as the calendar art of Raja Ravi Varma (Iyengar) were produced and promoted to draw the boundaries of the imagined *Bharat Mata* as exclusively upper-caste Hindu.[5] Furthermore, songs such as "Amra Nehat Gorib" ("We May Be Poor"), "Vande Mataram" ("Mother, I Bow to Thee"), and visual icons in the form of paintings, public performances, and Hindu

---

5   For more detailed analyses of such measures, see Dalmia for a religious, and Orsini for a linguistic approach.

iconography on coins and other mementoes were significant in naturalising the idea of an Indian nation as *Bharat Mata* (Goswami 257–62).

The nationalists adopted these themes into the nativist *Swadeshi* movement (1870–1907), which was the precursor of the later Quit India Movement, led by Gandhi, himself a latent Hindu nationalist (Frykenberg 139–41). With the establishment of the dominion of India after the British departure and partition of colonial India, upper-caste Hindu elites proficient in the Hindi language rose to capture the state machinery left behind by the British Raj. Although the institutional nationalists such as Nehru, who had actively participated in electoral politics under the tutelage of the British Raj (Chiriyankandath 39–63), became the face of independent India on the world stage, the kernel of post-1947 state nationalism remained resolutely Hindu and exclusivist. Thus, most of the earlier projections of the nation that the *Swadeshi* strand stood for were reified with active support from the state. To consolidate and reinforce the vision of a singular and territorial India, the majoritarian Hindu sentiment had to be tapped into and presented to the masses as monolithic. To this end, Hindu mythology and customs were abundantly used as a strategy to propagate the vision of a singular India and to neutralise pressures from competing visions of nationhood (Smith, *National Identity* 113).

As noted in the previous section, the process of making a national culture involves myths, such as 'land of the free, home of the brave' in the case of the United States of America, and 'unity in diversity' in the case of India. For a multinational state such as India, it becomes a matter of survival to weave into a coherent grand narrative the myths and symbols of all cultures thriving within the territorial unit. A vivid example is the incorporation of the Lion Capital of Ashoka as the state emblem of India (Vajpeyi 186). Through the appropriation of diverse cultural strands, historical figures, and music, a synthetic version of Indian culture, now touted as a source of the state's soft power (Thussu 127–53), is created. Through this synthetic culture, historical figures such as Buddha and Aryabhatta are appropriated and represented as part of a glorious Indian cultural heritage. Such subtle attempts are made to assign continuity to the idea of India as *pre*-India histories. The genesis blocks of Indian state culture are reiterated by a vast network of institutions and intelligentsia which further reify it and broaden its reach. One institution performing this function has always been the state-owned Doordarshan network of TV channels.

New communication technologies, TV in particular, made the dissemination of state culture easier, as the state enjoyed a monopoly over broadcasting. The establishment of All India Radio, also known as Akashvani, in 1936 and Doordarshan in 1959 opened new avenues for state culture to make its presence felt, "spread nationalist messages", and aid in maintaining the "territorial integrity, national integration, secularism, maintenance of public order, and upholding the dignity and prestige of Parliament, state legislatures and the judiciary" (Chakravorty 143–4). The role envisioned for Akashvani and Doordarshan by the Indian state is similar to the one the British state had outlined for the BBC, that is, to function as "an instrument of the national culture" to integrate "all the publics in the nation" into one organic whole and "serve the nation" (Hall, *Popular Culture* 376–8). Akashvani and Doordarshan, both owned and regulated by the state, remained the main avenues of entertainment, news, and infotainment for decades before cable TV and privately-owned radio stations became a reality in India. The capacity of Akashvani and Doordarshan to reach people on a massive scale made them the perfect platforms to disseminate state culture. However, such an endeavour could not be executed without the tacit support of intelligentsia and the professionals, particularly from the entertainment industry.

3 Broadcasting Bharat

Bollywood songs, as pointed out by Priya Jha, function as active agents involved in the construction of a monolithic national identity (43). According to Sumita Chakravarty, Indian cinema is both popular and antipopular (5). However, at the same time, post-1947 Indian cinema serviced a utopian view of a progress-oriented, yet spiritual nation (39–40). Chakravarty's lucid analysis of post-1947 to late-1980s Indian Hindi-language cinema highlights the ubiquity of nationalist themes such as projecting the nation's continuity, highlighting its supposed achievements, and finally its maturity and transition into an industrialised world. The movies, nevertheless, end up reifying upper-caste Hindu patriarchal culture (47).

The incorporation of nationalist themes in Indian cinematic forms is not a case of pure ideological alignment either. Such incorporation also appears to be motivated by the need to be "recognised" (15) as a worthy and valuable aspect of the national culture and strip off the notion of "profanity" (5) the cultural elite of India had attached to these cultural forms. However, after the late 1980s, Bollywood took a globalised turn and has since actively positioned itself as the "unofficial ideological apparatus" for the Indian state (Mehta 2).

Taking this into account, if we look at songs from Indian cinema from the early 1950s to the present, the kind of nationalism that has of late become virulent in India hardly comes to mind. The songs appear to allude to an accommodative Indian nationalism. However, upon taking a closer look at movie and music charts, it becomes clear that some of the biggest critical and commercial hits of Indian cinema are peppered with nationalist themes that mirror the parochial nativist discourse reminiscent of the *Swadeshi* era.[6] Furthermore, these themes are discursively entangled with the national security threat matrix of the Indian state, i.e. the shifting focus on perceived internal and external threats which invokes the global anti-terrorism discourse to justify its increasingly Orwellian nature.

Songs that invoke nationalist sentiments are called *Deshbhakti geet,* which literally translates to 'Songs of Nation Worship,' corroborating Ernest Gellner's assertion that "in a nationalist age, societies worship themselves brazenly and openly" (56). The nationalist themes that are generally invoked in songs from the early 1950s to the late 1980s are concerned with the necessity of working together to build the nation. These themes are compatible with the Nehruvian vision of nation-building, according to which dams are the temples ("Jawaharlal Nehru" n. pag.) of the new India. One of the most popular songs from the early 1950s is "Aao Bachho Tumhe Dikhaye" ("Come, Kids, Let's Show You") from the movie *Jagriti* (*The Awakening,* 1954). The music video is shot on a train which moves across the territorial confines of the Indian state to present a topographical image of the nation. The lyrics transform geographic features like the Himalayas into protectors of the nation in the North and appropriate the cultural heritage of former small Kingdoms such as Marathas, thus achieving what Margit Feischmidt and Gergő Pulay point out is "restoring the myth of the nation in lyrics" (316–9). The hook of the song, "Vande Mataram" ("Mother, I bow to thee"), is a reference to a late nineteenth-century nationalist hymn,[7] but it has over time become sloganised, and anyone who refuses to chant it is branded a traitor (Ashar n. pag.).

Grappling with the issue of transitioning towards an industrialised India during the Nehruvian era, songs such as "Chhodo Kal Ki Baatein" ("Let Go of Old Talk") from the movie *Hum Hindustani* (*We the Indians,* 1960) exemplify a utopian vision for the nation; however, the mythology invoked in this song speaks of India as being Ram's land, thus suggesting that the utopia is exclusively upper-caste Hindu. Other songs of this era such as "Tu Hindu Banega Na" ("You Will neither Become Hindu nor a Muslim") from the movie *Dhool Ka Phool* (*Flower of Dust,* 1959) speak of residents of India becoming Indian and not Hindu or Muslim, alluding to a rejection of sectarian identities in the

---

6 *Swadeshi* translates as country-made and refers to the stage in the anti-colonial movement in British India when people were encouraged to boycott English-made goods and instead opt for goods made by local industries.
7 See Goswami 259 for an elaboration on the symbolism and the themes of the original hymn as composed by the nineteenth-century nationalist B. C. Chattopadhyay.

project of nation-building. The plot of the movie revolves around the fate of a child born out of wedlock and brought up by a Muslim man in defiance of society's norms. Other songs praise the fertility of the national soil regarding agricultural, mineral, and intellectual produce, as, for instance, in "Mere Desh Ki Dharti" ("The Soil of My Nation") from the nationalist movie *Upkar* (*Beneficence,* 1967). The song subtly embeds Hindu nationalist themes of the nation as the mother in its lyrics and appropriates historical figures as sons of Mother India. Furthermore, only one Muslim figure features in the music video. He is disabled and comes into the frame while the lead figure, Manoj Kumar,[8] croons: "Yahan apna paraya koi nahi, Hai sub pe Maa upkaar tera" ("No one is a foreigner here, Mother you are beneficent to all," 3:54–4:07). The Muslim is depicted as a liability to a population actively working for the nation, subtly reinforcing the stereotype of the Muslim as a foreigner. The threats that are portrayed as stymieing the Indian nation from marching ahead in the lyrics and videos of these songs include corruption, poverty, and social taboos.

The Indian state fought a few wars with its neighbouring countries during this time, two wars with Pakistan (1965 and 1971) and one with China (1962). The cinematic adaptations of these wars portray India's actions as purely defensive, essentially parroting the narrative of the Indian state (Rasul and Mukhtar 22–2) being non-aggressive, which belies its ambitions of becoming a regional hegemon (Ayoob 420–2). Songs of Indian war-movies romanticise war casualties as martyrs who eagerly give their lives to protect the nation, and exhort the people of the nation not to forget the sacrifices of the martyrs. These themes are invoked in evergreen nationalist Hindi songs such as "Ae Watan Ae Watan" ("Oh Nation, Oh Nation") from the movie *Shaheed,* "Kar Chale Hum Fida" ("We Have Sacrificed") from *Haqeeqat* (*Reality,* 1964), "Jalwa Jalwa" ("Splendour, Splendour") from *Hindustan Ki Kasam* (*Swear on India,* 1999), and "Aye Mere Watan Ke Logo" ("Oh, People of My Nation"). Even though these songs are directed at all Indian nationals, the symbolism and iconography invoked in the lyrics as well as video frames are exclusively Hindu and support the concept of India as an essentially Hindu nation.

There are also movies that on the surface explicitly identify and appear to uphold the values of secularism and pluralism. For instance, the 1977 movie *Amar Akbar Anthony*, one of the biggest hits of the emergency era, has been interpreted as an example par excellence of the secular nature of India, which simultaneously reinforces religious hierarchies in the country (Elison et al.

---

8 Manoj Kumar starred in many nationalist movies such as *Puraab aur Paschim* (*East and West,* 1970), *Kranti* (*Revolution,* 1981), earning him the moniker Mr. Bharat (Rajadhyaksha n. pag.).

3–4). Similarly, the 1982 movie *Desh Premee* (*The Patriot*) attempts to service the 'unity in diversity' national myth through a sophisticated storyline. The movie portrays the Hindi-speaking protagonist, a former anti-colonial activist and a teacher by profession, as someone who instructs the four communities of *Bharat Nagar*,[9] two of them linguistic and two religious, i.e. Madrasi and Bengali, and Sikh and Muslim, about the virtues of living peacefully with one another. As representatives of their communities, the four men are simultaneously portrayed as internal threats to the nation as they are involved in criminal activity in the form of selling arms, drug trade, and other illegal activities. It is again noteworthy that the four communities are presented as if they were homogenous in their religious and ethnic composition.

Furthermore, at least two regions, Punjab and Madras, which these communities are shown to represent, were actively challenging the Indian state during the 1980s, providing yet another example of how pop culture comes to the aid of state nationalism in India. The role of the teacher as the national unifier is best captured in the title song of the movie "Mere Desh Premiyon" ("My Compatriots") where the protagonist urges the four enemies to shun their hatred and greed. The song also invokes the *Hindutva* theme of land as the mother and warns the four communities that if they do not stop their infighting, they will be dispossessed of their homes by a *bahar wala* (foreigner) (3:12-3:50). Another instance that exemplifies the attempt of the Indian state to reassert itself as a secular-plural tolerant polity is a multi-lingual song titled "Mile Sur" ("One Tune"). The song was strategically released on 15 August 1988 while Rajiv Gandhi was the Prime Minister ("Mile Sur" n. pag.). The song's purpose was to reassert national unity at a time when insurgencies in Punjab and the Northeast were still active, and a silent storm was gathering strength in Kashmir. The inclusion of different languages in this song and of the legal tender of the Indian state is meant to serve two purposes. First, it further projects India as a vibrant and plural democratic polity, and second, it grants token recognition to cultural and political communities to subsume them into the larger polity (Ingram 69–73). The token recognition, which usually takes the form of granting legal protections to the languages and heritages of these communities, is a tactic employed to deflect attention from the larger goal of self-determination, which many of these cultural and political communities (such as the people of Kashmir, Assam, and Nagaland) pursue.

---

9 India Enclave, the residential area's name, and its demographic composition is an allegory for the larger nation.

All the allusions to Hindu mythology, the metonymic substitution of *Bharat Mata* for India, the subtle othering of the non-upper caste Hindu might well be interpreted as the "mindless flags" (Billig 40) of the nation. However, such flagging does not remain mindless and benign forever; it metamorphoses into conscious action-oriented flagging targeting anyone perceived as a threat to the nation.

4   The Ever-Present *Tiranga*

National flags are one of the most potent symbols in the cultural repertoire of a state such that the emotional value ascribed to them is codified constitutionally and any act of disrespecting the flag is recognised as an offence deserving of legal punishment. It is therefore not surprising that flags, in the world of nation-states, have been sanctified and are no longer considered mere colourful pieces of fabric (Billig 2–3). The Indian state flag enjoys similar stature regarding emotional investment and legal sanctification. It is ubiquitous in Indian movies, be it atop a prison building in *Karma* (*Deed*, 1986) (Ghosh 134) or as a fluttering image on the cinema screen accompanied by the national anthem *Jana Gana Mana* (Beaster-Jones 17). Also, Doordarshan continues to be the broadcaster of most state ceremonies such as Independence and Republic Days. The parades on these days display cultural strands from each region of the Indian state in an orchestrated manner to service the 'unity in diversity' myth. Doordarshan offers live commentary on the parade with its logo coloured to complement the *Tiranga* (refers to the three colours of the Indian state flag). More recently, the channel began to include a miniature of the Indian national flag waving emphatically in the corner of the screen, usually above its logo, a practice that private channels have replicated. Until satellite antennae became ubiquitous across India, Doordarshan was the only medium that provided Bollywood movies, music, news, sports, and serialised dramas to millions of homes.

The affective premium that is put on the sacrosanct national flag is hard to miss in its appearances in Indian cinema. Take, for example, a scene from Mani Ratnam's *Roja* (*Rose*, 1992) where the protagonist risks his life to avoid the tricolour from burning (Hogan 97) or the scene from *Diljale* (*The Heart Burnt*, 1996) where the main character jumps to catch the flag just in time before it touches the ground. Another example is a scene from *Kuch Kuch Hota Hai* (*Something Something Happens*, 1998) where an ostensibly "Disneyfied 'Sunshine' summer camp … is ontologically transformed when the British Union flag is lowered, and the Indian flag is raised, and the portrait of Queen

Victoria replaced with that of the goddess Durga" (Basu, *Bollywood* 145). Apart from these banal, albeit emotionally laden, appearances of the *Tiranga*, the climactic scene from *Phir Bhi Dil Hai Hindustani* (*The Heart Remains Indian*, 2000) is particularly disturbing. In the scene, a policeman refuses to open fire on a marching crowd led by the roughed-up protagonist and says, "No, Sir. I can't shoot at my tricolour. I didn't join the police force to do that, Sir" (*Phir Bhi* 2:25:16–2:30:05). The subtle, yet profoundly disturbing connotation of the scene is that the *Tiranga* is above human life. Human life is protected as a consequence of the flag's sanctity, not because it is in itself worth preserving.

5 *Bharatvarsha* 2.0: Coming Soon?

The self-professed and embellished democratic secular image of the Indian state had been put to the test before the late 1980s; however, the tests were only to become more frequent and blatantly sectarian. Before 1988, the Indian state had weathered the storm of emergency rule and the anti-Sikh pogrom of 1984 in the wake of Indira Gandhi's assassination. Through pop culture, the state and the intelligentsia sought to reassert the supposed secular character of the polity as pointed out in the preceding section.

By the late 1980s, the *Hindutva* strand of Indian nationalism, which refers to India as *Bharatvarsha* (derived from ancient Hindu mythology meaning land of Bharat, an ancient King) and seeks to establish India exclusively as a Hindu state, had begun to openly assert itself.[10] Parallel to the bold assertion of the *Hindutva* brand of Indian nationalism in high politics emerged a reinvigorated interest of pop culture mavens in the dramatisation of mythological texts such as *Ramayana*[11] and *Mahabharata*.[12] Both were broadcast on Doordarshan and ran for over seventy episodes each. While it would be wrong to say that the dramatised versions of the epics fanned sectarian tensions in the country, their glorification and popularisation of Hindu iconography cannot be ignored, particularly in the context of the long history of minority othering in India. An unintended consequence of these televised epics, as Arvind Rajagopal points out, was the intensification and emboldening of the *Hindutva* (30).[13]

---

10 See Basu et al. for an in-depth analysis of the *Hindutva* ideology.
11 The Hindu epic poem that narrates the story of Hindu deities Ram and Sita.
12 An epic tale revolving around the Bharata dynasty.
13 The *Ramjanambhoomi* movement soon picked up steam and left a trail of carnage in its wake. This movement seeks to construct a temple in the same place where Babri Mosque once stood in Ayodhya. See Engineer for an incisive survey of the issue. The foundation of the temple was laid on 5 August 2020 by India's Prime Minister Narendra Modi.

In keeping with the realm of post-1992 high politics, Indian cinema has conspicuously flirted with the parochial nationalist vision and reproduced oriental stereotypes about minority communities, Muslims in general and Kashmiri Muslims in particular (Kabir 373–85; Khan 127–39; Rajgopal 237–46; Sharma 124–31), portraying them as a threat to the integrity of the nation in different ways (Dwyer n. pag.). Examples of such movies include *Roja* (*Rose*, 1992), *Sarfarosh* (*Ready to Die*, 1999), *Mission Kashmir* (2000), *Fiza* (*Ambience*, 2000), *Gadar: Ek Prem Katha* (*Mutiny: A Love Story*, 2001), *Indian* (2001), and *Farz* (*Duty*, 2001). The most obvious themes invoked in songs featured in these movies extol the virtues of being ready to sacrifice oneself for the nation, of holding the nation above everything, of aiding the nation against internal and external threats, and lastly to be loyal towards the nation unto death.

The symbiotic relationship of state and pop culture and, more particularly, electoral politics and pop culture became clear during the 2014 elections, as Narendra Modi sought to become the country's Prime Minister for the first time. In a bid to woo the urban, middle-class, and young voters, Modi's Bharatiya Janata Party (henceforth BJP) made use of pop cultural forms in a manner that India had never witnessed before. Modi's election slogans *Achchhey Din Aane Waley Hain* (Good days are coming) and *Abki Baar Modi Sarkar* (It is time for Modi's government) became household utterances because they were circulated through songs and advertisements. The video of the catchy song on the party's *YouTube* channel has attracted over 445,000 views, and both the song and the advert were aired on almost every TV channel and radio station during the election campaign. Once in power, the Modi administration stoked controversy as it went after what it dubbed as anti-national elements at Jawaharlal Nehru University. It was proposed that to inculcate nationalist sentiments amongst students, the national flag would be hoisted across university campuses in the country (Chaudhary n. pag.). Individuals who criticised this move as a tactic of enforcing the hegemony of Modi's party on public spaces were abused online and offline. University campuses across India, particularly in the National Capital Region (NCR) have had to deal with violence often instigated by the student wing of Modi's party (Shafi n. pag.). The Modi administration's use of pop culture did not stop there; the administration again made use of songs to propagate its supposed achievements at various points during its first tenure. One song titled "Mera Desh Badal Raha Hai" ("My Nation Is Changing") was released upon completing two years of Modi's first tenure. The song highlights the government's policies[14] such as the 'Make

---

14 Both policies have failed to achieve their objectives. Babu's and Kapur's online articles offer journalistic voices on the issue.

in India' campaign, the Modi government's push to kick-start manufacturing in India, and *Beti Padhao Beti Bachao* (educate daughters, save daughters), the Modi government's policy that purportedly addresses gender disparities through education schemes, to demonstrate that the administration was fulfilling its campaign promises. Mainstream Bollywood music director Shankar Mahadevan too eulogised the Modi administration in a rehashed version of his so-called breathless song titled "Non Stop India" (Modi). The lyrics of the song echo the talking points of Modi's administration and speak of the new respect India has earned under his leadership, for instance, a decrease in corruption levels, thus further evoking a positive image. By making use of these pop cultural forms, the Modi administration has attempted to, and to a large extent succeeded in dominating the public discourse with a version most suitable to its agenda and at the same time prevented any criticism of its policies. To further enamour himself to the millennials, especially those of the Non-Resident Indian (NRI) community, Modi undertook a series of high-profile foreign visits. A visit to the United States of America in 2014 was particularly hyped. Modi's entourage included many established names from the entertainment industry like Hugh Jackman, who joined the podium at New York's Madison Square Garden where Modi famously uttered the *Star Wars* catchphrase 'May the Force be with you' to applause and loud cheers from the NRI community affiliated with the Republican Hindu Coalition (RHC), a pro-Trump NRI organisation (Thobani 748). Modi's party went into hyperdrive while campaigning for the 2019 elections which saw Modi return to power with an overwhelming mandate. In violation of the country's election campaign laws, trailers of a biopic titled *PM Narendra Modi* were widely promoted, although the theatrical release of the movie was delayed due to a notice served to the producers by the country's Election Commission. The film glorifies Modi's journey from being a tea seller to the country's Prime Minister, portraying him as a selfless demigod tirelessly working for the progress of India. The movie personifies the cult around Modi to such an extent that the religious chant *Har Har Mahadev* (Everyone is Mahadev) was twisted into *Har Har Modi* (Everyone is Modi), equating Modi with the Hindu deity Shiva (Singh n. pag.). The soundtrack of the movie was, however, released in March 2019, two months before the biopic. It was a reflection of Modi and his party's ideology and subtly invoked themes of external and internal threats, suggesting that Modi was the only one capable of handling such dangers and ensuring that India rises to power and prestige on the world stage.

Given the ubiquitous flagging of Hindu nationalist themes in the realm of pop culture, a spillover effect that has shaped audiences' behaviour in the material world is hardly surprising. Aided with technology, high-speed internet, and the technical capacity required to graft these nationalist songs onto an assortment of images has opened the door for an average person to become an active producer. The intelligentsia and the cultural gatekeepers are no longer the sole producers of national culture; everyone now feels equally capable of showing his or her nationalism through pop culture. The baton of nationalism having passed from high culture to pop culture has produced some of the most egregious acts of violence and discrimination against the perceived threats by those who take themselves to be fulfilling a national duty, especially when such acts are rewarded. The meteoric rise of Tajinder Singh Bagga from a lone wolf heckler to a BJP spokesperson and an election contestant is one such example (Dutta n. pag.). The consequences of this coupling of pop culture and nationalism in contemporary India include disturbing acts committed by cow protection vigilantes, assaults on students and academics deemed seditious, heckling of people who do not stand up for the national anthem, as well as the overzealous initiatives of the Indian government to hoist the *Tiranga* in every university of the country. Another interesting development under the Modi government is that not only is India now taken as a Hindu nation by default, as imagined by the *Hindutva* parties, but also any criticism of the Modi government is quickly dismissed and labelled an anti-national activity. The consequences of this conflation have been disastrous for dissenters as free speech comes under attack (Prabhu n. pag.) and for the minorities in India as exemplified by the murder of noted scholar M. M. Kalburgi and public lynchings of Muslims and Dalits on the mere suspicion of having consumed beef (Nair n. pag.). I argue that these developments in the political landscape of India can only be fully understood when we take into account the role pop culture has played over the *longue durée* in reifying India in the popular imagination as exclusively Hindu and under threat. However, it would be wrong to impugn the agency of the masses and write them off as manipulated. As Sumit Sarkar has pointed out, when masses internalise past and newly invented prejudices, they become a force of hatred betraying their emancipatory potential, but not their agency.

6   Conclusion

This chapter argued that the Indian state has tapped into the potential of pop culture to propagate an upper-caste Hindu-centric national identity since the earliest years of its existence. Examples from different temporal junctures were used to substantiate this argument. The chapter also argued that the relationship between official nationalism and pop culture has acquired more urgency in contemporary India due to the emergence of new technologies and media. Successive governments in India have courted the entertainment industry and employed pop cultural forms to propagate and circulate a state-sponsored nationalism which portrays India as a homogenous Hindu nation facing internal and external threats. The only difference between the official nationalism of the Congress government and that of the current BJP government is that the former is subtle whereas the latter openly promotes an exclusivist upper-caste Hindu nationalist agenda. What remains to be seen is how far the Indian state is willing to tread down this slippery slope. Whether the trajectory will lead to the establishment of a Hindu state, the long-cherished goal of the Hindu right, or whether the Indian polity will make a course correction, only time will tell.

Works Cited

"Aao Bachho Tumhe Dikhaye." *YouTube*, uploaded by Shemaroo Filmi Gaane, 22 Sept. 2016, www.youtube.com/watch?v=XiiBsKU4z6c.

"Ae Watan Ae Watan." *YouTube,* uploaded by crazyoldsongs, 24 Mar. 2012, www.youtube.com/watch?v=ZeXHtLx2HI4.

Amar Akbar Anthony. Directed by Manmohan Desai, performances by Vinod Khanna, Amitabh Bachchan, and Rishi Kapoor, Hirawat Jain & Co., 1977.

Anderson, Benedict. *Imagined Communities: Reflections on the Origin and Spread of Nationalism*. Verso, 2006.

Ashar, Sandeep A. "Now It's Congress: Bharat Mata Ki Jai or Else." *The Indian Express*, 17 Mar. 2016, www.indianexpress.com/article/india/india-news-india/maharashtra-assembly-suspends-aimim-mla-for-not-saying-bharat-mata-ki-jai/. Accessed 23 Nov. 2020.

"Aye Mere Watan Ke Logo." *YouTube,* uploaded by Gyanvani Tube, 26 Jan. 2013, www.youtube.com/watch?v=f7G9iQR5uyU.

Ayoob, Mohammed. "India as Regional Hegemon: External Opportunities and Internal Constraints." *International Journal*, vol. 46, no. 3, 1991, pp. 420–48. doi: 10.2307/40202897.

Babu, M. Suresh. "Why 'Make in India' Has Failed." *The Hindu*, 20 Jan. 2020, www.thehindu.com/opinion/op-ed/why-make-in-india-has-failed/article30601269.ece. Accessed 23 Nov. 2020.

Basu, Anustup. *Bollywood in the Age of New Media: The Geo-televisual Aesthetic*. Edinburgh UP, 2010.

Basu, Tapan, et al. *Khaki Shorts and Saffron Flags: A Critique of the Hindu Right*. Orient Longman, 1993.

Beaster-Jones, Jayson. *Bollywood Sounds: The Cosmopolitan Mediations of Hindi Film Song*. Oxford UP, 2015.

Billig, Michael. *Banal Nationalism*. Sage, 1995.

Bourdieu, Pierre. *Outline of a Theory of Practice*. Cambridge UP, 2010.

Calhoun, Craig. *Nationalism*. Open UP, 1997.

Chakravarty, Sumita S. *National Identity in Indian Popular Cinema, 1947–1987*. U of Texas P, 2011.

Chakravorty, Pallabi. "Global Dancing in Kolkata." *A Companion to the Anthropology of India*, edited by Isabelle Clark-Decès, Blackwell, 2011, pp. 137–53.

Chaudhary, Shubhda. "Is a 270 ft National Flag in Central Universities the Answer?" *The Citizen*, 21 Feb. 2016, www.thecitizen.in/index.php/en/NewsDetail/index/8/6923/Is-A-270-Ft-National-Flag-In-Central-Universities-The-Answer. Accessed 23 Nov. 2020.

"Chhodo Kal Ki Baatein." *YouTube,* uploaded by Desi Chain, 4 Feb. 2016, www.youtube.com/watch?v=ZJ71CWqgvdY.

Chiriyankandath, James. "'Democracy' under the Raj: Elections and Separate Representation in British India." *The Journal of Commonwealth & Comparative Politics*, vol. 30, no. 1, 1992, pp. 39–63. doi:10.1080/14662049208447624.

Dalmia, Vasudha. *The Nationalization of Hindu Traditions: Bharatendu Harischandra and Nineteenth-Century Banaras*. Oxford UP, 2005.

Deol, Harnik. *Religion and Nationalism in India: The Case of the Punjab*. Routledge, 2000.

Desh Premee. Directed by Manmohan Desai, performances by Amitabh Bachchan, Hema Malini, Shammi Kapoor, and Parveen Babi, S. S. Movietone, 1982.

Dhool Ka Phool. Directed by Yash Chopra, performances by Mala Sinha, Rajendra Kumar, Nanda, and Ashok Kumar, NH Studioz, 1959.

Diljale. Directed by Harry Baweja, performances by Ajay Devgn, Sonali Bendre, Madhoo, Amrish Puri, Shakti Kapoor, and Parmeet Sethi, S. P. Creations, 1996.

Dutta, Nirmalya. "From Attacking Prashant Bhushan to Getting a BJP Ticket: The Rise of Tajinder Singh Bagga." *Free Press Journal*, 21 Jan. 2020, www.freepressjournal.in/india/from-attacking-prashant-bhushan-to-getting-a-bjp-ticket-the-rise-of-tajinder-singh-bagga.

Dwyer, Rachel. "Top Ten Muslim Characters in Bollywood by Rachel Dwyer." *Critical Muslim*, 1 Jan. 2013, www.criticalmuslim.com/issues/05-love-and-death/top-ten-muslim-characters-bollywood-rachel-dwyer. Accessed 22 Mar. 2020.

Elison, William, et al. *Amar Akbar Anthony: Bollywood, Brotherhood, and the Nation*. Harvard UP, 2016.

Engineer, Asgharali. *Babri–Masjid Ramjanambhoomi Controversy*. South Asia Books, 1990.

Eriksen, Thomas Hylland. "Nationalism and the Internet." *Nations and Nationalism*, vol. 13, no. 1, 2007, pp. 1–17. doi:10.1111/j.1469-8129.2007.00273.x.

Farz. Directed by Raj Kanwar, performances by Sunny Deol, Preity Zinta, Om Puri, and Jackie Shroff, Vishant International, 2001.

Feischmidt, Margit, and Gergő Pulay. "'Rocking the Nation': The Popular Culture of Neo-Nationalism." *Nations and Nationalism*, vol. 23, no. 2, 2017, pp. 309–26. doi: 10.1111/nana.12264.

Fiza. Directed by Khalid Mohammed, performances by Karisma Kapoor, Hrithik Roshan, and Jaya Bhaduri Bachchan, UTV Motion Pictures, 2000.

Foucault, Michel. *Archaeology of Knowledge and Discourse on Language*. Pantheon Books, 1972.

Foucault, Michel. *Discipline and Punish: The Birth of the Prison*. 1975. Penguin, 1991.

Frykenberg, Robert Eric. "Religion, Nationalism and Hindu Fundamentalism: The Challenge to Indian Unity." *Ethnic Studies Report,* vol. 11, no. 2, 1993, pp. 125–42.

Gadar: Ek Prem Katha. Directed by Anil Sharma, performances by Sunny Deol, Amisha Patel, Amrish Puri, and Lilette Dubey, Zee Telefilms, 2001.

Gellner, Ernest. *Nations and Nationalism.* Blackwell, 1983.

Ghosh, Tapan K. *Bollywood Baddies: Villains, Vamps and Henchmen in Hindi Cinema.* SAGE Publications India, 2013.

Goffman, Erving. "The Character of Total Institutions." *A Sociological Reader on Complex Organisations,* edited by Amitai Etzioni, Holt, Rhinehart & Winston of Canada, 1961, pp. 319–39.

Goswami, Manu. *Producing India: From Colonial Economy to National Space*. The U of Chicago P, 2004.

Greenfeld, Liah. *Nationalism and the Mind: Essays on Modern Culture*. Oneworld, 2006.

Guibernau, Montserrat. *The Identity of Nations*. Polity, 2007.

Hall, Stuart. "Notes on Deconstructing 'The Popular.'" *People's History and Socialist Theory*, edited by Raphael Samuel, Routledge, 2016, pp. 227–40.

Hall, Stuart. "Popular Culture and the State." *The Anthropology of the State: A Reader,* edited by Aradhana Sharma and Akhil Gupta, Blackwell Publishing, 2009, pp. 360–80.

Haqeeqat. Directed by Chetan Anand, performances by Dharmendra, Balraj Sahni, and Priya Rajvansh, Himalaya Films, 1964.

Hindustan Ki Kasam. Directed by Veeru Devgan, performances by Ajay Devgn, Amitabh Bachchan, and Manisha Koirala, Devgan Films, 1999.

Hobsbawm, Eric, and Terence Ranger. *The Invention of Tradition*. Cambridge UP, 2012.

Hogan, Patrick Colm. *Imagining Kashmir: Emplotment and Colonialism*. U of Nebraska P, 2016.

Hum Hindustani. Directed by Ram Mukherjee, performances by Sunil Dutt, Asha Parekh, and Helen, Filmalaya Pvt. Ltd., 1960.

Indian. Directed by N. Maharajan, performances by Sunny Deol, Shilpa Shetty, Rahul Dev, and Mukesh Rishi, Eros International, 2001.

Ingram, James. "Comment on Lawrence Blum." *Constellations*, vol. 5, no. 1, 1998, pp. 69–73. doi: 10.1111/1467-8675.00075.

Iyengar, Radhika. "In Literature and Art from over 100 Years Ago, Images of the Cow as Mother." *The Indian Express*, 5 Apr. 2017, www.indianexpress.com/article/research/literature-and-visuals-from-1880s-1940s-show-how-projection-of-gau-mata-became-symbolical-of-hindu-manliness-created-a-religious-rift/. Accessed 22 Mar. 2020.

Jagriti. Directed by Satyen Bose, performances by Abhi Bhattacharya, Ratan Kumar, and Rajkumar Gupta, Filmistan Ltd., 1954.

"Jalwa Jalwa." *YouTube*, uploaded by Tips Official, 20 Sep. 2011, www.youtube.com/watch?v=yRmnGwqyEJY.

"Jawaharlal Nehru (1889–1964): Architect of India's Modern Temples." *The Hindu*, 7 July 2003, www.thehindu.com/todays-paper/tp-features/tp-metroplus/jawaharlal-nehru-1889-1964-architect-of-indias-modern-temples/article28441764.ece. Accessed 22 March 2020.

Jha, Priya. "Lyrical Nationalism: Gender, Friendship, and Excess in 1970s Hindi Cinema." *The Velvet Light Trap*, vol. 51, 2003, pp. 43–53. doi:10.1353/vlt.2003.0007.

Kabir, Ananya Jahanara. "The Kashmiri as Muslim in Bollywood's 'New Kashmir Films.'" *Contemporary South Asia*, vol. 18, no. 4, Dec. 2010, pp. 373–85. doi: 10.1080/09584935.2010.526201.

"Kar Chale Hum Fida." *YouTube*, uploaded by oAzgarKhano, 8 July 2010, www.youtube.com/watch?v=n6yTCblgAQQ.

Kapur, Wamika. "Why the Beti Bachao Beti Padhao Scheme Has Failed on Several Counts." *The Wire Science*, 4 May 2017, www.science.thewire.in/education/beti-bachao-beti-padhao-scheme-failed/.

Karma. Directed by Subhash Ghai, performances by Dilip Kumar, Jackie Shroff, and Anil Kapoor, Mukta Arts Ltd., 1982.

Khan, Shahnaz. "Reading Fanaa: Confrontational Views, Comforting Identifications and Undeniable Pleasures." *South Asian Popular Culture*, vol. 7, no. 2, 2009, pp. 127–39. doi: 10.1080/14746680902920890.

Kranti. Directed by Manoj Kumar, performances by Dilip Kumar, Manoj Kumar, and Shashi Kapoor, 1981.

Kuch Kuch Hota Hai. Directed by Karan Johar, performances by Shah Rukh Khan, Kajol, Rani Mukerji, and Salman Khan, Dharma Productions, 1998.

Mehta, Rini Bhattacharya. "Bollywood, Nation, Globalization: An Incomplete Introduction." *Bollywood and Globalization*, by Mehta and Rajeshwari V. Pandharipande, Anthem P, 2010, pp. 1–14.

"Mera Desh Badal Raha Hai." *YouTube*, uploaded by DD News, 20 May 2016, www.youtube.com/watch?v=fZTPxkRBaoY.

"Mere Desh Ki Dharti." *YouTube,* uploaded by Virender Ajmani, 15 Aug. 2006, www.youtube.com/watch?v=vpqYjAHQtvI.

"Mere Desh Premiyon." *YouTube,* uploaded by Shemaroo Filmi Gaane, 12 Apr. 2021, www.youtube.com/watch?v=dBNh5gQwg5g.

"Mile Sur." *YouTube,* uploaded by oAzgarKhano, 9 Feb. 2010, www.youtube.com/watch?v=-jf6pwtPqCs.

"Mile Sur: The Unofficial Indian Anthem." *Financial Express,* 26 Apr. 2007, www.financialexpress.com/archive/Mile-sur-The-unofficial-Indian-anthem/105370/. Accessed 23 Nov. 2020.

Mission Kashmir. Directed by Vidhu Vinod Chopra, performances by Sanjay Dutt, Hrithik Roshan, Preity Zinta, Jackie Shroff, and Sonali Kulkarni, Vinod Chopra Productions, 2000.

Modi, Narendra. "Non Stop India." *YouTube,* uploaded by Narendra Modi, 15 Aug. 2019, www.youtube.com/watch?v=957HXVa_q2k.

Nair, Supriya. "The Meaning of India's 'Beef Lynchings.'" *The Atlantic,* 24 July 2017, www.theatlantic.com/international/archive/2017/07/india-modi-beef-lynching-muslim-partition/533739/. Accessed 23 Nov. 2020.

Nairn, Tom. *The Break-up of Britain: Crisis and Neo-Nationalism.* NLB, 1977.

Orsini, Francesca. *The Hindi Public Sphere 1920–1940: Language and Literature in the Age of Nationalism.* Oxford UP, 2009.

Phir Bhi Dil Hai Hindustani. Directed by Aziz Mirza, performances by Shah Rukh Khan, Juhi Chawla, Johnny Lever, and Paresh Rawal, Dreamz Unlimited, 2000.

PM Narendra Modi. Directed by Omung Kumar, performances by Vivek Oberoi, Manoj Joshi, Boman Irani, and Barkha Sengupta, Legend Global Studio, 2019.

Prabhu, Maya. "Is Free Speech under Threat in Modi's India?" *Al Jazeera,* 3 Aug. 2017, www.aljazeera.com/indepth/features/2017/07/free-speech-threat-modi-india-170712131837718.html. Accessed 15 July 2019.

Purab Aur Paschim. Directed by Manoj Kumar, performances by Ashok Kumar, Saira Banu, and Manoj Kumar, Vishal International Productions, 1970.

Rajadhyaksha, Radha. "The Enduring Nationalism of Mr. Bharat." *The Hindu,* 8 May 2016, www.thehindu.com/news/cities/mumbai/entertainment/the-enduring-nationalism-of-mr-bharat/article8572283. Accessed 15 July 2019.

Rajagopal, Arvind. *Politics after Television: Religious Nationalism and the Reshaping of the Indian Public.* Cambridge UP, 2004.

Rajgopal, Shoba Sharad. "Bollywood and Neonationalism: The Emergence of Nativism as the Norm in Indian Conventional Cinema." *South Asian Popular Culture,* vol. 9, no. 3, 2011, pp. 237–46. doi: 10.1080/14746689.2011.597953.

Rasul, Azmat, and Mudassir Mukhtar. "Bollywoodization of Foreign Policy: How Film Discourse Portrays Tension between States." *Journal of Media Critiques,* vol. 1, no. 5, 2015, pp. 11–27. doi: 10.17349/jmc115200.

Robb, Peter. "The Colonial State and Constructions of Indian Identity: An Example on the Northeast Frontier in the 1880s." *Modern Asian Studies*, vol. 31, no. 2, 1997, pp. 245–83. doi: 10.1017/S0026749X0001430X.

Roja. Directed by Man Ratnam, performances by Arvind Swami and Madhoo, Kavithalayaa Productions Pyramid, 1992.

Sarfarosh. Directed by John Matthew Matthan, performances by Aamir Khan, Naseeruddin Shah, Mukesh Rishi, and Sonali Bendre, Cinematt Pictures, 1999.

Sarkar, Sumit. "The Fascism of the Sangh Parivar." *Economic and Political Weekly*, vol. 28, no. 5, 1993, pp. 163–7.

Shafi, Showkat. "Nationalist Group ABVP Accused of Delhi Campus Violence." *Al Jazeera*, 27 Feb. 2017, www.aljazeera.com/indepth/features/2017/02/nationalist-group-abvp-accused-delhi-campus-violence-170226050247696.html. Accessed 15 July 2019.

Shaheed. Directed by S. Ram Sharma, performances by Manoj Kumar, Prem Chopra, and Anant Purushottam Marathe, PKK Movies, 1965.

Sharma, Alpana. "Paradise Lost in Mission Kashmir: Global Terrorism, Local Insurgencies, and the Question of Kashmir in Indian Cinema." *Quarterly Review of Film and Video*, vol. 25, no. 2, 2008, pp. 124–31. doi: 10.1080/10509200601074744.

Singh, Shekhar. "Har Har Modi, Ghar Ghar Modi Echoes". *The Pioneer*, 24 May 2019, www.dailypioneer.com/2019/state-editions/har-har-modi--ghar-ghar-modi-echoes.html. Accessed 15 July 2019.

Smith, Anthony D. *National Identity*. Penguin, 1991.

Smith, Anthony D. *Myths and Memories of the Nation*. Oxford UP, 1999.

Thobani, Sitara. "Alt-Right with the Hindu-Right: Long-Distance Nationalism and the Perfection of Hindutva." *Ethnic and Racial Studies*, vol. 42, no. 5, 2019, pp. 745–62. doi: 10.1080/01419870.2018.1468567.

Thussu, Daya. *Communicating India's Soft Power: Buddha to Bollywood*. Springer, 2013.

"Tu Hindu Banega Na." *YouTube,* uploaded by Venus, 14 Jan. 2015, www.youtube.com/watch?v=fgNa41wNxyw.

Upkar. Directed by Manoj Kumar, performances by Manoj Kumar, Asha Parekh, and Prem Chopra, Vishal Pictures, 1967.

Vajpeyi, Ananya. *Righteous Republic: The Political Foundations of Modern India*. Harvard UP, 2012.

"Vande Mataram." *YouTube,* uploaded by Shemaroo, 7 Aug. 2014, www.youtube.com/watch?v=WfqMmypbACg.

CHAPTER 7

Meet the 'Holy Family': From Multicultural Australia to Enforced Reconciliation in Baz Luhrmann's *Australia* (2008)

Hanna Teichler

1   Introduction

> [T]oday we honour the Indigenous [sic] peoples of this land, the oldest continuing cultures in human history. We reflect on their past mistreatment.
>
> We reflect in particular on the mistreatment of those who were Stolen Generations – this blemished chapter in our nation's history.
>
> The time has now come for the nation to turn a new page in Australia's history by righting the wrongs of the past and so moving forward with confidence to the future. (Rudd n. pag.)

With these solemn words, on February 13, 2008, former Australian Prime Minister Kevin Rudd apologized on behalf of the government and the Australian nation at large for the forcible removal and cultural re-education of Australia's Aboriginal people. This gesture of remorse marked a culmination point in the struggle to come to terms with Australia's troubled history of systematically eradicating indigeneity through a state-run foster system. Since the 1990s, indigenous lobbyists, politicians, human rights activists, and many others called for institutionalized processes to foster a process of reconciliation between indigenous peoples and the Australian nation, specifically arguing that the legacies and results of this system of forcible removal required a public working-through. As a result, the government launched an inquiry into the forcible removal of Aborigines and Torres Straight Islanders. Its final report, the *Bringing Them Home* report published in 1997, remains the most widely read government publication until the present day and had a tremendous influence on how the issue of Aboriginal cultural re-education was perceived by the wider public. The inquiry came to the conclusion that the system and its effects were genocidal. Among its key recommendations was a public apology to Australia's Aboriginal peoples and the payment of reparations.

However, it took Australia another ten years to implement some of the report's findings: Kevin Rudd's election campaign was built on the realization that the political and social climate had significantly changed in recent years; the public's eyes and ears were sensitized to Aboriginal issues and human rights violations. Rudd thus spearheaded his election campaign with the promise of an apology, and so he eventually delivered.[1]

The public apology and the increased visibility of the Stolen Generations – a term coined for the victims and survivors of the foster system – shed a spotlight on how Australia was forced to reconcile the idea(ls) of a multicultural society with this history of systematic human rights abuse at the hand of the state and courts. Australian national identity and nationalism are built on a specific legacy of British colonialism: despite its arguably humble origins as a penal colony, it transformed into a blossoming crown dominion, and today is considered a 'First World' country, economically successful and politically stable. Moreover, after the Second World War, multiculturalism became national state policy and reason of state to account for Australia's status as an immigrant country. This idea of an Australian society that is welcoming and inclusive to outsiders stands in utter contrast to the practices of forcible removal of Aboriginal people and thus challenges the narrative of multicultural Australia.

Among the many arenas in which Australian nationalism was challenged and reassessed, the sphere of cultural production proved particularly engaged with the vexed questions of how reconciliation would challenge the nation's sense of self. The release of Baz Luhrmann's filmic epos *Australia* (2008) almost coincided with Rudd's apology and the new wave of solidarity with the Stolen Generations that came with it. Interestingly, *Australia* is the third most successful movie in the history of Australian cinema in terms of revenue.[2] *Australia* taps into this specific identity-political climate of National Sorry Days and public apologies, seeking to provide an all-encompassing account and productive re-evaluation of the country's ambivalent history, as director Baz Luhrmann describes:

> I started the project with six months of researching general Australian history. I was looking for the canvas to play out a story, so really the film could have been set at any point – at one stage I was looking at the First

---

[1] An earlier version of this chapter was originally published in my monograph *Carnivalizing Reconciliation* (2021).

[2] *Australia* earned a revenue of $211 million; its economic success is only surpassed by public cinema milestones such as *Crocodile Dundee* (1986), directed by Peter Fairman, and *Mad Max: Fury Road* (2015) by David Miller.

Fleet [the eleven ships that set sail from Britain in 1787 to set up the first colony in New South Wales] – but there were a few specific issues I wanted to explore. One was our relationship with England, the parent country, and why, when Australians have self-confidence in so many areas, do we not have the confidence for self-governance? Another was to do with Australia's indigenous population. (Luhrmann n. pag.)

Here, Luhrmann sets up a direct and almost teleological connection between the act of first settlement, which for some remains the original sin, the subsequent emancipation from the colonial motherland, and the lasting attachment to the Crown. Although somewhat framed in cringe-worthy terms, he decidedly introduces the issue that "was to do with Australia's indigenous population" into his version of Australian national identity. In this spirit, this feature film traces how the country – in Luhrmann's terms – has come to realize, to become aware of, itself. *Australia* is framed as a national epos: the film covers historical ground ranging from British imperialism to the World Wars, from the Stolen Generations to representing Australia's own version of national identity post reconciliation. In alignment with the epic genre, *Australia* sets out to tackle the 'big questions' as it grapples with the many controversial facets of Australian history within two hours and forty-five minutes, in particular with the difficult legacy of enforced cultural re-education of its Aboriginal peoples.

As this chapter argues, the effects that this feature film produces with its decidedly identity-political angle are ambiguous: Australian national identity after reconciliation is allegorized as the Holy Family. Lady Ashley, the British aristocrat turned Australian, marries the personification of Australianness, the Drover, and adopts the Aboriginal child to incorporate all Aborigines metonymically and symbolically into the national fold. The outback as the formative space where Australian identity is produced becomes a space of empowerment for its underdogs: Lady Ashley grows into a female Drover, thus challenging the paradigm of the male rural worker as the central representative of an imagined Australian national identity. Nullah, the half-caste with his deep, mythic connection with the outback, marks it as an Aboriginal space. *Australia* thus deconstructs the formative image of an outback that is male and white, and reorients it towards historically and practically marginalized voices. In this manner, *Australia* pursues alternative myth-making by pluralizing Australian nationalism.

Luhrmann's movie seems to have found the perfect recipe to smooth over the tensions and inequalities that national myths bring with them. *Australia*'s bright and gay colors, its parodic elements, and its schematic characters support the impression of a self-contained universe, a filmic world that forms a merry entity in which all falls into place in the end. Luhrmann's epic feature film engages with pertinent aspects and contested issues of and within Australian history, such as colonialism, independence, and the forcible removal of Australia's Aboriginal children. It ostensibly tries to empower Aboriginal peoples – Nullah is the main narrator for a good part of the movie – but eventually imagines a nation that culminates in the figure of the Australian mother who adopts Aboriginal children, thus symbolically re-integrating indigeneity into the national fold. Luhrmann's feature film quite convincingly pluralizes restrictive national myths – as will be analyzed in this chapter – and creates a version of Australian nationalism that is much more aligned with Australia's idea of multiculturalism. By the same token, its rather simplistic take on Australian reconciliation, one that rests on a segmentary, happy-go-lucky multiculturalism, prevents it from unfolding a truly subversive potential. It is, after all, an odd take on the prospects of reconciliation if all turmoil over history is solved by framing an Englishwoman as Mother Australia who adopts the country's stolen child, a constellation that re-establishes colonial power hierarchies. *Australia* strives to counter difficult historical legacies with a song and a smile, but it places a sugary coat on national narratives and formative myths. Luhrmann's agenda to include, even center, indigeneity in his Australian epos leads to the movie giving consent on behalf of the Aboriginals to be part of this national narrative. *Australia,* consequently, is not the voice of, but a voice for the Aboriginals. Moreover, *Australia*'s rendering of indigeneity consolidates a specific stereotypical image of the Aboriginal as the 'noble savage.' As I outline in this essay, Luhrmann's vision of reconciliation seems driven by the imperative to arrive at a sense of closure, of reconcilableness. This strategy takes its toll on *Australia*. The narrative and its aesthetics ache under the heavy framework of Luhrmann's enforced reconciliation – to borrow a term from Theodor W. Adorno – and thus, in the end, (re)produces the opposite effect to its benevolent political agenda. If read at face value, the national allegory of the Holy Family exemplifies how hierarchies not only persist, but are reinvigorated. The movie's solution to Australia's struggle over historical burdens and national identity post reconciliation is that settler Australia – as represented by Lady Ashley – remains the central reference value and focal point of this post-reconciliation brand of Australian nationalism.

In the following, I will provide a brief overview of the events that led to Rudd's apology, which aspects of Australia's national history came to intersect through the discourse and practice of reconciliation, and how Luhrmann's movie relates to these issues. A detailed analysis of what *Australia* sets out to achieve will be juxtaposed by its shortcomings, thus pointing towards the fallacies embedded in the promise of reconciliation. With regard to the framing perspective of this volume – nationalism and the postcolonial – *Australia* marks an interesting case study, for it sheds light on the pitfalls of Australian reconciliation: within the diegetic universe of Luhrmann's epos, reconciliation serves national unity under the auspices of settler Australia, much rather than to enable anything remotely resembling indigenous political agency, and does not seek to destabilize these received hierarchies. Reconciliation becomes a short-lived moment of empowerment to Australia's indigenous peoples because their stories, their fates come to be seen. Yet, in the overarching logic of this version of Australian nationalism, Aboriginals are effectively asked to assume their position as 'children' of the reconciled Australian nation – neither at the margins, scolded and silenced, nor as responsible, self-governing, mature people.

2   In "a Land Far, Far Away"

As it has already been stated, the release of Luhrmann's feature-epos coincided with former Australian Prime Minister Kevin Rudd's official apology to the Aboriginal population, and to the Stolen Generations in particular. He offered this acknowledgement of a government-run system of forced relocation and re-education: Australia's Aboriginals and Torres Strait Islanders were subject to enforced relocation to reserves, whereas their children – the ones of mixed descent in particular – were taken from their families and kin. This foster system designed to enable cultural re-education of Aboriginal children in an ultimately European image was in place until the mid-1970s. Rudd's gesture of atonement to Australia's Aboriginal peoples formed an integral part of what Jeffrey Olick has termed the "politics of regret" (1): in an attempt to grant recognition to and engage with their traumatic experiences, the official inquiry into the legacies of the system was launched, and its final *Bringing Them Home*-report was received as a milestone in Australia's struggle for reconciliation.[3] These performances in the shape of governmental apologies and official inquiries were supposed to fulfil several objectives, among which is the empowerment of indigenous peoples through granting them a stage to tell their stories. However, as one can imagine, to challenge and reframe Australian identity in light of the stories of the Stolen Generation led to contention on the part of non-indigenous citizens. Danielle Celermajer notices a "backlash

---

3 For a more detailed and theoretical analysis of the concept of reconciliation (theological, judicial), see Teichler 2017.

of resistance [against the rhetoric and practices of reconciliation], provoking some Australians to protest what they saw as an unjust accusation, an imputation of guilt and responsibility for actions they did not personally commit" (153). The self-image of Australia as a liberal and inclusive nation was under attack; the construction of a new national narrative which included indigenous resistance and suffering posed a threat to well-established notions of Australian identity.

In resonance with the processes of reconciliation and Rudd's apology, a critical re-evaluation of the image of Australian identity unfolded, and two national narratives came into conflict. On the one hand, Australia takes pride in having become a culturally and economically established community, especially with regard to its "inauspicious origins" as a penal colony (Wimmer 3). As a crown dominion, Australia later 'successfully' participated in the two World Wars and was among the first nations to ratify the genocide convention. During the 1970s, Australia increasingly became aware of its status as an immigrant country and promoted multiculturalism as national policy. Yet the system of cultural 're-education' – which was deemed genocidal – blemishes the celebratory image of Australian history.

Baz Luhrmann sets out to solve this conundrum concerning Australian national identity, and as I have already argued, the outcome is quite ambiguous: Marcia Langton, professor of Australian indigenous studies, praises *Australia* and its agenda for having "given Australians a new past," and "a myth of national origin that is disturbing, thrilling, heartbreaking, hilarious, and touching" (n. pag.). To meet this task, *Australia* not only engages with the discourse of distancing (from imperial dominance) and approximation (i.e. finding a distinct Australian identity) but seeks to balance out these issues. One of the driving forces of Luhrmann's filmic epos is the aspect that Australia still maintains an ambiguous relationship to its imperial mother Britain. How to include and how to negotiate the remnants of this 'Anglo-Celtic' heritage in Australian national narratives is still a matter of contestation. Adi Wimmer remarks with respect to this tension that "the British [were] enviously perceived as calm and self-assured about their identity," whilst in Australia, identities and certainties were in flux after the First World War (1).

Australia picks up on this formative struggle between Britishness and an emerging sense of Australianness. Set in 1939, English aristocrat Lady Ashley (Nicole Kidman) travels to the distant colony Australia to check on her husband, a known philanderer. Lady Ashley is introduced to the viewer as stereotypically British, enjoying the occasional tea party and horse ride through the lush meadows of her vast property. Upon arrival in Australia, she meets the independent cattle drover, played by Hugh Jackman, who throughout the movie is simply referred to as 'the Drover.' The contrast between the two protagonists could not be more pronounced. He is a jack-of-all-trades, outback-savvy and weather-beaten, and, naturally, a man of few words. Lady Ashley, by contrast, brings silk dresses and the proverbial stiff upper lip to the Australian desert. As this odd couple arrives at the failing cattle farm, Lady Ashley finds her husband murdered, supposedly by an Aboriginal elder called "King George" (David Galpilil). King George is quickly established as the uncanny force, always lurking in the background, hovering over his grandson Nullah and his fate. In situations of crisis, he intervenes in an almost God-like manner. Nullah (Brandon Walters) is the son of Daisy, an Aboriginal housemaid (Ursula Yovich), and the villainous farm foreman Neil Fletcher (David Wenham) – he is the product of rape. Daisy loses her life in an attempt to save Nullah from the Australian authorities who have come to take him away. This half-caste boy is also the one who informs Lady Ashley about the cattle theft and points her towards Fletcher as the culprit. Infatuated with Nullah and having her mind set on saving *Faraway Downs,* Lady Ashley dares to risk a cattle drive through the perilous outback. The Drover and Nullah are the prime enablers of this risky adventure. While the Drover assembles a colorful team to drive the cattle, including a Chinese cook, a British accountant, and Drover's best friend Magarri (David Ngoombujarra), Lady Ashley begins to transform from the English aristocrat stranded in the unforgiving outback, into the female drover. In a sense, she does not simply become a drover's wife as she marries the Drover in the end, but claims her right to become a national emblem, a national allegory: Australia's mother. When the couple adopts Nullah and allow him to go on the walkabout, an Aboriginal coming-of-age ritual, the ruptures and rifts within the Australian national narrative are neatly resolved. They become Australia's Holy Family.

The outback becomes the stage on which to negotiate a sense of Australianness. In this manner, the film taps into the discourse of the outback as a space where Australia comes to be. In the process of distinguishing Australian national identity from Britain's, the outback became the quintessential space of projection, negotiation, and imagination of what it means to be Australian, as Russel Ward famously outlines in *The Australian Legend* (1966). At the heart of this 'bush myth' was the question of who inhabits and cultivates the land, and out of this proprietary scheme, an identity was born: the bush myth imagines a noble bushman, virtuous, practical, resilient, and determined, as Graeme Davison similarly argues: "Like American pioneers, bushmen entered and conquered the alien landscape. They tamed the hostile environment, made it human, and thus performed a central civilizing, nation-building function" (31). Accordingly, the outback was promoted as distinctly, characteristically

Australian, and its physique captured the uniqueness of Australia. It was both mythicized and idealized. Along with it, as both Ward and Davison deduce, the bush and its hero, the drover, became 'real Australians.' In the bush myth, the Australian rural worker is often pitted against the decay and decadence of either the Australian city or British Imperial culture and its corruption. Inevitably, 'membership' in this 'Australian club' was rather exclusive, as critics Liz Conor, Odette Kelada, and Laleen Jayamanne have argued in their analyses of Luhrmann's film. Excluded from this definition of Australianness were women, indigenous peoples, other ethnic minorities, and town or city people. In this sense, the bush myth and the drover as its representative are racialized and misogynist images of Australian national identity.

However, within *Australia,* this 'strange' country is not referred to as 'the land far, far away,' as the name of Lady Ashley's cattle farm, *Faraway Downs*, might suggest; it is England that is invoked as the alien place far, far away from Australian civilization.[4] The audience's first encounter with Lady Ashley is accompanied by Nullah's voice-over that introduces her as the "strangest woman" who is not from this country, Australia, but from a "country far, far away" – England (*Australia* 0:04:43). This is clearly a reference to the realm of fairy tales, further sustained by repetitive allusions to 'storytelling' as the primary human condition.[5] In this spirit of storytelling, *Australia* does not shy away from contesting the seminal national narrative of the bushman and the outback by addressing the nation's structural racism.

Consider, for example, whom *Australia* sends into the outback on the hazardous cattle drive. At one point, the survival of the cattle farm can only be secured if the cattle are sold in Darwin. This means that 1,500 animals have to be guided through the outback. In the aftermath of Fletcher's demise,[6] the farm is mal-staffed for such a perilous undertaking, and in dire need of capable people to enable the drive. Nullah hurries to fetch the Drover, whose second appearance in the movie frames him as a reproduction of the Australian legend outlined above: on horseback, he rushes to the farm to assess the situation and to eventually remedy it. The Drover is portrayed as the noble, but slightly

---

4 Nullah introduces himself and the history of Aboriginal dispossession within the first twelve minutes of the film.
5 Nullah and King George are able to sing 'magic songs' in reference to Aboriginal storytelling practices, and Lady Ashley consoles Nullah after the death of his mother with the famous song "Over the Rainbow."
6 Farm manager Neil Fletcher is fired by Lady Ashley because he repeatedly misbehaved towards Nullah and the other Aboriginal staff on *Faraway Downs*. Fletcher's behaviour worsens after Nullah uncovers his treachery (*Australia* 00:30:00–00:35:42).

'savage' hero, the enabler that the lost aristocrat Lady Ashley has been waiting for (*Australia* 00:35:42–00:41:20). The Drover's re-entry forms a connection to another frontier existence related genre: the Western. Panoramic shots and upward camera angles make the Drover appear larger than life and properly heroic. He becomes one with the landscape that he is literally performing on. Fast-paced cuts create suspense that culminates in Lady Ashley convincing the Drover that the drive can actually be managed by the 'impossible 7:' Lady Ashley, Nullah, the Drover, an Aboriginal woman, the Drover's Aboriginal friend Magarri, the Chinese cook, and the alcoholic farm accountant, Kipling Flynn, embark on this perilous journey. Thus conceived, *Australia* breaks open the male, misogynist, and racist discourse of the bush myth, and transforms it into a testimony to multicultural Australia. Moreover, in the tradition of revisionist history writing, this particular framing pluralizes and corrects the bush myth. The Australian outback indeed becomes a place where 'dreams do come true,' as the song "Over the Rainbow" famously suggests. This special group of drovers symbolizes an act of empowerment within *Australia,* for it writes and imagines marginalized groups right onto the canvas where Australianness is seemingly already precluded – the outback. Australia's blatant racism towards its Aboriginal peoples, its anti-British and anti-aristocratic attitude, and the marginalization of other ethnicities (like the Chinese) are projected onto the outback where they are temporarily overridden. *Australia* inscribes the marginalized into the mainstream national discourse. The seven drovers (six after Kipling's death) represent the cultural compartments which comprise multicultural Australia and thus become agents of an imagined reconciled Australia.

Furthermore, Nullah plays a significant role in this setting, for he, along with his grandfather King George, becomes the primary enabler of this dangerous endeavor, the cattle drive. Fletcher and his villains wreak havoc on the group because they scare the animals into a stampede (*Australia* 1:00:00–1:07:29). With fires, they force the rampaging cattle towards a cliff. Nullah gets in front of the stampede, standing close to the edge of the cliff. He is forced to watch how Kipling Flynn is trampled to death under the hooves of the herd, yet unleashes his 'magic' onto the animals. The film frames his magic intervention as a mixture of song and incantation, summoning and spell. He gesticulates, hums, and sings the stampeding cattle until they mysteriously come to their senses and stop right at the edge of the cliff. With this heroic act, the Aboriginal child not only saves the cattle herd, the driving party, and by extension also *Faraway Downs,* but also becomes the main facilitator of the 'Australian Dream' that Lady Ashley dares to imagine. Although this dream is still a 'white' one, *Australia* changes the paradigms of this story.

3   In the Loving Embrace of "Missus Boss"

Consider, for example, how the scene described above ends (*Australia* 1:00:00–1:07:29). Nullah, who has just saved the entire endeavor by calming the cattle, loses consciousness over this enormous task and falls into Lady Ashley's arms, who assures him that he is safe with her. The Drover rushes to their side and remains with the two long enough for the viewer to capture the representation of a Holy Family. The impression of a nuclear family is evoked by an upward camera angle, rendering them almost divine apparitions. The Drover fades into the background of the arrangement to give all the narrative and visual space to Nullah and Lady Ashley. Odette Kelada points out that this scene establishes an intertextual link with Charles Chauvel's famous 1955 melodramatic film *Jedda* – a movie which was not only the first Australian film to be shot in color, but also the first one to feature two Aboriginals as leading actors (88). In *Jedda*, the eponymous Aboriginal girl becomes an orphan and is adopted by the family of the station boss, the McCanns. Sarah, the wife, seeks to assimilate Jedda into white Australian society and to raise her according to European values. All traditional Aboriginal ways are forbidden to Jedda, but as she grows older, she meets Marbuck, an Aboriginal man from the bush, and they fall in love. The filmic narrative suggests that Marbuck abducts her from the McCanns' home. However, Marbuck's tribe further impedes the growing love between the two, for Jedda is deemed unworthy of him because of her light skin color. In the end, the two commit suicide. Marbuck jumps off a cliff with Jedda in his arms. *Australia* cites this cliff scene, as Nullah is on the verge of falling off the cliff, before he is saved by Lady Ashley. In contrast to this rendering in *Australia*, Jedda's fall suggests the impossibility of assimilation of the 'savages' and also precludes a return to the Aboriginal community. Kelada remarks:

> The cinematic juxtaposition could be read as suggesting that rather than symbolically falling between the abyss of assimilation politics and what was conceived as 'traditional' tribal Indigeneity, a brighter post-apology future can be imagined now for 'Jedda'/indigenous peoples. Luhrmann's homage to Jedda revives and rescues the ghost of this Aboriginal child figure by performing a retrieval from the cliff face and salvation in the familial arms of Lady Ashley and Drover. This fits neatly with a fantasy epic for Australia past and present. (86–7)

Yet what was meant as a nod to *Jedda* and its heritage ultimately becomes part of an odd colonial power hierarchy in *Australia.* Liz Conor refers to *Australia*'s "reference-saturation" in this context and remarks that the "entrenched cultural habit of referencing reality through the 'image bank' ... of modernity" is one major narrative strategy of Luhrmann's movie (97).[7] *Australia* attempts to challenge *Jedda*'s stance on the impossibility of Aboriginal assimilation. The scene consequently does not reframe Jedda's suicide as Nullah's self-empowerment. Although Nullah saves the cattle and becomes, in a sense, 'superhuman' through this deed, *Australia*'s re-arrangement of the cliff scene centralizes Lady Ashley's motherhood and her prowess as a child-saver, distorting the moment of Aboriginal empowerment into emphasizing the dependence of Australia's indigenous populations on the white settlers. Lady Ashley once again becomes the point of reference. As Kelada suggests,

> It is important to note that this white mother is a *good* mother. She effectively rescued the 'Jedda'-like figure from the fatal descent off the cliff and *clasps* the child to her, with Drover appearing in time to construct a familial embrace. This white mother is one who questions the authorities when they parrot 'bad' ideas of the period claiming that Aboriginal mothers did not care for their children. ... Lady Ashley's protest provides contrast with such 'bad' colonialists and presents her as a progressive *good* white person, identifiable and likable/consumable for a contemporary audience. Underlying this, ... the movie still plays out how the bond between Aboriginal mother and child can be severed with disturbing ease. (88, emphases in original)

Kelada refers to a peculiar binary opposition that *Australia* constructs. On the one hand, the viewer encounters Lady Ashley as a progressive female protagonist. Her character seems to be far ahead of her contemporaries, both in terms of the way she perceives herself and the attitude she holds towards other socially and/or ethnically marginalized people. She fights against male dominance and refuses to be reduced to her status as a woman – which would restrict her to the domestic sphere and limit her agency. In this sense, she is a

---

[7] One of the most widely referenced intertextual connections is the link to the American musical fantasy film *The Wizard of Oz* (1939). Despite the proclivity to interpret it as a filmic adaptation of a children's book, some scholars point to the strong subversive qualities of the (original) narrative, as exemplified by e.g. Henry Littlefield (1964) or Hugh Rockoff (1990). *Australia* draws on L. Frank Baum's *The Wonderful Wizard of Oz* and its filmic adaptation. It is the silhouette of *Faraway Downs* that emerges through the mist as the viewer is introduced to the story, and it is the invocation of a 'land far, far away' that sets the tone for this intertextuality. This land, Oz, which is a well-established nickname for Australia, will be healed by the mysterious woman from 'far, far away.'

modern version of *The Wizard of Oz*'s Dorothy who has come to an unknown land to make it accessible to her.

Daisy, Nullah's mother, is silenced and marginalized by the overarching narrative of *Australia*. Whilst it is true that female Aboriginals held the weakest position in the hierarchy of the marginalized, Daisy appears solely as the facilitator of Lady Ashley's motherhood 'by accident.' Daisy only has a few words to say before she accidentally drowns in the water tank. In an act of revenge, recently fired Fletcher tells the authorities about Nullah's existence on *Faraway Downs* (*Australia* 00:41:45). Consider how the movie interweaves two narrative strands through parallel montage: a police car appears and an officer questions Lady Ashley about the existence of a "half-caste fella." The scene is introduced by one of the formative panoramic shots which descend on the scene, and the camera lingers on an Aboriginal tracker who is complicit in the child-removal endeavor (00:43:33). The words "Run, Nullah, run!" interrupt this otherwise picturesque scene where Lady Ashley is shown in her first foray into cattle-driving. In an attempt to escape the policemen, Daisy and Nullah hide in the giant water tank. An officer starts the pumping mechanism to wash his face – which *Australia* marks as a deliberate act based on the assumption that someone could have hidden in the water tank. The water level rises as Lady Ashley tries to appease the officers and to convince them to leave the premises. At some point, Daisy is unable to stay above water anymore, for she cannot swim. Although Drover and the others rush to help her as soon as the police drive away, Daisy drowns in the tank, while Nullah survives (00:46:44). Daisy's death is the prerequisite and enabler of *Australia*'s narrative of reconciliation. The rise of Lady Ashley is contrasted with the fall of Daisy. Only through her disappearance as a mother-figure can Lady Ashley take her place and commence her quest to save the country, as Nullah predicted in his opening remarks (00:01:30). Kelada further suggests that

> [w]hile Daisy's death is powerfully performed and depicts a grand maternal bond, it is contradicted by Nullah's quick recovery from grief after such a terrible climax. The scene with Lady Ashley [singing 'Over the Rainbow'] that follows his mother's death plays out the notion of disposable emotional bonds between an indigenous mother and a child . ... The soothing nature of singing and bonding may have worked as a healing scene. However, what is anomalous is that as Nullah is coaxed from his tears and looks up at Lady Ashley in wonder, he becomes strangely invested in the white woman's goal: the objective of transporting her cattle for sale. (88–90)

Although Lady Ashley later insists that she "is not good with children," Drover settles the matter by pointing out that a child needs a mother (*Australia* 00:48:20). Lady Ashley replaces Daisy, while Drover will, in the long run, replace Fletcher as Nullah's absent and evil father (Conor 163). As both Kelada and Conor aptly remark, other Aboriginal (and female) family members are out of the question as surrogate mothers. On the contrary, although we know that Drover was married to an Aboriginal woman, *Australia* lets him utter the inappropriate remark that Aboriginal women are very easy to get along with, and the suggestive potential of this comment is supported by a shot on his groins, to which Drover actually points while talking. This scene is an example of *Australia*'s overplayed aesthetics that risk evoking the opposite of its benevolent intentions. With this scene, the position of female Aboriginals as the furthest away from the center is strengthened rather than contested, and bizarrely, the colonial assumption that Aboriginals are unfit to take care of children is taken up again. *Australia*

> conveniently expunges the kinship network into which Nullah and his ongoing care and education would have ordinarily been inextricably woven. This is clumsily masked by the exception of King George, who himself references the 'King Billy' type. He is a 'magic man', asserting his right to educate Nullah, who tells Lady Ashley that Nullah too is 'magic'. King George's claim on Nullah centres on his responsibilities as an elder to initiate the boy, but his status as accused murderer leaves his claim and authority as grandfather and educator unsubstantiated until he is exonerated. (Conor 163)

As Nullah falls into her arms by the cliff, Lady Ashley seals her maternal bond with the exclamation: "You're safe with me" (*Australia* 01:05:20). After Daisy's death, Nullah becomes the facilitator of Lady Ashley's endeavor rather than a distinct individual in Luhrmann's national allegory. In this sense, Conor speaks of a "domesticated form of Aboriginality" (104). Although Nullah introduces himself as a person who belongs to no-one and is situated between two cultural poles, he becomes the common property of Luhrmann's reconciliation narrative. *Australia* starts off promisingly when Nullah's magic capacities are gradually revealed. The connection to the supernatural is evoked prominently when Nullah 'senses' and accompanies the death of Lord Ashley. Humming and gesticulating, Nullah waves Lady Ashley towards her dead husband's body that is laid out in the living room (*Australia* 01:05:20). Nullah's and Lady Ashley's first encounter amplifies this impression: Nullah has just told the viewer that the country will be saved by this "strange woman," and that he will sing her to him (00:23:20).⁸ The camera blends over to Lady Ashley's room, and a strange, but not frightening, female and childlike voice hums a soothing melody. Lady Ashley appears to be afraid of this supernatural apparition. The uncanny mood is supported by billowing curtains, preparing the audience for a ghost.

Further on, the mystery dissolves into relief, because Nullah physically enters the scene. In the beginning, he is mildly irritating, but turns out to be loveable. The uncanniness is cleared by comic relief, and Nullah returns to the human realm when he cracks a joke about "wrong-side business," a reference to sexual encounters (00:25:40). Nullah tells the sad story of his origins – Fletcher frequently raped his mother, and she became pregnant with him – yet the film turns it into a joke, and Nullah into a 'black fella' fool. The idea of "wrong-side business" reappears when Drover kisses Lady Ashley for the first time, and Nullah catches them, inquiring as to whether they would now also engage in such business (01:12:50). It is Nullah's role to disrupt the (melo-)dramatic with the wits of a child. Nullah is represented as a young wizard in Oz, transcending the boundaries between nature and culture. These are ultimately colonial tropes and racially biased representations. King George – *the* Wizard of Oz – and Nullah both are framed as exotic. It is the colonizers' fantasy of Aboriginality that manifests itself in the conception of *Australia*'s Aboriginal characters. Conor argues that Nullah is even closely associated with the piccaninny child, a racist and derogatory caricature that was, for example, found in art, on tableware and household items. She writes:

> From the 1910s to the 1960s the 'piccaninny' became a common household ornament through the enormously popular ceramics of Brownie Downing ... [,] the Martin Boyd Pottery company, the children's books of Elizabeth Durack and Jane Ada Fletcher ... [,] the watercolours and fabric designs of Peg Malty ... and the nature writings and photography of Charles Barrett and Axel Poignant. Yet the popularity of the 'piccaninny' peaks as the policy of assimilation, which rested on child removals, intensified across each of the states, as Aboriginal children became the principal target for colonial states' governance of Indigenous populations. The 'piccaninny' came to embody an 'Aboriginality of childhood' ... that through their removal came to inscribe a white Australian future. (99)⁹

---

8   Nullah repeatedly refers to his capacity to connect with someone through his singing, usually over a vast distance. He is able to sing someone to him.

9   Conor further outlines how the "term 'piccaninny' migrated from Britain and the United States via seamen in the early decades of settlement" and how "the use of Aboriginal motifs in settler art was first encouraged by the Australian artist Margaret Preston in a series of four articles in *Art and Australia* between 1925 and 1941. She urged that Aboriginal art should

Although Nullah tells most of the film's story – frequently he is the voice-over – he also becomes an object that settler Australia desires (104). As Conor puts it, the "trans-colonially and trans-nationally" circulated piccaninny child is once more subjected to "a distinctly British acquisitive impulse over the colonized, racialized child," and *Australia* translates this impulse into giving consent for the Aboriginals to be part of Luhrmann's reconciliation epos (104).

It is in this vein that Nullah remains on the sidelines when Lady Ashley becomes the Drover's wife, and thus turns Australian. *Australia* thus establishes another intertextual connection to a seminal bush myth text: Henry Lawson's "The Drover's Wife" (1892). Although Lawson's short story centers on and represents the perspective of a drover's wife, it is regarded as a key narrative of the bush myth, as Liesl Hermes and Christine Vandamme have outlined. There are two key scenes to Lady Ashley's transformation. The cattle drive party returns to their camp after Nullah has successfully bewitched the herd, but they find their camp in shambles (*Australia* 1:07:30–1:14:58). Fletcher and his villains have destroyed all the belongings that Lady Ashley brought on the trip. This is precisely the moment when the aristocratic Lady Ashley finally becomes a female version of a drover: she regrets that she has brought "all those things" (commodities, luxury items, clothing) to the outback, as they now seem ridiculously out of place to her (1:07:30). Simultaneously, the Drover discloses that he was married to an Aboriginal woman who died of tuberculosis because the doctors would refuse to treat Aboriginals (1:12:50). Lady Ashley confesses that she is unable to have children. Nullah, however, remains absent from this scene, and only plays "Over the Rainbow" on Kipling's harmonica, marking the completion of Lady Ashley's transition and indicating that King George's prophecy has come true – this woman has come to save this land. The most powerful representation of Lady Ashley's transformation and her acceptance into the fold is the second bar scene (1:24:26–1:25:27). In the first bar scene, Drover was marked as marginalized and unwelcome in society, while the Aboriginal Magarri and women were altogether excluded from the bar. These tropes are taken up again in the second bar scene which follows the successful cattle drive. Lady Ashley is welcomed into the fold of rural Australia(n men) because she has proven herself to be a 'true Australian' bush-woman. Her joining of the club is marked by her "deserv[ing] a drink like any man." This collective eventually opens its doors once more and broadens the frame

---

become the foundation and inspiration of a modern, national Australian art. Preston's art …, is construed from an " 'alliance between art, anthropology, modernism and nationalism' " (99–100). Conor also mentions a Darwin woman who refers to Nullah as a piccaninny in *Australia*.

of who, according to *Australia*'s vision of the nation, belongs to multicultural Australia. In the third bar scene, Australia's structural racism is finally overcome because Magarri is allowed to enter the bar and to have his drink in the company of his friends. Aboriginal men, thus conceived, are also incorporated into Luhrmann's national narrative.

4 Conclusion

Notwithstanding Nullah's and Magarri's introduction into the national fabric, Luhrmann's vision of reconciliation consequently culminates in the quintessential trope of the Australian Holy Family with its central mother figure. Not foregrounding and imagining an independent notion of indigeneity, *Australia* is satisfied with assimilating the Aboriginals into the Australian national narrative. They are an integral part of Australian national identity post reconciliation, but they do not receive structural agency that reaches beyond stereotypical uncanny traits. *Australia* is astonishingly straightforward in transporting rather simplistic solutions and characters, precisely because the melodramatic aesthetics, the emphasis on comic relief and parodic exaggeration are *not* subordinated to *Australia*'s identity politics. Luhrmann's movie seeks to make a very important, pro-indigenous point about Australian history and strives to incorporate the major rifts in Australian history into one perfect whole. This endeavor to construct a pluralized brand of Australian nationalism results in oversimplifications which eventually turn against Luhrmann's benevolent intentions. *Australia* is arguably the most pertinent example of the paradox of reconciliation: whilst the movie longs to empower indigenous peoples and aspires to include their histories into the national narrative as an act of justice and respect, it produces the opposite effect. This national narrative is teleological and linear to the extent that this Australia is colorful but segmented and ultimately hierarchical. The Australian nation as imagined in this movie is reconciled with its troubled history (the country's origins as a penal colony under the British thumb) and the legacy of the Stolen Generations (as *Australia*'s Aboriginal protagonists merge into the national fabric and take their place as facilitators of, and not equal partners in, this Australian success story).

In the process, Aboriginal Australians are simply incorporated into the national framework, and the legacy of forcible removal is reconciled with Australian history by the allegorical act of Lady Ashley adopting Nullah. The lost children are repatriated, returned into the national fold, and reconciliation is enforced on Australia's indigenous peoples, thus presupposing their 'consent' to have reconciliation imposed on indigenous notions of history, identity, and futurity.

Works Cited

Adorno, Theodor W. *Noten zur Literatur*, edited by Rolf Thiedemann, Suhrkamp, 1991.

Australia. Directed by Baz Luhrmann, performances by Nicole Kidman, Hugh Jackman, and Brandon Walters, 20th Century Fox, 2008.

Baum, Lyman Frank. *The Wonderful Wizard of Oz*. 1900. Wirton Arvel, 2016.

Celermajer, Danielle. "The Apology in Australia: Re-covenanting the National Imaginary." *Taking Wrongs Seriously: Apologies and Reconciliation*, edited by Elazar Barkan and Alexander Karn, Stanford UP, 2006, pp. 153–84.

Conor, Liz. "A 'Nation So Ill-begotten': Racialized Childhood and Conceptions of National Belonging in Xavier Herbert's *Poor Fellow My Country* and Baz Luhrmann's *Australia*." *Studies in Australasian Cinemas,* vol. 4, no. 2, 2010, pp. 97–113. doi: 10.1386/sac.4.2.97_1.

Crocodile Dundee. Directed by Peter Fairman, performances by Paul Hogan, Linda Kozlowski, and John Mellon, Paramount Pictures, 1986.

Davison, Graeme. "Rethinking the Australian Legend." *Australian Historical Studies*, vol. 43, no. 3, 2012, pp. 429–51. doi: 10.1080/1031461X.2012.706625.

Hermes, Liesel. "Henry Lawson's 'The Drover's Wife' in the Australian Short Story." *Global Fragments: (Dis)Orientation in the New World Order*, edited by Anke Bartels et al., Rodopi, 2007, pp. 301–12. doi: 10.1163/9789401204224_021.

Jedda. Directed by Charles Chauvel, performances by Rosalie Kunoth-Monks, and Robert Tudawali, Columbia Pictures and Umbrella Entertainment, 1955.

Jayamanne, Laleen. "The Drover's Wives and Camp Couture: Baz Luhrmann's Preposterous National Epic." *Studies in Australasian Cinema*, vol. 4, no. 2, 2010, pp. 131–43.

Kelada, Odette. "Love Is a Battlefield: 'Maternal' Emotions and White Catharsis in Baz Luhrmann's Post-Apology Australia." *Studies in Australasian Cinema*, vol. 8, no. 2–3, 2014, pp. 83–95. doi: 10.1080/17503175.2014.939428.

Lawson, Henry. "The Drovers Wife." 1892. *The Drover's Wife and Other Stories* by Henry Lawson, edited by Alan Brissenden, Hodder & Stoughton, 1974, pp. 8–16.

Littlefield, Henry M. "The Wizard of Oz: Parable of Populism." *American Quarterly*, vol. 16, no. 1, 1964, pp. 47–58.

Luhrmann, Baz. "How We Made the Epic of Oz." *The Guardian*, 2 Nov. 2008, www.theguardian.com/film/2008/nov/02/baz-luhrmann-nicole-kidman-australia. Accessed 12 Nov. 2017.

Mad Max: Fury Road. Directed by George Miller, performances by Tom Hardy, Charlize Theron and Nicholas Hoult, Warner Bros., 2015.

National Inquiry into the Separation of Aboriginal and Torres Strait Islander Children from their Families. *Bringing them Home Report*, 1997, www.humanrights.gov.au/sites/default/files/content/pdf/social_justice/bringing_them_home_report.pdf. Accessed 20 Aug. 2020.

Olick, Jeffrey K. *The Politics of Regret: On Collective Memory and Historical Responsibility.* Routledge, 2007.

Rudd, Kevin. "Apology to Australia's Indigenous People." *Government of Australia,* www.australia.gov.au/about-australia/our-country/our-people/apology-to-australias-indigenous-peoples. Accessed 23 Mar. 2020.

Rockoff, Hugh. "The *Wizard of Oz* as Monetary Allegory." *Journal of Political Economy,* vol. 98, no. 4, 1990, pp. 739–60.

Teichler, Hanna. "Aspirin or Amplifier? Reconciliation, Justice, and the Performance of National Identity in Canada." *Postcolonial Justice,* edited by Anke Bartels et al., Brill, 2017, pp. 317-32.

Teichler, Hanna. *Carnivalizing Reconciliation. Contemporary Australian and Canadian Literature and Film beyond the Victim Paradigm.* Berghahn, 2021. (forthcoming).

The Wizard of Oz. Directed by Victor Fleming, performances by Judy Garland, Ray Bolger, Jack Haley, Bert Lahr and Margaret Hamilton, Metro-Goldwyn-Mayer, 1939.

Vandamme, Christine. "'The Drover's Wife': Celebrating or Demystifying Bush Mythology?" *Commonwealth Essays and Studies*, vol. 38, no. 2, 2016, pp. 73–81.

Ward, Russel. *The Australian Legend.* Oxford UP, 1966.

Wimmer, Adi. *Australian Film: Cultures, Identities, Texts.* Wissenschaftlicher Verlag Trier, 2007.

CHAPTER 8

Intersections of Race, Sexuality, and National Identity in BioWare's *Mass Effect*

Theresa Krampe

1   Introduction: On the Political Aesthetics of Playing Queer[1]

Fiery comets rain down on the city, setting skyscrapers ablaze like giant torches. The sky is dark, heavy with ashes and smoke. Large, coleopteran machines move between multi-storey buildings, trampling everything in their way and tearing through concrete walls with beams of red light. The air resonates with the thunder of distant explosions. Despite the futuristic architecture dominating the remaining skyline, the city looks disturbingly familiar. The camera zooms in between the houses to reveal dark streets lined with burning cars and piles of rubble. Soldiers take cover behind half-torn walls and abandoned military vehicles, entrenching themselves between the facades of Georgian houses and office buildings with shattered windows. In a fortified part of the streets, we encounter two men, both heavily armed, mid-conversation. "Guess we're old soldiers, eh, Shepard?", the speaker, whose name is Kaidan, addresses the other officer. "Brothers in arms. We know the score." Then, quietly, he adds: "We know this is goodbye." The camera pans to the destroyed office buildings. Beyond glass and concrete, the grey sky is visible. "I'm not afraid to die," Kaidan continues. "But how are you doing? Scared?" "Damn straight I'm scared," Shepard answers. "But that fear is gonna keep me alive long enough to strike these bastards right through the heart." "Yeah. Exactly," the other agrees, apparently lost for words. "So. Take care, Major," Shepard says, turning to leave. Kaidan catches him by the arm. They kiss. "Stay safe," Kaidan says, voice breaking. "Yeah." The camera pans over burning tanks in the background. Fade to black.

With much pathos and melodrama, the scene could fit into any generic post-apocalyptic science fiction movie, albeit the kiss between the soldiers puts an unexpected spin on the patriotic trope of the war hero saying goodbye to wife and kids. In reality, the paragraph above novelises an audio-visual rendering

---

[1] This chapter builds on my previous research on queerness and hegemonic masculinity in *Mass Effect* (Krampe n. pag.).

of narrative and cinematographic affordances contingent on player choice. In other words, it retells an interactive cutscene from the videogame *Mass Effect 3*, released by the Canadian developer BioWare in 2012. Undetected by some, video gaming has long outgrown its status as a pastime for 'geeky' adolescents, and developers and publishers of so-called AAA-games[2] invest huge sums of money in their games and reach considerable audiences. According to its publisher Electronic Arts, *Mass Effect 3* alone sold close to a million copies within the first twenty-four hours after its release in the US (Thier n. pag.). Indeed, videogames have come a long way from the moving dots that was *Spacewar!* (1962).[3] Nowadays, numerous adventure and role-playing games (RPGs) offer immersive and complex storytelling experiences. At the same time, videogames suffer from a significant inertia effect when it comes to the diversification of representation, both within the games themselves and in a working environment in which the overwhelming majority of game designers identify as straight white men (Schallegger 44).[4] What is more, even though the fictional worlds of videogames have been associated with a temporary suspension of the rules of 'real life' and thus an almost utopian potential for transgressive behaviour (e.g. Consalvo 180), they remain embedded in the logics of nationalism, imperialism, and global capitalism. Science fiction and fantasy RPGs in particular often challenge normative identities and traditional notions of national belonging but, in the end, seem unable to escape their own ideological and economic entanglements.

It is imperative, then, that the humanities devote as much attention to videogames as to literature and film. This is a difficult task, as any comprehensive approach to videogames also needs to account for medium-specific characteristics such as a game's rule system, its mechanics and gameplay, or its interactive dimension. In this chapter, I hope to meet this challenge by offering a critical reading of BioWare's *Mass Effect* (hereafter: *ME*).[5] Unlike the majority of AAA-games, *ME* emphasises character diversity and the representation of

---

2 The meaning of the acronym is disputed. AAA-games (pronounced "triple A"), the game-industry's equivalent of blockbuster movies, are typically produced with a large budget and development team.

3 *Spacewar!* was, at the time, of course, impressive. Designed to show off the abilities of the computer, it also contained a simulation of physical laws.

4 Videogame journalism, for instance, increasingly addresses the lack of racial (as well as gender and sexual) diversity among videogame protagonists and game designers (e.g. Ong n. pag.; Sheikh n. pag.; Ramanan n. pag.).

5 By *ME*, I principally mean the original *Mass Effect* trilogy, consisting of three games: *ME1* (2007), *ME2* (2010), and *ME3* (2012). In 2017, the spin-off *Mass Effect: Andromeda* was released, featuring mostly different characters and settings.

minoritised identities while abandoning differentiations along national, racial, or gendered lines. Overt allusions to national identity are nearly absent and seem to have lost their meaning and divisive force in the game's futuristic intergalactic society. A careful analysis of the complex intersections of national, racial, and sexual, individual and collective identities, however, reveals how *ME* remains firmly grounded in the ideologies governing twenty-first century societies, including more subtle but no less powerful forms of nationalism and imperialism.

While *ME* resists simplified and unambivalent interpretations, I suggest that through an integrated and intersectional analysis of the game's affordances for the construction of non-hegemonic male identities, it is possible to decode the complex mechanisms of power and knowledge informing the game's representational politics. A queer game studies approach, as outlined by Bonnie Ruberg and Adrienne Shaw, lends itself well to such an endeavour, as it focuses on the transgressive potential entailed in moments of 'queer play' in games. For the purposes of the following game analysis, queerness as a concept includes but is not limited to the study of non-heteronormative sexualities. Rather, following Judith Butler, it is understood as an interrogative paradigm: "a site of collective contestation, the point of departure for a set of historical reflections and futural imaginings" (173). The specificities of the medium furthermore demand that I take into account how videogames create meaning through a complex interplay of narrative, audio-visual aesthetics, gameplay mechanics, and socio-political context. Reading the game space of *ME* as a sandbox for the negotiation of a specifically Canadian brand of Western national and cultural identity discloses an ideology of neoliberal, multicultural globalisation at the heart of the game. I argue that contrary to initial appearances, *ME* showcases nationalism's continued sway over Western popular culture well into the twenty-first century.

2 Game Studies and Cultural Studies

That videogame studies are only now receiving widespread recognition as a legitimate field of study does not mean that there have not been earlier attempts at conceptualising games and play. The classic reference for studying the role of games in society is Johan Huizinga's 1938 *Homo Ludens*.[6]

---

[6] *Homo Ludens* was first published in Dutch in 1938. A subsequent English translation, published by Routledge & Kegan Paul in 1949, is based on the 1944 German translation as well as the author's own English translation.

Developing a cultural theory of play, he describes it as a voluntary activity, constrained by binding rules, perceived as different from everyday life, and evoking strong emotions in the player (28). He also coined the expression 'magic circle,' now commonly used as a shorthand to describe the spatiotemporal frame of the game, liberated from the confines of ordinary social life. Games may also be experienced as storyworlds by players of narrative games (Adams 44; Schallegger 47). Brenda Laurel, as early as 1993, famously conceptualised computer programmes, including games, as a form of drama in *Computers as Theatre,* and, in 1997, Janet Murray heralded the dawn of a new medium of storytelling in *Hamlet on the Holodeck.*

In the early 2000s, the young discipline of game studies increasingly focused on the relation between games and their socio-political contexts, addressing questions related to representation and identity politics. Female gamers and videogame protagonists received attention early on, for instance in Justine Cassell and Henry Jenkins's now seminal *From Barbie to Mortal Kombat: Gender and Computer Games* (1998). With regard to LGBTQ* representations in videogames, the work of Adrienne Shaw, including her often-cited 2009 article "Putting the Gay in Games: Cultural Production and GLBT Content in Video Games," has been crucial to mapping the field. Major BioWare franchises such as *Star Wars: Knights of the Old Republic* (2003–16), *Dragon Age* (2009–ongoing), and *Mass Effect* (2007–17) have been received as milestones with regard to character diversity in general and queer representation in particular and have consequently been subject to several analyses from queer studies perspectives (e.g. Greer; Condis; Ruberg and Shaw).

Inquiries into the representation of Black or Asian queer subjectivity, by contrast, are rare, possibly due to the scarcity of Black and Asian game characters.[7] Notable exceptions include Anna Everett's critique of racist ideologies and practices in the gaming context (e.g. Everett; Everett and Watkins) or the work of Lisa Nakamura on the significance of racialised identities in virtual space (see also Malkowski and Russworm 5). Furthermore, more research on the intersection of in-game sexuality and other factors such as race, nationality, or even genre conventions is needed. Two recently edited volumes, Ruberg and Shaw's 2017 *Queer Game Studies* and Jennifer Malkowski and TreaAndrea M. Russworm's *Gaming Representation: Race, Gender, and Sexuality in Videogames* (also 2017) have done much to emancipate discussions of identity

---

7 In AAA-games, characters of colour are rare, protagonists even rarer. If they do appear, it is usually either as superficially designed sidekicks or as typecast athletes and gangsters, for example in the *Grand Theft Auto* series (Mafe 90).

politics from the 'margins' of game studies (Malkowski and Russworm 1) and bring them to prominence in academia as well as in critical discourses online.

Building on this pioneering work, I will use an intersectional queer studies approach in this chapter in order to address the strategies of representation and the mechanisms of power at work in ME. Coined by legal scholar Kimberlé Crenshaw in her 1989 landmark essay "Demarginalizing the Intersection of Race and Sex" as a way of conceptualising black women's double marginalisation, intersectionality can be used to engage a wide range of identity categories such as nationality, race, class, sexuality, ability, religion, geography, or historical era, highlighting how their combined action produces and legitimises complex matrices of oppression (Carbado et al. 304–5; Lutz et al. 3; Manalansan 532).

3 Queer Intersections: Identity Politics in ME

ME is a science fiction shooter RPG series taking place in the not-too-distant future of the twenty-second century. Players assume the role of Commander Shepard, who is Captain of the spaceship *Normandy*, on his[8] quest to save the world from a sentient machine race determined to wipe out all organic life in the galaxy. The world of ME is vast and detailed. On their quest to save the galaxy, players encounter a variety of alien species, each associated with a distinct social and political system as well as cultural peculiarities. The most iconic of these is perhaps the migrant fleet, a diasporic community living almost self-sufficiently on spaceships.

While the main story arcs of ME as well as other BioWare franchises such as *Dragon Age* tend to be archetypal quest plots, the game's innovative quality lies in its development of unique and well-rounded non-player characters (NPCs) whose personalities, individual storylines, and relations to other characters constitute a major part of narrative and gameplay (Jørgensen 317). Indeed, the investment in characters on the part of both designers and audiences has developed into a trademark characteristic of BioWare RPGs (Adams 45). While some NPCs have exclusively narrative functions, others, referred to as squad

---

8   Shepard is, to a certain extent, customisable; i.e. players can choose either a male or female version of Shepard, alter their physical appearance and skin colour, and choose from several personal backgrounds. The default version suggested by the game and its promotion material, however, is a white male in his early thirties; tall, broad-shouldered, and with a military style buzz cut on a quest to save the world and rescue a number of damsels in distress in the process.

mates in *ME,* are also game pieces. These typically have unique narrative arcs in the form of optional side quests which explore their personalities, motivations, and relations to the player character (PC). Although the game can be finished without extensively interacting with any of the characters, engagement with the squad mates is encouraged through ludic (i.e. gameplay-related) and narrative rewards. Completing their personal quests effects significant changes in approval, which may, for instance, unlock new skills or romantic potential. Conversely, failing to engage with the NPCs has negative consequences. Squad members may even die, choose to abandon the player, or not be recruited in the first place, thus reducing the narrative content that can be explored and weakening the team's combat strength. The most extreme case is perhaps *ME2,* where the entire squad, including the PC, may be killed in action if the player does not gain everyone's loyalty by completing their personal missions (Krampe n. pag.).

Interaction between the player/PC and the NPCs is mediated through dialogue. Even though most character-developing conversations are optional, it is safe to assume that most players will roleplay them due to the narrative and ludic benefits mentioned above. The *ME* games use a dialogue wheel to simulate conversations. The wheel presents the player with paraphrases of the PC's actual answers which will then be delivered by professional voice actors. Visual cues, such as colour codes, symbols, or the position in the dialogue wheel, provide information about the tone of the PC's answer. Typically, answering modes include a diplomatic 'paragon,' a more aggressive 'renegade,' and a neutral or humorous answer. In some situations, these may be supplemented by dialogue options for flirting. Choosing the latter may set flags for later dialogue, thus activating romantic subplots (n. pag.).

ME's gameplay, especially its mixing of at least two game genres, is crucial to the analysis of its identity politics. *ME*'s shooting and cover mechanics, on the one hand, are reminiscent of the third-person shooter (Patterson 211). The use of ranged weapons such as the sniper rifle even causes a switch into the first-person perspective at the precise moment of taking the shot. These shooter-elements emphasise the military theme in *ME,* which is traditionally associated with the archetype of the able-bodied, straight, white, male hero. On the other hand, the complex system for level-ups and skill distribution and the frequent use of dialogue wheels are derived from the RPG genre. Concerned with modelling human interaction and relationships, the RPG-elements allow for the playful construction and acting out of various identities in *ME*'s military setting, including counter-hegemonic 'queer' identities. Indeed, as the *ME* series progresses, it challenges the hegemony of the military hero archetype. This is evident, for instance, in the affordance of non-heterosexual romance subplots in the second and especially third games, and the inclusion of a character with disability (Krampe n. pag.).

The first ME title sees non-white characters, such as Shepard's mentor Captain Anderson, in supporting roles with little screen time. It is only in the second instalment that ME introduces Jacob Taylor as the first squad mate of colour, presumably of African-American origin. However, as game designer anna anthropy, game scholar TreaAndrea Russworm, and others have rightfully pointed out, merely ticking off "gay" as a "checkbox on a character sheet" (anthropy) or the token inclusion of blackness without the engagement of surrounding discourses and histories of signification should not be confused with a nuanced, diverse representation (Russworm 109–10). Accordingly, Jacob's reception among gamers is mixed, and he is frequently accused of being "the token black guy" (UnholyDemigod n. pag.) who is only included in the game for the sake of claiming greater ethnic diversity. As a player under the username Xathos comments:

> What does Jacob have combat wise [sic]? Nothing too spectacular really. ... I never got a good grasp as to what kind of person he was. ... Oh, and that romance of his? Whew. ... Possibly the worst one in the series (and even his abs don't save it). ... I didn't connect with it [his narrative arc] at all like I did [sic] the others. (n. pag.)

Human skin colour and 'ethnicity' remain unmarked in the in-game dialogue and narration. This does not mean that racism and colonial power relations are absent from the games, though. Quite the contrary, racialised discourses are merely displaced to human-alien relations. In line with the games' 'progressive' pedagogy, overt displays of racist attitudes, such as human squad member Ashely's slurs against non-humans throughout *ME1*, are met with disapproval by other characters, and the player is restricted from voicing similar sentiments through the PC. However, race relations and imperialist ideologies are also engrained in the game's narrative and ludic system in subtler and arguably more profound ways that threaten to undermine the game's cosmopolitan message. The intergalactic division of labour, for instance, follows a racialised logic and race becomes a critical factor in the player's management of in-game intercultural (read: interspecies) relations. While humans stand out as neutral points of reference and successful allrounders, aliens are marked as other, each associated with a race-specific set of biological markers, abilities, and personality traits. The majority of Salarians, for instance, are socially awkward scientists, while Krogans are warriors and mercenaries whose lack of intellect is repeatedly emphasised. Gameplay mechanics train the player to pay attention to race through the repetition of combat scenarios in which race equals opponent type. When facing Krogan enemies, for instance, the player will learn by trial and error to take them out from a distance to avoid their devastating melee attacks. Salarians, by contrast, are more vulnerable to physical damage and can thus be taken on in close combat. Racial differentiation and stereotyping are rewarded by the game system, tied to ludic success or failure.

As the series progresses, it increasingly affords romance arcs for non-human squad mates. However, like same-sex relationships, these are subordinate to the 'desirable' heteronormative choices. Queer and xenophilic romances are afforded later in the series, receive less screen time, and are presented in a way that is less 'sexy' than the heterosexual romance choice (in the sense that less erotic content is shown). The exception are the Asari who are universally sexualised in the games. "The alien is loved and hated, fetishised and feared, enigmatic and infective," MacCormack asserts (117), and indeed *ME*'s discourses of biological alterity tap into a plethora of anti-gay and anti-immigrant sentiments reminiscent of the early years of the AIDS pandemic (Manalansan 532): the sexual and racial Other is constructed as a carrier and propagator of disease. This interpretation is even more pronounced when playing a female PC, who will be warned of the health risks involved in sexual activity with a non-human squad mate (Østby 210–4). The alien is constructed as a threat to 'our' race and culture, preying on women as biological and ideological reproducers (Anthias and Yuval-Davis 8–10). In the end, though *ME*'s dialogue choices discourage overt racism, several aspects of its gameplay as well as its narrative and cinematography intertwine racial, social, economic, and cultural discourses to form a racist and frequently also sexist matrix. This line of inquiry allows for a counter-reading of *ME*'s affordance of interracial and interspecies romances as a form of playground in which unconscious desires can be satisfied and the dominance and identity of the white male is reaffirmed in and through his relationship with various Others all of whose bodies are placed and organised in social hierarchies (hooks 22).

4 The Closeted Nationalism(s) of *Mass Effect*

In a 2016 publication, literary and media scholar René Reinhold Schallegger offers a much more optimistic view on the state of representational diversity in games, proposing a reading of BioWare's 2014 *Dragon Age: Inquisition* as not only a "game changer" (60) in terms of progressive and inclusive representations of sexual diversity in videogames but also a "most Canadian reply" (56) to the industry's ongoing marginalisation of disenfranchised groups.

He convincingly shows how leitmotifs of Canadian culture, such as survival against the dual threat of internal disintegration and external colonisation but also the centrality of compromise between groups and identities, reappear in the diegetic universe of the game. Thedas, the world of *Dragon Age,* thus becomes a platform for a what-if scenario simulating a social order based on "the principle of diversity and respect for the Other" (55).

A similar case can be argued for *ME*. In a way, the franchise's entanglement with actual-world discourses is even more overt because of the game's borrowings from genres with strong traditions of social criticism, such as dystopian science fiction. The specific Canadianness of *ME*, however, warrants further clarification since, at first glance, the game seems to dispense with group formation along familiar national lines. The gameworld's political organisation is no longer dependent on the nation-state but is centred on the "Alliance" (*ME*), a panhuman representational body which is integrated into the galaxy's intergovernmental organisation. References to the characters' national identities, by contrast, are virtually absent from the games. Interestingly, this changes in *ME3*. The third game's narrative opens in Vancouver, remodelled into a futuristic metropolis but retaining several of its present-day landmarks like Stanley Park or Canada Place, which also serve as backgrounds for ludic scenarios (Kuling 45). The strong element of galactic exploration during gameplay in combination with Shepard's heroic masculinity and the use of Canadian accents for the voice acting lend themselves to a reading of the avatar as a distinctly Canadian version of the hegemonic male, the "strong, courageous, honourable man of the Frontier" (Grace 185-6). In the most recent instalment in the *ME* series, *Mass Effect: Andromeda* (2017), the motifs of exploration and colonisation feature even more strongly since the PC/player is tasked with finding new worlds suitable for human settlement. *Andromeda,* through the introduction of the Angara species native to these potential new homes, also adds the aboriginal element that Schallegger identifies as a typical representation of Canadianness (55–60).

Peter Kuling suggests how the experience of Canadian national identity can be likened to queer sexuality: similar to members of the LGBTQ* community, Canadians "pass" as Northern Americans unless "coming out" along national lines (45). Indeed, *ME3* connects Canadianness and queerness through the trope of coming out of the closet in the story arc revolving around the NPC Kaidan Alenko (45–6). While Kaidan has been around since the first game – he is, in fact, the first NPC to join Shepard's squad – his identification as Canadian and his possible identification[9] as queer is only made explicit in the third game. Meeting Shepard at a restaurant, Kaidan expresses his desire for a "[s]hot of

---

9   If the player plays as a female Shepard, she can enter into a romantic relationship with Kaidan as early as the first game. Within the spatiotemporal frame of a single playthrough,

whisky and a good old Canadian lager" – both of which turn out to be unavailable – before reminiscing about his childhood home: "At my parents' place in Vancouver, (*laughs*) drank [sic] more than a few beers on their balcony looking over English Bay. Yeah. Beautiful view." The references to Canadian places and beverages become part of Kaidan's nostalgic yearning for home as he associates Canada's national culture and geography with the filial ties to his family. The cherished memories of his childhood and youth in times of peace contrast sharply with the wartime settings dominating the game.

Kaidan's coming out as Canadian is temporally and thematically linked to his coming out as queer. Provided that Shepard is male and the player has made the corresponding choices while interacting with Kaidan earlier in the game, Kaidan will follow up his description of Vancouver with a proposal of a romantic nature: "We've been friends a long time, Shepard. ... Maybe what I've never found, what I want is, something deeper with someone that I already care about. (*looking at Shepard*) That's what I want." Kaidan's national identity and romantic interest in Shepard are thus revealed in a single scene: the 'outing' as Canadian functions as a transition into a more intimate conversation in the course of which Kaidan confesses his feelings for Shepard (see also Kuling 44–6). Through an analogy between queerness and Canadianness, the romantic subplot transposes the transgressive utopian potential inherent to queerness to Canadian national and cultural identity. Like queerness in the broader sense, Canadianness is characterised precisely by its indefinability, a certain blurriness that opens up the possibility of challenging conventional categories of identity formation. Often defined by what it is not (almost American, but not quite), Canadianness can act as a foil upon which to project desires and utopian visions (Szatanik 59–60, 63). Covertly, the scene thus features a third outing: that of the *ME* franchise as a closeted Canadian game.

Similar to Schallegger's reading of *Dragon Age*, *ME3*, by creating an analogy between queerness and Canadianness, formulates a cosmopolitan version of Canadian national identity in line with cultural ideals such as multicultural tolerance and the peaceful resolution of conflict. *ME*'s emphasis on team cooperation, engagement with sociocultural difference, and invocation of the harmonious coexistence of various species in the galaxy's major political and economic centres indeed seems to advocate a post-nation state order based on democracy, mutual respect, and intercultural cooperation (Patterson 208). Gameplay, though focused on combat, is team-based and tactical. Typically, the player controls two NPCs in addition to the PC. There is little room for

---

the romance arc may then 'pass' as heteronormative.

individual power fantasies, but success is dependent on collective efforts. In *ME3*, Shepard's main task is to forge alliances among the various races comprising the galactic community. The game system assigns numerical value to those alliances. This number determines endgame outcomes such as the degree of Earth's destruction caused by enemy attacks or the survival of PC and NPCs. In other words, in order to ludically beat *ME*, the player must achieve interplanetary and interracial cooperation. Defeating the alien invaders can thus also be read as an allegory: the utopian vision of overcoming a history of aggressive nationalism and racist segregation in favour of transnational cosmopolitanism. As Kuling observes, "[q]ueerness and Canadianness become models for cosmopolitan and progressive world views in videogames that are overtly American, heterosexist, and masculinist" (47). Anti-essentialist, democratic, "and distinctively queer identity formation" (44) perpetuates a national myth associating Canada with the liberal values of multicultural as well as sexual tolerance (46–7).

However, the 'inclusive' interpretation is time and again troubled by the game's unruly meanings that threaten to subvert this utopian moment and that lend themselves to deconstructive readings. *Mass Effect*'s game mechanics, in particular the game goals, are not devoid of ideological implications. Quite the contrary, they serve to elicit conformity with a very specific – namely neoliberal – value system in the player; a value system no less, which carefully hides its own ideological nature. In *ME3*, the player, mediated through the PC, is put in the role of the multiculturalist umpire (Patterson 207, 214). In order to win the game, she must manage ethnic and cultural difference to cajole or coerce an "imposed racial harmony" (214). Shepard's actions not only steer the galactic community's political process, but player decisions, which frequently involve moral dilemmas, may even determine the fate of entire peoples, including the possibility of genocide. Shepard, by default a hegemonic Western male, becomes what Slavoj Žižek has termed the "privileged empty point of universality" ("Multiculturalism" 44), a purportedly neutral ideological and ethical position from which and through which all other (marked) genders, ethnicities, and nationalities must be managed (see also Hall 228–9).

Žižek argues that multiculturalism is "the ideal form of ideology of [contemporary] global capitalism" ("Multiculturalism" 44), a kind of cultural self-colonisation which derives its power "from a kind of empty global position" (44) – empty because it is devoid of positives. The discourse of liberal multiculturalism presents itself as universal; independent of cultural or ethnic roots or historical context ("Tolerance" 667), while local cultures and situated discourses appear "caught in their specific culture" (667). This logic depends on a paradoxical form of doublethink. Liberal multiculturalism functions as the new nationalism that makes use of much the same tropes and strategies as traditional nationalism. At the same time, however, it needs to deny any allegiance – national or otherwise – to maintain its purported neutrality. In turn, and in line with the logics of Othering so pervasive in traditional nationalism, the specificity of anything but liberal multiculturalism is constructed along conventionalised topoi. These are also evident in *ME*: the portrayal of the Krogan race, for instance, buys into stereotypes of the barbarian Other while the depiction of the Angara in *Andromeda* idealises 'native' culture as 'more natural and authentic.' The logic, problematically, is that of the civilising mission. Tolerance is put in the service of a flawed multiculturalist ideology intent on the policing of racialised others and on regulating the global order (Žižek, "Tolerance" 662).

In this context, Kyla Wazana Tompkins's relativisation of the virtues and leverage of activist agency from within the nation-state is crucial. As a disciplining apparatus, the state only allows for very limited forms of political intervention. According to Tompkins, the affordance and visibility of queer performativity in a military setting is not inherently subversive but may "become part and parcel of the new militarized normal, which is then deployed against … [internal and external] racialized others" (179). In other words, the game's representation of queer diversity, discursively connected to neoliberal value systems, may reaffirm, rather than challenge, traditional nationalisms and the master narrative of Western cultural hegemony. Roderick A. Ferguson makes a similar point: "queerness is put in the service of a hegemonic rationality that conveniently regards queerness as a satellite for citizen ideals and as a lever for the state's regulation of racial difference" (115). Paradoxically, the game's advocacy of values of queer inclusivity and multicultural tolerance is ultimately what sustains white male authority. If, according to the logic of liberal multiculturalism, "true tolerance is fully possible only in individualist Western culture" (Žižek, "Tolerance" 662), it follows that fighting the intolerance and backwardness of the other, if necessary by violent means, becomes justifiable. Intolerance is legitimised in the name of tolerance. In the end, *ME3*'s creation of an equivalence of queer inclusivity, multicultural tolerance, and Canadianness perpetuates nationalist discourses of progress and exceptionalism which legitimise and sustain Western cultural hegemony.

5   Conclusion: The Game, the Player, and the Critic

This chapter owes its existence to two well-matched passions: my love for BioWare's single-player RPGs, and my conviction that videogames are worth studying and can encourage critical engagement with media and culture in the broadest sense. Representation in games, just as in novels or films, is never neutral but warrants careful critical attention to questions of voice and agency, silencing and marginalisation. Games shape and are shaped by the discourses that surround them. They can be complicit in the reproduction of oppressive power structures that regulate the socio-political context of their production and reception, or they can resist the naturalised reproduction of the orthodoxies of said context. Perhaps most crucially in our contemporary reality of resurging nationalisms and regionalisms, videogames remain entangled with strong concepts of nation and empire, sometimes as overt allies, as in grand strategy games, sometimes in more complex and subtle forms, as in the *Mass Effect* series.

Analysing videogames from critical queer, intersectional, and postcolonial perspectives is a challenging but crucial endeavour, and much remains to be done. The ME games being the extensive and complex games that they are, there are countless aspects and themes that could not be addressed in this chapter: the way mapping and geography cohere with orientalist cliché to transpose imperialist power imbalances between centre and margin into the gameworld, for instance, the absence of First Nation perspectives from the *Mass Effect* trilogy's invocation of Canadianness, or the way colonisation recurs as a motif in contradictory ways throughout ME. Furthermore, different player choices, beginning with their choice of avatar, may yield very different gaming experiences and allow for different readings of its content. Playing as a female character of colour, for example, engages multiple discourses ranging from the empowerment of minoritised subject positions to such problematic practices as high-tech blackface.

As has become evident from the sample analysis offered in this chapter, the ME games are in the world and of the world in the sense that they negotiate contemporary anxieties and discourses within fictional space. The inclusion and character depth of BioWare's non-hegemonic characters marks a significant development of RPG gaming towards greater representational diversity. Queer play and its utopian potential can be found in the ways the games encourage the player to try on different identities, to form bonds with diverse characters, and to imagine a different world order. It also pervades subtle moments in which the game challenges its players' power fantasies. Yet heteronormativity and hegemonic masculinity remain the dominant modes of representation, nationalism and imperialism its prevalent ideologies. Even though national identity is rarely mentioned explicitly, the game remains infused with latent nationalism. Allusions to empire are virtually omnipresent, be it in the player's playful exploration and exploitation of distant planets, or in the positioning of the avatar as an umpire with the power to govern all racialised Others.

The intersectional and anti-essentialist approach followed here is particularly useful when it comes to investigating the complex ways in which worldly discourses interact to reinforce or undermine hegemonic power relations. Such a reading, then, discloses a myth of neoliberal, multicultural globalisation at the heart of the game. It challenges the master narrative of progress reinforcing Western cultural hegemony that acquires legitimacy through the invocation of tolerance and cosmopolitanism.

Works Cited

Adams, Meghan Blythe. "Renegade Sex: Compulsory Sexuality and Charmed Magic Circles in the *Mass Effect* Series." *Loading …: The Journal of the Canadian Game Studies Association*, vol. 9, no. 14, 2015, pp. 40–54.

Anthias, Floya, and Nira Yuval-Davis. Introduction. *Woman-Nation-State,* by Anthias and Yuval-Davies, MacMillan, 1989, pp. 1–15.

anthropy, anna. "Now We Have Voices: Queering Videogames." *YouTube*, uploaded by IndieCade, 19 Dec. 2016, www.youtube.com/watch?v=QrTKHHzzt1A. Accessed 02 Oct. 2020.

BioWare. *Dragon Age.* Electronic Arts, PC, 2009–14.

BioWare. *Mass Effect.* Electronic Arts, PC, 2007.

BioWare. *Mass Effect 2*. Electronic Arts, PC, 2010.

BioWare. *Mass Effect 3*. Electronic Arts, PC, 2012. Extended cut, released 26 June 2012.

BioWare. *Mass Effect: Andromeda.* Electronic Arts, PC, 2017.

BioWare, et al. *Star Wars: Knights of the Old Republic.* Electronic Arts et al. 2003–14.

Butler, Judith. *Bodies That Matter: On the Discursive Limits of 'Sex.'* 1993. Routledge, 2011.

Carbado, Devon W., et al. "Intersectionality: Mapping the Movements of a Theory." *Du Bois Review,* vol. 10, no. 2, 2013, pp. 303–12. doi: 10.1017/s1742058X13000349.

Cassell, Justine, and Henry Jenkins, editors. *From Barbie to Mortal Kombat: Gender and Computer Games.* The MIT Press, 1998.

Condis, Meghan. "No Homosexuals in *Star Wars*? BioWare, 'Gamer' Identity, and the Politics of Privilege in a Convergence Culture." *Convergence,* vol. 21, no. 2, 2014, pp. 1–15. doi: 10.1177/1354856514527205.

Consalvo, Mia. "Hot Dates and Fairy-Tale Romances: Studying Sexuality in Video Games." *The Video Game Theory Reader,* edited by Mark J. P. Wolf and Bernard Perron, Routledge, 2003, pp. 171–94.

Crenshaw, Kimberlé Williams. "Demarginalizing the Intersection of Race and Sex: A Black Feminist Critique of Antidiscrimination Doctrine, Feminist Theory and Antiracist Politics." *University of Chicago Legal Forum,* no. 1, 1989, pp. 1241–99.

Everett, Anna. *Digital Diaspora: A Race for Cyberspace.* State U of New York P, 2009.

Everett, Anna, and Craig Watkins. "The Power of Play: The Portrayal and Performance of Race in Video Games." *The Ecology of Games: Connecting Youth, Games, and Learning,* edited by Katie Salen, The MIT Press, 2008, pp. 141–166. doi: 10.1162/dmal.9780262693646.141.

Ferguson, Roderick A. "The Relevance of Race for the Study of Sexuality." *A Companion to Lesbian, Gay, Bisexual, Transgender, and Queer Studies,* edited by George E. Haggerty and Molly McGarry, Blackwell, 2007, pp. 109–24.

Grace, Sherill E. *Canada and the Idea of North.* McGill-Queen's UP, 2007.

Greer, Stephen. "Playing Queer. Affordances for Sexuality in *Fable* and *Dragon Age.*" *Journal of Gaming & Virtual Worlds,* vol. 5, no. 1, 2013, pp. 3–21.

Hall, Stuart. "Conclusion: The Multicultural Question." *Un/Settled Multiculturalisms: Diasporas, Entanglements, Transruptions,* edited by Barnor Hesse, Zed, 2000, pp. 215–41.

Huizinga, Johan. *Homo Ludens: A Study of the Play Element in Culture.* 1949. Routledge, 1980.

hooks, bell. *Black Looks: Race and Representation.* South End Press, 1992.

Jørgensen, Kristine. "Game Characters as Narrative Devices: A Comparative Analysis of *Dragon Age: Origins* and *Mass Effect 2*." *Eludamos. Journal for Computer Game Culture,* vol. 4, no. 2, 2010, pp. 315–31.

Krampe, Theresa. "No Straight Answers: Queering Hegemonic Masculinity in BioWare's *Mass Effect.*" *Game Studies,* vol. 18, no. 2, 2018, n. pag.

Kuling, Peter. "Outing Ourselves in Outer Space: Canadian Identity Performances in BioWare's *Mass Effect* Trilogy." *Canadian Theatre Review,* vol. 159, 2014, pp. 42–7.

Laurel, Brenda. *Computers as Theatre.* 2nd ed., Addison-Wesley, 2014.

Lutz, Helma, et al. Introduction. *Framing Intersectionality: Debates on a Multi-Faceted Concept in Gender Studies,* by Lutz et al., Ashgate, 2011, pp. 1–22.

MacCormack, Patricia. "Queer Posthumanism: Cyborgs, Animals, Monsters, Perverts." *Queer Interventions,* edited by Noreen Giffney and Michael O'Rourke, Ashgate, 2009, pp. 111–28.

Mafe, Diana Adesola. "Race and the First-Person Shooter: Challenging the Video Gamer in *BioShock Infinite.*" *Camera Obscura* 89, vol. 30, no. 2, 2015, pp. 89–123. doi: 10.1215/02705346-3078336.

Malkowski, Jennifer, and TreaAndrea M. Russworm, editors. *Gaming Representation: Race, Gender, and Sexuality in Video Games.* Indiana UP, 2017.

Manalansan, Martin F. "Queer Intersections: Sexuality and Gender in Migration Studies." *The Routledge Queer Studies Reader,* edited by Donald E. Hall and Annamarie Jagose, Routledge, 2013, pp. 529–46.

Murray, Janet H. *Hamlet on the Holodeck: The Future of Narrative in Cyberspace.* Free Press, 1997.

Nakamura, Lisa. *Cybertypes: Race, Ethnicity, and Identity on the Internet.* Routledge, 2002.

Ong, Sady. "The Video Game Industry's Problem with Racial Diversity." *Newsweek,* 13 Oct. 2016, www.newsweek.com/2016/10/21/video-games-race-black-protagonists-509328.html. Accessed 14 Aug. 2017.

Østby, Kim Johansen. *From Embracing Eternity to Riding the Bull: Representations of Homosexuality and Gender in the Video Game Series* Mass Effect *and* Dragon Age. 2016. Universitetet i Oslo, PhD dissertation. *DSpace,* urn.nb.no/URN:NBN:no-58062.

Patterson, Christopher B. "Role-Playing the Multiculturalist Umpire: Loyalty and War in BioWare's *Mass Effect* Series." *Games and Culture,* vol. 10, no. 3, 2015, pp. 207–28.

Ramanan, Chella. "The Video Game Industry Has A Diversity Problem – But It Can Be Fixed." *The Guardian,* 15 Mar. 2017, www.theguardian.com/technology/2017/mar/15/video-game-industry-diversity-problem-women-non-white-people. Accessed 02 Oct. 2020.

Ruberg, Bonnie, and Adrienne Shaw, editors. *Queer Game Studies.* U of Minnesota P, 2017.

Russell, Steve, et al. *Spacewar!* Steve Russell, PDP-1, 1962.

Russworm, TreaAndrea. "Dystopian Blackness and the Limits of Racial Empathy in *The Walking Dead* and *The Last of Us.*" *Gaming Representation: Race, Gender, and Sexuality in Video Games,* edited by Jennifer Malkowski and TreaAndrea M. Russworm. Indiana UP, 2017, pp. 109–28.

Schallegger, René Reinhold. "Game Changers – Representations of Queerness in Canadian Videogame Design." *Zeitschrift für Kanada-Studien,* vol. 36, 2016, pp. 42–62.

Shaw, Adrienne. "Putting the Gay in Games: Cultural Production and GLBT Content in Video Games." *Games and Culture,* vol. 4, no. 3, 2009, pp. 228–53. doi:10.1177/1555412009339729.

Sheikh, Rahil. "Video Games: How Big is Industry's Racial Diversity Problem?" *BBC Asian Network,* 20 Dec. 2017, www.bbc.com/news/technology-42357678. Accessed 02 October 2020.

Szatanik, Suzanna. "Crisis House: Metaphors of Queer Depression." *Out Here: Local and International Perspectives in Queer Studies,* edited by Dominika Ferens et al. Cambridge Scholars, 2006, pp. 56–67.

Thier, Dave. "*Mass Effect 3* Ships 3.5 Million Units." *Forbes,* 9 Mar. 2012, www.forbes.com/sites/davidthier/2012/03/09/mass-effect-3-ships-3-5-million-units/#19e8b61d58fd. Accessed 15 Nov. 2018.

Tompkins, Kyla Wazana. "Intersections of Race, Gender, and Sexuality: Queer of Color Critique." *The Cambridge Companion to American Gay and Lesbian Literature*, edited by Scott Herring. Cambridge UP, 2015, pp. 173–89.

UnholyDemigod. "Re: For Those Who Haven't Noticed that Jacob is Kanye." *Reddit, 7 Apr. 2012*, www.reddit.com/r/masseffect/comments/rx8xg/for_those_who_havent_noticed_that_jacob_is_kanye/. Accessed 20 Apr. 2017.

Xathos. "Re: Poll: Most Reviled Mass Effect Squad Mate?" *Escapistmagazine*, 21 Jan. 2013, www.escapistmagazine.com/forums/read/9.398967-Poll-Most-reviled-Mass-Effect-squad-mate?page=4. Accessed 20 Apr. 2017.

Žižek, Slavoj. "Tolerance as an Ideological Category." *Critical Inquiry*, vol. 34, no. 4, 2008, pp. 660–82.

Žižek, Slavoj. "Multiculturalism, or, The Cultural Logic of Multinational Capitalism." *New Left Review*, vol. 1, no. 225, 1997, pp. 28–51.

PART 4

Nationalisms in Postcolonial Literatures

∴

CHAPTER 9

Blind Spots: Nationalism and the Photographic Gaze in Teju Cole's *Every Day Is for the Thief*

Ralf Haekel

1 Nationalism, Museums, and Photography

In Teju Cole's *Every Day Is for the Thief*, the nameless protagonist and narrator travels from New York to visit his hometown Lagos for the first time in years. In the course of this "travelogue-like novella" (Rippl 472), he also visits the Nigerian National Museum. His high hopes, fuelled by the images he has preserved in his memory since he was a child, however, are utterly disappointed by the exhibition itself:

> The galleries, cramped, are spatially unlike what I remember or had imagined, and the artifacts are caked in dust and under dirty plastic screens. The whole place has a tired, improvised air about it, like a secondary school assignment finished years ago and never touched since. The deepest disappointment though, is not in presentation. It is in content. I honestly expected to find the glory of Nigerian archaeology and art history on display here. I had hoped to see the best of the Ife bronzes, the fine Benin brass plaques and figures, Nok terra-cottas, the roped vessels of Igbo-Ukwu, the art for which Nigeria is justly admired in academies and museums the world over. It is not to be. (Cole, *Every Day* 73)

This passage is indicative of a main tendency of *Every Day Is for the Thief*: the protagonist's negative reaction synecdochally mirrors his disappointment in Nigeria as a whole, which is described almost exclusively in terms of corruption and bribery right from the start. Everybody in Lagos seems to take bribes on every occasion. This small-scale everyday criminal activity is contrasted with the nostalgia of grandeur associated with the museum and, by implication, the world of national culture and art. As a symbol of political power and physical embodiment of nationalism, a national museum not only represents the body politic; it also directs the view and thus induces a specific way of seeing which is met by a gaze that is always already shaped by expectations and models. Cole's novella, I argue, critically reflects this gaze. Having left Nigeria for the United States of America early in his life, the protagonist and narrator has taken on the point of view of the outsider – and his attitude is now, in part, colonial: "My recent experience of Nigerian art at the Metropolitan Museum in New York was excellent. The same had been true at the British Museum, as well as at the Museum für Volkerkunde [sic] in Berlin" (74).

By taking these national museums – embodiments of colonial exploitation and Western imperialist self-representation – as role-models, the narrator finds himself caught in an ideological trap:

> I am aware of the troubled history of the collecting of African art, the way colonial authorities had carted off treasures to their capitals in the nineteenth and early twentieth centuries. But I also know how rich Nigerian museums had been as recently as the 1960s and '70s, when the British archaeologists Frank Wilson and John Wallace had been curators here. (74)

As this passage shows, the protagonist is well aware of the history of national museums and the ideology behind them; yet at the same time he still speaks from a position that is similar to the point of view of a coloniser.

Museums, especially national museums, are instrumental in the establishment of national identity, as Andrew McClellan maintains:

> National consciousness, this identification with the imagined community, is the product of state-sponsored social engineering or education, and it is here that the interests of the state and the function of the museum intersect. If identity presupposes the collecting of objects ..., it is no coincidence that the foundation of a national museum has been a high priority of many newly founded nation-states. (29)

In order to achieve this aim of constructing national identity, a national museum, as a rhetorical device, has to be part of an established semantic network: "The national museum, then, operates within a larger context of national symbol systems, all working to persuade individuals that they share an identity with thousands or millions of others" (Weiser 119). The close ties between nationalism and museums in a postcolonial context are highlighted by Benedict Anderson. In *Imagined Communities*, Anderson argues that "museums, and the museumizing imagination, are both profoundly political" (182). Furthermore, he shows how the colonial practice of establishing museums to further national identity construction is continued in a postcolonial context: "It is probably not too surprising that post-independence states, which exhibited marked continuities with their colonial predecessors, inherited this form of political museumizing" (187). In and through a museum, Anderson suggests, the religious and aesthetic objects on display change their function and can be utilised for the political and profane aims of the nation-state: "Museumized this way, they were repositioned as regalia for a secular colonial state" (186). It is little wonder, then, that the functions of the museum and of photography – both visual and rhetorical media – intersect. Allan Sekula, for instance, argues for "a close link between photography and nation" (29). Both, museum and photography, are and can be used to construct national consciousness. Yet, whilst a museum is static and singular, photography is, as a technologically reproducible medium, necessary for the proliferation of nationalist ideology, as Anderson, with a nod to Walter Benjamin, asserts: "a characteristic feature of the instrumentalities of this profane state was infinite reproducibility, a reproducibility made technically possible by print and photography" (186). This, in turn, also implies that by exposing the "hypermediacy" (Bolter and Grusin 34) of the medium, i.e. by making the medium visible through distortion, remediating both the museum and photography, as Teju Cole does in his novella, can serve to expose how they construct national identity and how they aim at manipulating the gaze of the onlooker.

The link of nationalism and colonialism to the topics of representation and vision, which is conjured up in the fourteenth chapter of *Every Day Is for the Thief*, is therefore central to the work, and the visit to the National Museum betrays a key aspect of the book: Teju Cole's novella consciously plays with a set of conventions and expectations, aiming at estranging its readers, leading them astray, or even making them complicit. In this chapter, I argue that two features of the novella create and, at the same time, undermine the discourse of nationalism: first, the use of genre and, second, the inclusion of photography. *Every Day Is for the Thief* evokes a wide range of generic forms of Western literature, partly following their conventions and connotations but also subverting them. At the centre of the book is, furthermore, the topic of vision, as epitomised in the National Museum of Lagos. The gaze is of particular importance here, especially the complex use of photography in the novella itself and the interplay of text and image. In what follows, I will look at, first, the role of genre in the construction of nationalism in *Every Day Is for the Thief* as well as in Cole's other writings, before then turning to the topic of photography. I wish to show how these images play with, but eventually run counter to and undermine, the narrative and cultural foundations of Western nationalism, and how Cole uses the medium of photography to criticise and throw into sharp relief the narrative representational forms of nationhood and nationalism within a postcolonial context.

2   The Uses of Genre in *Every Day Is for the Thief*

Every Day Is for the Thief is not a plot-driven novella. It follows the logic of a fictitious travel narrative, with each of its twenty-seven chapters presenting a snapshot-like view on a given topic. Beginning at the Nigerian consulate in New York, the narrator re-visits the places, family, and friends he left behind in Lagos when he emigrated to the US in his youth. Nationalism does not present itself as an obvious topic. Yet the text is anything but a solely subjective account of the voyage; rather, it presents itself as an essayistic reflection on perception, point of view, alterity, and identity. That these issues regarding the gaze are always related to Nigeria as a nation becomes obvious in the second chapter:

> Disembarkation, passport control, and baggage claim eat up more than an hour of our time. The sky outside fills with shadows. One man argues with a listless customs official about the inefficiency. – This is an international airport. Things should be better run. Is this the impression visitors should have of our nation? (Cole, *Every Day* 10)

In order to achieve this characteristic blend of personal reflection and detached analysis, Cole employs a sophisticated use of several different genres and plays with the expectations that are attached to each generic category. Hence, Cole's writings are hard to pin down with the use of traditional tags. Like his first internationally published novel *Open City*,[1] *Every Day Is for the Thief* is a generic mixture, a feature that Birgit Neumann describes as follows: "Consciously crossing multiple generic borders and questioning the validity of standardized Western literary categories, the book [*Every Day Is for the Thief*] is as much a fictional autobiography as it is a novella, a travelogue, a diary and a collection of essays" (317). In accordance with his other publications, Cole uses and alludes to a wide range of genres, mainly of the Western traditional canon, yet cannot be said to follow any one convention in a strict sense. By writing in the tradition of travel literature, this tendency is stressed even further, since travel writing is, by definition, a "literary form that draws on the conventions of other literary genres" (Youngs 3). This play with traditions and styles destabilises any simple and one-dimensional reading of Cole's works, especially regarding politics in general and nationalism in particular. The conscious and ironic stance

---

[1] A first edition of *Every Day Is for the Thief* predates the publication of *Open City* by four years. First published in Nigeria in 2007, Cole issued a revised international edition with Faber & Faber in 2014 after *Open City* became an international bestseller in 2011.

towards fixed categories also renders the classification of Cole as 'Afropolitan' rather pointless,[2] as neither traditional nor fashionable recent categories seem to be apt to characterise his writings. Indeed, Cole's works are political in the sense that they evade any given and fixed definition.

I first want to contextualise the question of politics in Cole's works before returning to a discussion of politics in *Every Day Is for the Thief*. During the Q&A session after a talk entitled "A Quartet for Edward Said" he gave in Berlin in April 2018, Cole was asked about the importance of politics in his writings. In his answer, he admitted that, while being openly political in his journalistic and essayistic writings, he tries to be more nuanced and neutral in his fiction. Which is not to say, he claimed, that his fictional work is apolitical, far from it. His novels just make easy interpretations and allegiances difficult and complicated. In order to illustrate this argument, he pointed to a passage in *Open City* which refers to Edward Said:

> You see, Said was young when he heard that statement made by Golda Meir, that there are no Palestinian people, and when he heard this, he became involved in the Palestinian question. He knew then that difference is never accepted. You are different, okay, but that difference is never seen as containing its own value. Difference as orientalist entertainment is allowed, but difference with its own intrinsic value, no. You can wait forever, and no one will give you that value. (Cole, *Open City* 104–5)

Often interpreted as representing his own position, Cole stressed in the Q&A session that this passage is uttered by Farouq, a former student from Morocco working in Brussels in a telephone shop. Farouq, who is openly political in his thinking, also states: "I wanted to be the next Edward Said! And I was going to do it by studying comparative literature and using it as a basis for societal critique" (128). However, Julius, the narrator and protagonist of *Open City* who is presented as a sympathetic character until a crucial plot twist reveals a much darker side to him, is less easy to pin down regarding his political leanings. He is interested in the conversation but ultimately indifferent to any ideology or political position. The protagonist's abysmal character traits only become fully apparent towards the end of the novel. In New York, Julius meets Moji, whom he presents as an old, nearly forgotten acquaintance. At first, she seems to be

---

[2] Cole merely refers to the term in a rather sarcastic manner: "I'm an Afropolitan, a pan-African, an Afro-pessimist, depending on who hates me on any given day. I embrace all those terms. However, labels: they always apply, except when they don't" (qtd. in Pahl 73). For a discussion of the concept of Afropolitanism, see Ede.

just a girl he knew in his youth, but in the course of the narrative it turns out that Julius, when he was fourteen and Moji fifteen years old, raped her at a party. Presumably suppressing his shame, he subsequently 'chose to forget' his crime until Moji confronts him almost two decades later:

> I don't think you've changed at all, Julius. Things don't go away just because you choose to forget them. You forced yourself on me eighteen years ago because you could get away with it, and I suppose you did get away with it. But not in my heart, you didn't. I have cursed you too many times to count. And maybe it is not something you would do today, but then again, I didn't think it was something you would do back then either. It only needs to happen once. (245)

Cole thus undermines any easy form of identification – political or personal – especially with the main characters of the novels. Although both texts – *Every Day Is for the Thief* and *Open City* – differ on various levels, they are both remarkably similar in their use of a semi-autobiographical protagonist and narrator. Like Cole himself, both were born in the United States, grew up in Lagos, and, in their late teens, left Nigeria for the US again to attend university. These narrators invite the readers to identify them with Cole himself, to sympathise with them, to share their opinions and political views. Yet, sooner or later, both narrators betray aspects to their characters that render such a shared understanding highly problematic. Julius in *Open City* only gradually accepts his guilt as a sexual predator, a guilt that he had safely stowed in his subconscious. In *Every Day*, this dubious side to the main character shows in the fact that he, a native Nigerian, has taken on the point of view typical of Western colonisers, and his opinions and judgements of Nigeria are characteristic of a colonial rather than a postcolonial or anticolonial attitude. This is all the more intricate since the narrator knows, and reflects on, the fact that he is simultaneously a native and a foreigner:

> Night descends with no warning. I am breathing the air of the city for the first time in a decade and a half, its white smoke and ocher dust which are as familiar as my own breath. But other things, less visible, have changed. I have taken into myself some of the assumptions of life in a Western democracy – certain ideas about legality, for instance, certain expectations of due process – and in that sense I have returned a stranger. (*Every Day* 16–7)

Concerning the common history of European fiction and European nationalism, on which Cole's novella can and should be regarded as a comment, this situation is significant.

Given the fact that Western literature, and especially the genres of eighteenth- and nineteenth-century novels and travelogues, not only reflect the development of nationalism but are actually instrumental in creating and fostering it (Said 80–97), the ambiguity of *Every Day Is for the Thief* is a political statement in its own right. The background is the following: Joep Leerssen argues that "all nationalism is cultural nationalism" and that "cultural preoccupations do not passively 'reflect' or 'follow' social developments or political movements, but ... they tend to anticipate them ... Nationalism stands out amidst other ideologies in that it formulates a political agenda on the basis of a cultural ideal" ("Nationalism" 562).

Narrators in fiction are instrumental in the development of cultural nationalism in that they take on the role of mediators, negotiating between a national self – the implied readers – and an 'other' that is only created in the process – the described object. In the history of European nationalism and imperialism, the genre of travel writing is particularly important as it represents the Western political position assuming dominance by actively taking on an outsider's point of view, thus creating an alterity which is at the heart of the colonial discourse.[3] Yvonne Kappel states that Cole's novella makes use of the generic distinction between the traditional and the postcolonial travelogue, a distinction that the text constantly blurs:

> The postcolonial travelogue deals primarily with defining a home by articulating experiences that are removed from dominant Western concepts, thereby setting itself apart from the traditional travelogue. Teju Cole's protagonist, however, depicts his journey to his home country Nigeria by applying Western cultural concepts to an African environment. He thereby reproduces the colonial discourse ... However, by reproducing this discourse, he does not affirm its validity but rather questions it by highlighting its limitations. By thus drawing on these categories, Teju Cole's travelogue highlights the ambivalences of categories that build on binary oppositions. His appropriation in fact problematizes the very essence of these categories and their applicability to non-European contexts. (68)

---

3 On the importance of genre in this context, see Said 59, and, referring to this passage in Said, Döring 13.

Every Day's narrator resembles the mediating narrator figure of the traditional Western travelogues in that he also "no longer identifies with the country which is represented, but becomes an intermediary, an exteriorized, detached observer" (Leerssen, *Remembrance* 34). He differs, however, regarding the political function of this narrator: whilst the traditional Western intermediary figure in history helped to create nationalism in the first place, Cole's narrator exhibits the very role of this medial figure. Cole constructs his narrator as unreliable, and thus exposes the cultural construction of nationalism in a postcolonial setting *as a construction*. The novella follows a strategy to first make the reader complicit, and then it undermines the narrator's own position, questioning the validity of any nationalism and construction of nationhood in general – a tendency that is further supported by Cole's use of photography.

3 Photography, Glass, and Vision

Every Day Is for the Thief not only alludes to the Western canon as being instrumental in the development of nationalism, but also to a wide range of other contemporary works. Among the works *Every Day* refers to are Michael Ondaatje's *Running in the Family* (1982) or Chinua Achebe's *No Longer at Ease* (1960), novels that are associated with homecoming and reclaiming one's own past. In what follows, however, I will focus on the intertextual and intermedial references and cross-references which are concerned with the novella's use of photography. Most of the chapters are shot through with photographs. Yet, as I aim to show, these photographs do not serve to illustrate the narrative, but rather act as companion pieces to the text, subtly unsettling the recipient.

The use of photography links Cole's works with those of other novelists. *Open City*, for instance, bears strong intertextual links to the works of W. G. Sebald, especially *Austerlitz*, and Sebald's use of images in his works. The use of photography in *Every Day Is for the Thief* further stresses these close connections to the German author. The first photographs in *Austerlitz* are images of a gaze (Sebald 11). The four pairs of eyes – of two owls and of the painter Jan-Peter Tripp and the philosopher Ludwig Wittgenstein – do not primarily illustrate the text but rather accompany it: they are "key to an aesthetic reading of the novel" (Gnam 40), a meta-medial and meta-fictional reference to the general topic of seeing. Thus, they bring up the question of perspective within the text.

The first two photographs in *Every Day* also thematise the topic of seeing, adding, however, yet two further layers: mediation and blindness (see Figures 9.1 and 9.2).

FIGURES 9.1 AND 9.2   Photographs taken from Teju Cole's *Every Day Is for the Thief*

Without any apparent immediate relation to the text, these pictures nonetheless serve as aesthetic keys to the novella. Both photographs show windows. The first depicts a cracked window through which we see the back of a man, apparently waiting, presumably in conversation with two other men. The second picture from the end of chapter two is taken from the back of a taxi cab; the windscreen is wet and thus only partly transparent. Both photographs have in common that they make visible what is usually crystal clear – vision thus appears as obstructed. Gabriele Rippl describes the distancing quality of these photographs: "[T]he blurry surfaces of this second set of examples do not invite us into the picture; they keep us at a distance. When we gaze at such pictures, they remain mere surfaces without pictorial depth; instead of alluring the onlooker, she is thrown out of the picture" (478). What is more, the two photographs, focusing on the windows rather than on what is visible through or behind them, raise the issues of point of view and of mediation. We should be able to see what is behind the glass; it should mediate what is to be seen, i.e. the glass should be invisible. Yet the splintered and the clouded windows refer to our use of media that determine our point of view, and thus we are shown to be usually unaware that our vision is directed, led, or even misled. The blurred and cracked medium emphasises blindness rather than vision.

Glass is a topic that Cole regards to be a central subject matter in the history of photography. In an article on the 2017 mass shooting in Las Vegas, he reflects on the role of press photographers in the wake of the massacre – and the fact that broken glass and broken windows are at the core of what has been pictured. He reads this as connoting "the abysmal void beneath our way of life, from which a bewildering violence erupts incessantly" (Cole, "History of Photography" n. pag.). Turning away from the terrorist attack and broadening the view towards a more general reflection, he states:

> Glass is everywhere in photography. From Eugène Atget's reflective vitrines to Lee Friedlander's sly self-portraiture, photographers have long been in thrall to the visual complications glass can inject into a composition. Glass is present not only as photography's seductive subject but also as its physical material. Photographs were commonly made on wet-plate negatives (glass coated with photosensitive emulsion) in the 19th century, and then on the improved and portable dry-plate negatives, before film was manufactured at a sufficient strength in the 20th century to serve as a transportable medium for photographic emulsion. Sometimes the very glass of the negative becomes part of the photograph's story. (n. pag.)

When windows break, however, it is not only the object that falls apart. Breaking glass also immediately refers back to the very medium of photography. Just as every window is an accident waiting to happen, any transparent and invisible medium is waiting to be seen and to be recognized as an interruption. Cole concludes his article: "An intact window is interesting mainly for its transparency. But when the window breaks, what intrigues us is the brittleness that was there all along" (n. pag.).

Metaphorically, the meta-medial use of photography in *Every Day Is for the Thief* thus points back at the reader who is looking at the object of this travelogue: Lagos, Nigeria. By blurring the vision, readers and spectators are made aware that any subject matter of a travelogue is not just there to be described, but first and foremost an object created in and through a medium. With the invisibility of the glass taken away, the point of view is shown to be anything but innocent; the object in view is presented as constructed, and constructed as an *other*. Thus, these photos also refer to the narrative itself. The narrator, because of his absence of fifteen years, is, just like a typical Western recipient of a travel narrative, also an outsider. His perspective is neither neutral nor immediate, but blurred and blinded by convention, in this case blind to Western generic conventions of travel writing and the ghost of nationalism. Just like in the Said reference quoted above, the narrator sees Nigeria's otherness, but he fails to understand its "difference with its own intrinsic value." He turns out to be yet another orientalist.

4 Blind Spots

The topics of vision and blindness play a significant role in Cole's other writings as well. The final essay of his 2016 collection *Known and Strange Things* is entitled "Blind Spot." In this text, Cole relates, and reflects on, a period when he suffered from partial blindness. The essay sets in with Cole reflecting on staying up late in order to finish reading Virginia Woolf's diary. The next morning, he gets up "with a gray veil right across the visual field of my left eye" ("Blind Spot" 379). Metaphorically, the essay suggests that Cole was losing his vision not merely as a result of a certain medical condition, but because he was indeed blinded by Woolf's writings: "But the pages held a radiance too, because of Woolf's prose, the intensity of her attention to life, and the epiphanic moments that intermittently illuminated the gloom. I went to sleep in the glare of her words" (379). Thus, light, vision, and narrative and textual perspective are interlinked and mutually inform each other. This loss of sight, which turns out to be non-permanent, leads to a reflection on vision and blindness in art and particularly the art of fiction. Blindness in the text is present in two different ways, a literal and a figurative one. It has an immensely aesthetic quality, calling up writers, artists, and art itself:

> Glasses, inconvenient as they are, are also an occasion for gratitude at not having to live life in an impressionistic blur. But blindness was another matter. Blindness happened in literature and films, it happened to blues musicians, to mythical figures, to those unfortunates one encounters on the streets of Lagos or on the subways of New York. (380)

In the course of his medical examination, he is even further blinded, this time by the light the ophthalmologist uses to look at the retina:

> She tested my vision on the alphabet charts, irrelevantly, I thought, since I wasn't there to have new glasses made, and then, dilating both pupils with mydriatic drops, examined each eye with a powerful lamp. She looked closely. In the vision-cancelling intensity of the lamp, my gray veil became a thick red cloud of pure vision, and I imagined I could see my own optic nerve. (381)

Blindness in this text turns out to be not the absence, but rather a heightened form, of vision, a precondition for self-reflection, for looking inside oneself. The medical condition that Cole suffers from in the essay – papillophlebitis – is caused by a haemorrhage within the eye. Thus, the eye itself resembles the mediality of the blurred or cracked window-panes in his fiction; whilst trying to see through or beyond the obstacle, the viewer is only made aware of the mediation rather than what is to be mediated. The onlooker *sees* the blind spot rather than is being hindered by it in their attempt to see the world.

After leaving the medical practice, Cole's incapacity to see the street renders the world outside somewhat unreal, and it becomes a way of seeing the streets as if through the medium of photography:

> My body made its way down the bright street, mystified and almost inadvertent. The journey took a long time, twice as long as it should have taken, and I was afraid I'd get knocked down at one of the intersections. Each house looked much the same as the next, polygonal, almost flat, neither more nor less substantial than the sky above, each successive block glowing like the built landscape in the very first street photograph, the view from Niépce's country house in Le Gras in 1826. (382)

The partial blindness has a contrary effect: it heightens the very act of seeing; and the association of blindness with photography emphasises this act of learning to see again and to see more clearly. The reference is to the very first street photograph and thus to the invention of the medium which inaugurated a new way of seeing the world. This reference to the self-reflexive character of photography eventually leads to thoughts about writing as such:

> When we write fiction, we write within what we know. But we also write in the hope that what we have written will somehow outdistance us. We hope, through the spooky art of writing, to trick ourselves into divulging truths that we do not know we know. *Open City* ... is in part an examination of the limits of sensitivity and of knowledge. (383)

This passage indicates that the importance of the metaphorical field of blindness and vision spans Cole's entire works.

Quite tellingly, his latest book publication is also called *Blind Spot*. Each page shows a photograph from a city around the world; yet the images are not ordered accordingly. Thus, the book hints at a cosmopolitan world but does not resemble a teleological travel account. The tripartite arrangement is rather reminiscent of a rhetorical emblem book (Rippl 4) with each double page consisting of a *motto*, *pictura*, and *subscriptio*.[4] As each *motto* refers to the specific

---

4 On the relationship between these three structural elements and their rhetorical dimension, see Neuber.

place where the photo was taken, the book intimates the tradition of rhetorical topology, since a *topos*, a place, is where topics are found in order to create and arrange a speech. Cole takes this ancient Greek rhetorical tradition of ordering and rearranges it. For instance, the picture called "Rhinecliff" shows a window covered with what is presumably soap to prevent people from seeing through the glass. Again, Cole uses a picture of a stained window to block the view in order to signify an inability to see that verges on blindness. This meta-medial picture, reminiscent of the two discussed previously, conjures up the topic of mediation, a topic that is then taken further in the *subscriptio*, i.e. the accompanying text: "My eyes were technically fine, but for weeks I saw nothing worth photographing" (Cole, *Blind Spot* 222). This *subscriptio* is remarkable because it turns the hierarchy of mediation on its head: instead of looking at art as a mirror to nature, looking at nature – seeing – becomes an act that is only fulfilled when it becomes art – photography.

I want to combine this *topos* of blindness with the genre of travel writing. In one of the several pictures bearing the motto "Lagos," the text of the *subscriptio* runs:

> All the cities are one city. What is interesting is to find, in this continuity of cities, the less obvious differences of texture: the signs, the markings, the assemblages, the things hiding in plain sight in each cityscape or landscape: the way street lights and traffic signs vary, the most common fonts, the slight variations in building codes, the fleeting ads, the way walls are painted, the noticeable shift in the range of hues that people wear, the colour of human absence, the balance of industrial product versus what has been made by hand, greater or lesser degrees of finish, the visual melody of infrastructure as it interacts with terrain: wall, roof, plant, wire, gutter: what is everywhere but is everywhere slightly different. (200)

Cole stresses the continuity of places, the similarity of pattern rather than alterity and opposition. This very cosmopolitan approach to places stands in stark contrast to the point of view of the semi-autobiographical narrator of *Every Day Is for the Thief*, who assumes the position of an outsider, thus creating Lagos and Nigeria, his former home, through othering. The *subscriptio* also hints at the aesthetic function of the images in the travel narrative. While the position of the narrator is textually fixed, the openness of the photographs reveals a much more cosmopolitan viewpoint. Running counter to the text, they demonstrate how the textual element of the travel narrative is ordered and structured by traditional types, genres, and value judgements. The photographs, on the contrary, by stressing mediation, self-reflexively point back to themselves *and* to us as viewers, questioning our attitudes and political opinions, thus also questioning the binary opposition of identity and alterity of traditional nationalist narratives.

5   Conclusion

Photography undermines the narrative voice in *Every Day Is for the Thief* by unsettling the recipient's point of view. These photographs expose a blind spot: however hard one looks, there is always something that one does not, that one cannot see. By highlighting the topic of mediation, these pictures do not complement, but run counter to, the narrative. Chapter fourteen, in which the protagonist visits the National Museum in Lagos, is, quite tellingly, not accompanied by a photograph. The narrator only bemoans the poor state of the museum, stressing the importance of memory. But this lament only exposes how very much the point of view is always already structured. The narrative betrays a form of Western othering which is also complemented by the history of the institutions themselves: national museums have developed out of cabinets of curiosity, *Wunderkammern*, which are themselves rhetorical ordering systems of the world, thus instruments and metaphors of power during the early stages of nationalism. *Every Day Is for the Thief* thus questions the history of power and nationalism. Rather than perpetuating the narrative of alterity on which nationalism is ultimately based and which is represented by the protagonist, the use of photography in the novella subtly undermines any such grand narrative. The images stress that every view of the world is necessarily mediated and characterised by blind spots.

Works Cited

Achebe, Chinua. *No Longer at Ease*. Fawcett, 1960.

Anderson, Benedict. *Imagined Communities: Reflections on the Origins and Spread of Nationalism*. Verso, 1991.

Bolter, Jay David, and Richard Grusin. *Remediation: Understanding New Media*. MIT P, 1999.

Cole, Teju. "A Quartet for Edward Said." Edward W. Said Days, 4 Apr. 2018, Pierre Boulez Saal, Berlin.

Cole, Teju. *Blind Spot*. Random House, 2017.

Cole, Teju. "Blind Spot." *Known and Strange Things*. Faber and Faber, 2016, pp. 379–85.

Cole, Teju. *Every Day Is for the Thief*. Faber and Faber, 2014.

Cole, Teju. *Open City*. Faber and Faber, 2012.

Cole, Teju. "The History of Photography Is a History of Shattered Glass." *New York Times Magazine*, 15 Nov. 2017, www.nytimes.com/2017/11/15/magazine/the-history-of-photography-is-a-history-of-shattered-glass.html. Accessed 2 Jan. 2019.

Döring, Tobias. *Caribbean-English Passages: Intertextuality in a Postcolonial Tradition*. Routledge, 2002. doi: 10.4324/9780203166901.

Ede, Amatoritsero. "The Politics of Afropolitanism." *Journal of African Cultural Studies*, vol. 28, no. 1, 2016, pp. 88–100. doi: 10.1080/13696815.2015.1132622.

Gnam, Andrea. "Fotografie und Film in W. G. Sebalds Erzählung *Ambros Adelwarth* und seinem Roman *Austerlitz*." *Verschiebebahnhöfe der Erinnerung: Zum Werk W. G. Sebalds*, edited by Ingo Wintermeyer and Sigurd Martin, Königshausen & Neumann, 2007, pp. 27–48.

Kappel, Yvonne. "Re-Membering the Travelogue: Generic Intertextuality as a Memory Practice in Teju Cole's *Every Day is for the Thief*." *Zeitschrift für Anglistik und Amerikanistik*, vol. 65, no. 1, 2017, pp. 67–83. doi: 10.1515/zaa-2017-0006.

Leerssen, Joep. "Nationalism and the Cultivation of Culture." *Nations and Nationalism*, vol. 12, no. 4, 2006, pp. 559–78. doi: 10.1111/j.1469-8129.2006.00253.x.

Leerssen, Joep. *Remembrance and Imagination: Patterns in the Historical and Literary Representation of Ireland in the Nineteenth Century*. Cork UP, 1996.

McClellan, Andrew. "Nationalism and the Origins of the Museum in France." *The Formation of National Collections of Art and Archaeology*, edited by Gwendolyn Wright, UP of New England, 1996, pp. 29–39.

Neuber, Wolfgang. "Locus, Lemma, Motto. Entwurf zu einer mnemonischen Emblematiktheorie." *Ars memorativa. Zur kulturgeschichtlichen Bedeutung der Gedächtniskunst 1400–1750*, edited by Jörg Jochen Berns and Wolfgang Neuber, Niemeyer, 1993, pp. 351–72. doi: 10.1515/9783110941593.351.

Neumann, Birgit. "Verbal-Visual Configurations in Teju Cole's *Every Day Is for the Thief*: Practices of Transition and Moments of Re-Vision." *Literatur in Wissenschaft und Unterricht*, vol. 47, no. 4, 2014, pp. 317–34.

Ondaatje, Michael. *Running in the Family*. McClelland & Stewart, 1982.

Pahl, Miriam. "Afropolitanism as Critical Consciousness: Chimamanda Ngozi Adichie's and Teju Cole's Internet Presence." *Journal of African Cultural Studies*, vol. 28, no. 1, 2016, pp. 73–87. doi: 10.1080/13696815.2015.1123143.

Rippl, Gabriele. "Picturing Lagos: Word-Photography Configurations in Teju Cole's *Every Day Is for the Thief* (2007/2014)." *Social Dynamics*, vol. 44, no. 3, 2018, pp. 472–84. doi: 10.1080/02533952.2018.1501545.

Said, Edward W. *Culture and Imperialism*. Vintage, 1994.

Sebald, W. G. *Austerlitz*. Hanser, 2001.

Sekula, Allan. "Photography and the Limits of National Identity." *Grey Room*, vol. 55, 2014, pp. 28–33. doi: 10.1162/GREY_a_00143.

Weiser, M. Elizabeth. *Museum Rhetoric: Building Civic Identity in National Spaces.* Pennsylvania State UP, 2017.

Youngs, Tim. "Introduction: Filling the Blank Spaces." *Travel Writing in the Nineteenth Century: Filling the Blank Spaces*, edited by Youngs, Anthem P, 2006, pp. 1–18.

CHAPTER 10

Emotional Nationalism in the New Nigerian Novel

Hannah Pardey

1   Introduction: Investigating the New Nigerian Novel's Authors and Readers

In her book chapter "Citizens of the World: Reading Postcolonial Literature" (2007), C. L. Innes describes the result of postcolonial studies' notorious neglect of audiences in terms of a reductive dichotomy: "most critical analyses of postcolonial writing implicitly or explicitly presume that the reader is either a member of the writer's nation, as in Benedict Anderson's *Imagined Communities* (1983) ... or, more frequently, a generalized cosmopolitan Westerner" (200). Her critical assessment of scholarly presumptions about 'the' postcolonial reader gains particular significance with regard to a flourishing literary phenomenon that oscillates between notions of the national and the global: the new Nigerian novel. Usually employed to highlight contemporary Nigerian authors' cosmopolitan consciousness, the term not only bespeaks a drastic deviation from earlier writers' political commitment to the postcolonial nation (Adesanmi and Dunton vii–xii). Moreover, the contemporary jet set of Nigerian literary production, which is best epitomized by Taiye Selasi's fancy self-stylization as 'Afropolitan,' entertains strong relations to various Western institutions in order to ensure its "unapologetic membership in the global elite" (McPherson 260).

This aspiration does not necessarily contradict the generic structures of various new Nigerian novels.[1] Their narrative focus on the nation has created an extensive critical debate about Nigerian writers' relations to Nigerian audiences. Focusing on Chimamanda Ngozi Adichie's *Half of a Yellow Sun* (2006), for instance, Hamish Dalley draws on statements by the author to demonstrate how she fashions herself as "a public intellectual who demands that the national community" of Nigerian readers "confronts its troubling past" (126–7). While acknowledging the new Nigerian novel's function of reconciling

---

1 Similar to the two novels investigated in this chapter, Sefi Atta's *Everything Good Will Come* (2005), Chinelo Okparanta's *Under the Udala Trees* (2015), and Ayòbámi Adébáyò's *Stay with Me* (2017) are generic hybrids that combine elements of the *Bildungsroman* and the historical novel.

national audiences with Nigeria's colonial legacies, this chapter shifts focus to the second aspect of Innes's finding by reading two historical novels by contemporary Nigerian authors, Adichie's *Half of a Yellow Sun* and Helon Habila's *Measuring Time* (2007), alongside a selected sample of online reviews on *Amazon* and *Goodreads*. More precisely, it takes up Innes's critique that postcolonial scholarship makes "little differentiation between different kinds of Western readers" (200) by specifying the second grouping and exploring its relation to Anderson's notion of 'imagined communities.'

The chapter's research endeavour requires a precise look at the new Nigerian novel's writers and audiences. Arguably, the definition of authors and readers in spatial terms is particularly unsuited in postcolonial – and increasingly digitized – contexts where writing and reading "are frequently activities involving mobile, exilic and diasporic" (Benwell et al. 1) agents. Even more crucially, the assumption of Western or Westernized agents constructs Nigerian authors as market-driven tools and their audiences as equally passive stooges who are "duped by ... neo-colonial ideologies" (3–4). Such a construction severely curtails the agency of both parties and, in effect, disregards or disguises the cultural work of the new Nigerian novel. Instead of presupposing a 'universal' Western reader, this chapter draws on Pierre Bourdieu's notion of 'capital' to argue that the writers and readers of the two novels share (the pursuit of) a particular social formation or class affiliation that manifests itself most visibly in their online practices on social media platforms.

In the last couple of years, the emergence of an affluent middle class of African writers has been hotly debated in African cultural and literary studies. In his article "The Global Program Era: Contemporary International Fiction in the American Creative Economy" (2018), Kalyan Nadiminti shows how their education in creative writing programmes instructs postcolonial authors in developing "a globalizing middle-class voice" (377) and discusses the aesthetic consequences in terms of a "bourgeois sociolect" (382). Emphasizing their novels' entanglement with the US-American university, Nadiminti gives attention to the structural, systematic quality of contemporary postcolonial production which, I contend, is further augmented by another vast system or network that conditions the new Nigerian novel: the internet. Postcolonial digital humanities scholar Roopika Risam cautions to theorize the internet as a free space or "blank slate" and instead suggests to focus on the interest groups "that are actively constructing the medium of the digital cultural record" (6). Both the media-savvy authors and audiences of the two novels under consideration in this chapter, I argue, employ their economic capital to turn digital platforms into public arenas of middle-class self-fashioning and thus increase their affective capital (Bourdieu 241–58; Gohrisch 11–23).

The following investigation of *Half of a Yellow Sun* and *Measuring Time* develops against the backdrop of their authors' and readers' engagement in what I call the digital affect: an affective online community that connects producers and consumers in their (aspiration towards) membership in global capital market structures.² The subsequent pages demonstrate how the new Nigerian novel's market conditions inscribe themselves in the literary texts. Adopting a narratological perspective, the chapter shows that both novels use textual strategies that can be subsumed under the umbrella term 'emotional nationalism' and materialize in the two aesthetic principles of allegorical and disenchanted realism.³ The concluding section looks beyond the novels and conceptualizes emotional nationalism as a reception strategy to consider how the digital age refashions ideas of the nation.

2   Allegorical Realism: Adichie's *Half of a Yellow Sun* (2006)

At first glance, Adichie's second novel suggests the continuation of a national writing tradition established by earlier Nigerian novelists. To start with, the novel's title constructs a direct link to the Nigerian Civil War. As explained in the story, it refers to the Biafran flag: "swaths of red, black, and green and, at the centre, a luminous half of a yellow sun" (Adichie 163). Set in various parts of Nigeria before and during the war, the novel focalizes Biafra's secession and collapse through three protagonists who highlight that "class, gender, and race" constitute "significant variables" (Dalley 124) in the perception of national change. Ugwu, an adolescent village boy from Opi, moves to Nsukka to work for the mathematics lecturer Odenigbo. Olanna, the beautiful daughter of newly rich Igbo parents and the twin of Kainene, joins her partner and his new houseboy to deploy her degree from London at Nsukka University's sociology

---

2   Exploring the conditions of writing, distributing, and reading the new Nigerian novel in the digital age, my PhD project, tentatively titled "Postcolonial Middlebrow: The New Nigerian Novel," builds on a self-constructed corpus of more than 30,000 documents including author interviews and audience responses on *Amazon*, *Goodreads*, and *YouTube* for twenty novels. The eleven reviews mentioned above represent the findings of my linguistic analysis and literary-sociological interpretation: the digital affect's excessive expression of emotions functions to simultaneously embrace and resist global capitalism.
3   I thank Jana Gohrisch who suggested the term 'emotional nationalism.' My subsequent considerations primarily developed from regular discussions with my colleagues at Hannover University. I am particularly indebted to Jana Gohrisch and Ellen Grünkemeier who have been and continue to be most generous with their time and expertise in the process of supervising my MA thesis and PhD project that this chapter is based on.

department. Richard, a British expatriate and journalist, seeks to write a book about Igbo-Ugwu art and engages in a relationship with Kainene.

Although the title and the choice of focalizers indicate the novel's positioning towards Nigeria and one of its central historical events, the following paragraphs focus on the text's plot construction and focalization techniques to demonstrate how they create affective perspectives on the nation. More precisely, I draw on and go beyond Hamish Dalley's notion of 'allegorical realism' to argue that *Half of a Yellow Sun* represents national turmoil "through the language of domestic melodrama" (134) in order to invite affective modes of historical knowledge. Offering an emotional understanding of the Biafran War by allegorizing it through "metaphors of sexual insecurity, personal betrayal, family breakdown, and survival" (138), the novel renders the postcolonial nation available for international readers' appropriation and thus participates in the construction of an affective online community.

I substantiate my claim by exploring the novel's inverted chronological structure and the focalizing characters' exceedingly "psychologized and subjectivized" (Jameson 71) approaches to the nation. Olanna represents war through the lens of middle-class domesticity, while Ugwu negotiates historical change through the ideological foil of middle-class progress. The fact that the novel constructs his rite of passage in close parallel to Biafra's move to independence and "juxtaposes the making of a single person against the destruction of national hope" (Andrade 93) in its final pages points to the text's larger discourse of humanity that invariably prioritizes the personal destinies of the characters over national events.

The plot's "back-and-forth chronology" (Dalley 124) forms a key component of the novel's aesthetics of emotional nationalism. Divided into four parts, *Half of a Yellow Sun* alternates between the pre-war and war years. Parts one and three, set in "The Early Sixties," centre on the novel's domestic sphere. Infected by "post-independence euphoria" (123), the characters forge friendships and romantic attachments that are later unhinged by various breaches of trust. Parts two and four, by contrast, are set in Biafra in "The Late Sixties" and consequently stress the political developments leading to secession and war. Forced to leave their homes and resettle over and over again, the characters witness three years of air raids, economic embargos, and starvation before they return to Nsukka to embrace their futures as "permanent outsiders" (Strehle 653).

The transposition of parts two and three subordinates the national hi/stories represented in parts two and four to the domestic hi/stories of parts one and three. The national upheavals referred to in the novel's second part – two coups, a series of Igbo massacres in the Muslim-dominated north, Biafra's secession, and the onset of the war – fly below the radar of more pressing concerns relating to the characters' personal bonds. Who are the parents of Baby, given Olanna's conviction that she and Odenigbo "did not conceive a child" (Adichie 107)? Why did Richard stop visiting the couple (168)? What does "the incident with Olanna" (151) refer to? Why does Ugwu try to blank out "those weeks before Baby's birth" (200)? Why did Richard revise his first book title (137)? And "what happened to the manuscript" (107), why did Kainene destroy it (182)? Arguably, the novel's inverted plot construction complicates an understanding of the depicted political processes, particularly for the reader who "kn[ows] very little about Biafra" (Melissa McCauley, *Amazon*). As a consequence, the online community's desired knowledge about "the groups of people involved and their motives" (Melissa McCauley, *Amazon*) presupposes its members' willingness to empathize with the characters (Dalley 136–37; Strehle 661).

The novel's continuous focus on the characters' subjective vantage on national conflict further shapes the reader's felt understanding of the political events depicted and promises the kind of 'emotional truth' that is announced on the author's website and in the novel's paratext. While all focalizers "call for empathetic witnessing and affective response" (Dalley 132) and thus function as exemplary "vehicles for lessons in Nigerian history" (Sally Howes, *Amazon*),[4] I will concentrate on Olanna in the subsequent sections because it is primarily her perspective that takes the novel's language of domesticity to another level so as to include explicit descriptions of sexual intimacy. Principally, I take issue with scholarly readings of Olanna's emphasis on the individual body as a cross-border strategy that, according to Zoe Norridge, renders the character "quintessentially human" (19). By contrast, I contend that Olanna's middle-class viewpoint undermines such inclusive notions and rather reveals the belief system of the affective online community. Instead of "paint[ing] the

---

4 Dalley (137–9) offers two other examples of how the novel's focalizers emotionalize national conflict. During an involuntary stop at Kano airport, Richard witnesses the killing of an Igbo staff member. As Nnaemeka's "chest [blows] open, a splattering red mass" (Adichie 153), Richard drops Kainene's love note he was reading when Hausa soldiers stormed the terminal. The simultaneity of events suggests an overlap between the public and the personal. More precisely, Richard's perspective subordinates Nnaemeka's murder, a significant public event, to the personal anxieties of an Englishman who fears that the massacre will have severe consequences for his love relation to Kainene (167–8). Framed through questions of personal belonging, the mediation of national politics is emotionalized. Ugwu's focalization of Olanna and Odenigbo's wedding ceremony functions in a similar way. The Nigerian air raid, which brings the festivities to an abrupt stop, is primarily rendered through the houseboy's worries about his family's security. Threatening his surrogate parents' "seal of stability" (202), Ugwu reads the bombs that fall from the sky as signalling impending domestic conflicts, not national breakdown.

human condition" (mtnmike, *Amazon*), the character's curious entanglement of materialist and sexual discourses encourages the emotional domestication of unfamiliar experiences and thus reinforces the community's "democratic fantasy of its own universal appeal" (Aubry 4).

In her discussion of Olanna's function for international audiences, Norridge remarks that the novel's explicit depictions of sexual intercourse invite an "embodied form of reading" (35) that enables both character and reader to "explore conflict" (18) and to negotiate experiences of pain and loss. For instance, on returning from Kano where she saw the havoc wreaked by a second wave of massacres, Olanna remembers the dead bodies of her relatives lying around "like dolls made of cloth" (Adichie 148). The traumatic experience causes severe effects on her body. Unable to move her legs, she stays in bed for several days and gives in to what she calls her "Dark Swoops" (156). Sex with Odenigbo not only helps her overcome her paralysis but offers an adequate approach to processing her trauma:

> She knew he didn't want to, that he touched her breasts because he would do whatever she wanted, whatever would make her better. She caressed his neck, buried her fingers in his dense hair, and when he slid into her, she thought about Arize's pregnant belly, how easily it must have broken, skin stretched that taut. She started to cry. (160)

Explored through and expressed by sexual intimacy, Olanna's compassionate identification with her murdered cousin Arize may allow for the reader's "corporeal knowledge" (Dalley 132) about the atrocities of the Nigerian Civil War. However, further examples clearly suggest that the individual body is no universal category.

In fact, the examples highlight that Olanna's body is a middle-class body that reacts to material – and, by implication, sexual – deprivation. A daughter of wealthy Igbo parents, Olanna enjoyed a Western education at Nigerian boarding schools and European universities. While she struggles with this privileged background and "being a part of the gloss that was her parents' life" (Adichie 34) at the outset of the novel, her perception of national turmoil as both material and sexual sacrifice presumably encourages the online community to conceptualize her as a close "friend" (Consumer, *Amazon*) and to embrace her position of privilege.

For instance, following the evacuation of Nsukka, the family resettles in rural Abba. The "slower and simpler" (Adichie 185) life that awaits Olanna here soon turns into a source of worries, particularly concerning the upbringing of Baby (184). Problems to fit in with the women of her sewing group hinge on perceived class differences. While they cannot relate to Olanna's shortage of "her books, her clothes, her china, her wigs, her Singer sewing machine, the television" (185), *Amazon* reviewer Caradee Wright suggests no such barriers: "I cannot imagine having to leave my house and my possessions instantly never to return." Oscillating between empathy for the Biafrans and condescension on their pathetic lives, Olanna's patronizing gestures such as giving classes in the courtyard that "teach [the poor children] to speak perfect English" (Adichie 291) or sharing food with the mother of a kwashiorkor-stricken child (327) further underline her approach to the nation as a caring yet detached charity lady who, like her sympathetic online audiences, glances with disgust at "the liquid-looking boils on [a girl's arm]" (327) or the greedy crowds who queue for food at the relief centre (167).

Against this backdrop, the intimate vocabulary of Olanna's focalization effectively emotionalizes national change to stimulate the online community's desire for self-realization through empathic suffering from a safe distance. The family's movement to ever smaller and more uncomfortable accommodations inhibits Olanna's pleasure of sex expressed earlier. On arrival at a wretched one-room apartment in Umuahia, she looks dolefully at "the bed, two yam tubers, the mattress that leaned against the dirt-smeared wall" (337), and cannot picture herself "mak[ing] love" (326) there. Consequently, she and Odenigbo "sle[ep] with their backs turned to each other" (327). Her partner, equally petrified by their bleak circumstances, refuses her occasional advances: "he shrugged her hand off and said, 'I'm tired, *nkem*.' She had never heard him say that before" (382, emphasis in original).

While Olanna's perspective allegorizes national upheaval through middle-class conflict, Ugwu represents the creation and breakdown of the nation through an allegory of middle-class progress. Reading his strand of the story as a *Bildungsroman*, I argue that the child protagonist functions as "a particularly apt vehicle" (Hron 28) to introduce the affective online community to Nigerian social and political issues. The growing proximity between character and audiences culminates in Ugwu's authorship of a national narrative that alleviates the community members' "embarrassment of having known nothing" (Samadrita, *Goodreads*) about the Biafran War. Accordingly, I look at the character construction of and focalization through Ugwu to demonstrate how they provide an opportunity for social distinction through the middle-class educational ideal of self-improvement.

Ugwu's representation as "the ignorant, wide-eyed African" (Cousins 146) initially inhibits middle-class identification. The patronizing yet sympathetic distance evoked in the chronologically earlier chapters is created by a rift between the novel's figural narrator and focalizer. Emphasizing the character's thoughts, the narrating instance recedes into the background and only makes his or her presence felt through rare textual markers such as phrasal conjunctions which illustrate that the focalizer's perceptions are not simply represented but filtered and evaluated. The narrator's judgmental impetus gains particular significance with regard to Ugwu who, contrary to Olanna and Richard, is not fluent in the novel's language.[5]

For example, the first chapter frequently hints at the translation process at work (the phrase "in English" appears nine times) or has the houseboy admire the 'foreign' tongue (Adichie 20). Ugwu's limited knowledge of English implies that the representation of his consciousness requires a switch in linguistic code. Opening a divide between narrator and focalizer, this shift produces humorous effects. The divide manifests itself in particular in a stylistic technique that Daria Tunca calls "underlexicalization" (71), which means that the narrator holds back the English terms for the objects Ugwu sees. For example, Ugwu marvels at "the alien furniture" (Adichie 5) in his new middle-class home and discovers, among other things, a "metal box studded with dangerous-looking knobs" (5, a radiogram), "something that look[s] like a woman's coat" (9, a dressing gown), or "the white thing, almost as tall as he was" (6, a fridge). Accordingly, the online audiences are invited to align with the narrator to "pok[e] fun at the boy's unfamiliarity" (Tunca 71) with the household items.

Apart from occasioning condescendingly benevolent responses (Cousins 146–7), other instances of underlexicalization gesture towards proximity between the ignorant houseboy and the reading community. When Odenigbo provides "a wide piece of paper" (Adichie 10, a world map), he not only familiarizes Ugwu with "the strange places" (10) he points out with his pen but also the novel's international readers. As Ugwu's limited understanding of Nigeria equals that of his curious observer, Odenigbo's lessons in the "rubbish" (11) colonial discourses invite character and reader to revise some of their stereotypical assumptions. The lecturer's creed that "[e]ducation is a priority" (11) aligns Ugwu and his audiences in the novel's large-scale educational project and promises knowledge through empathic identification.

In fact, Ugwu quickly notices that he is "not a normal houseboy" (17). His surrogate parents not only provide "a comb and a shirt" (47–8) or teach him how

---

5 Daria Tunca (68) points to the phrasal conjunction 'as if' in examples concerning the mediation of Olanna's thoughts while queueing for food at a relief centre: "She felt as if she were doing something improper, unethical" (Adichie 267) and "It was as if they all shoved her aside in one calculated move" (268). Contrary to the narrator's representation of Ugwu's perceptions, the rift works in favour of Olanna. Expressing sympathy rather than distance, the narrator's use of the phrasal conjunction suggests that Olanna's worries are unfounded.

to cook with an adequate amount of oil (48) but ensure his schooling and supply plenty of "excellent" (17), i.e. British, books and newspapers. Consequently, Ugwu develops a sense of pride that rests on his distinction from the inhabitants of his village whom he seeks to "impress ... with his English, his new shirt, his knowledge of sandwiches and running tap water" (86). The houseboy gradually comes to cultivate precisely those middle-class values (or pretensions) that his master and mistress exemplify. During a visit to his village in "The Late Sixties," for instance, he finds that "[h]is mother's food [is] unpalatable" and thus craves "to get back to Nsukka and finally eat a real meal" (119). Unlike his sister Anulika, he is further determined to "not marry until he ha[s] become like Master, until he ha[s] spent many years reading books" (176). The country's political upheavals offer abundant opportunity to further consolidate his intellectual superiority over his relatives. As Biafra's secession approaches, he begins to "read the newspapers more carefully" (142). Similar to the affective online community, Ugwu understands that education generates the cultural capital that buys social distinction.

Eventually, Ugwu develops a perspective on national turmoil which closely resembles that of Olanna. On the family's arrival in Umuahia, he expresses the same sense of deprivation that dominates the experience of his role model: "the compound," he notices with disgust, is "ugly with its stubby grass and cement blocks piled in corners" (196–7). Similarly, he cannot endure that "the neighbours' houses" stand "so close" that he can smell "their greasy cooking" (197). The fact that Olanna involves him in her schooling project and turns him into a teacher suggests that Ugwu has by this time achieved a level of education that renders the narrator's judgments obsolete: the narrator increasingly retreats, encouraging the reader's more immediate and undisturbed emotional identification.

Ugwu's educational self-fulfilment is best substantiated by his authorship of the novel's metatext "The Book: The World Was Silent When We Died." Locating this metatext within the critical 'writing back' paradigm, various scholars agree that it offers a "narrative from the perspective of below" (Gehrmann 228) or marks "the exit of the Western subject [i.e. Richard] from narrative control" (Novak 40).[6] I contend that such perspectives neglect that the metatext constitutes the final product of Ugwu's middle-class progress and therefore

---

[6] Despite my alternative reading of Ugwu's authorship, I consider the character of Richard a significant metafictional comment in that he encourages both the online community and the novel itself to critically reflect on their strategies of emotional nationalism. See Cousins for an excellent examination of Richard as a stand-in for the novel's "American and British readers" (149).

compromises the novel's "revisionist dimension" (Gehrmann 228). Instead of challenging the online community's desire for emotional education, the eight sequences of the book-within-the-book provide a straightforward historiographic account of Nigeria to supplement the emotional reading experience of the main narrative and alleviate the online audiences' sense of ignorance concerning international politics.

3   Disenchanted Realism: Habila's *Measuring Time* (2007)

Gesturing beyond "the prevailing realist tone of [Adichie's] novel" (Bryce 63), Habila's second novel has unanimously been discussed as a postmodern masterpiece. Anindyo Roy, for instance, contends that the novel's representation of national history challenges realism's effect of "achiev[ing] a totalizing vision" (18). Similarly, Frank Schulze-Engler points to the novel's explicit exploration of the "parallels between writing fiction and writing history" (264) to conclude that the protagonist arrives at "a new concept of historiography" (277). Mamo's efforts at writing local history arguably entail metafictional aesthetic means that exceed the predominantly realist conventions of Adichie's text. Instead of representing a war-stricken nation, *Measuring Time* provokes the protagonist's imaginary occupation with the history of his village and thereby ponders a range of ethical implications resulting from the writing of national narratives. Accordingly, the text has frequently been conceptualized as a metahistorical novel because it openly "reflects on the possibilities to reconstruct the past" (Gehrmann 231).

Mamo's attempts to recreate the past imply the revision of (fictional) "documentary material" (Nünning 365). Thus, the main narrative, divided into four parts and moving in chronological succession, is interspersed with a plethora of intratexts which suggest a "multiplicity of histories" (Roy 5), ranging from the letters his twin LaMamo writes from the trenches of various African civil wars and excerpts from Mamo's biographical history *Lives and Times* to Reverend Drinkwater's *A True History of the Peoples of Keti* and diary entries by his wife, Hannah. In its "montage of texts" (Nünning 366) and its constant foregrounding of the historian's interpretive task, *Measuring Time* even comes close to what Linda Hutcheon famously labels historiographic metafiction, i.e. fiction which "problematizes the entire notion of historical knowledge" (89) about the postcolonial nation.

Probing into scholars' emphasis on the novel's postmodern playfulness, I use the following paragraphs to argue for the text's adherence to realist narrative conventions as a case of emotional nationalism. Contrary to Adichie's novel, *Measuring Time* employs realist techniques of narrating the nation that I call disenchanted: a kind of realism that deliberately evokes the magical realist strategies of earlier national narratives to demonstrate their failure.[7] Paying special attention to the construction of Mamo, I illustrate how his sickle-cell anaemia functions as a principle of structuring the novel's representation of time and space to invite the online community's affective understanding of post-civil war Nigeria. In a second step, I explore the 'raw realism' of his twin's letters as a further strategy of emotionalizing the nation to offer readerly contentment.

Comparing the *Bildungsroman* structure of *Half of a Yellow Sun* to the distinct developments of the twins, the lessons Mamo and LaMamo learn are gloomily 'real' ones. In an early scene in the novel, Mamo stays in bed to recover from one of his exacerbations. He listens to his Auntie Marina's fantastic stories that "slowly work ... their magic in his veins, keeping him alive" (Habila 23). In an excerpt from his *Lives and Times*, he compares her to the storyteller of *The Arabian Nights*: "*She was a magician, a witch with words. She could conjure up mountains and undersea kingdoms with words. I stayed alive from day to day just to hear her next story. She was Scheherazade, I was the king, but she told stories to save my life, not hers*" (21–2, italics in original). It is only in retrospect that Mamo realizes how the telling of stories serves personal interests: Auntie Marina wanted to escape loneliness, Mamo wanted to assure his "immortality" (25).

The first painful lesson in 'reality' follows only moments after Mamo's recovery. "This was the year they killed the old witch's dog" (27), the narrator imparts. The twins rub the dog's rheum into their eyes to invoke the "distant places, underwater people, and spirits" (27) from their aunt's stories. The result is both comical and educational. Stories, the episode teaches, are an illusion: they literally "glue ... [the twins'] eyelids shut" (33) and provoke horrible nightmares. The dog's rheum blurs their clear vision and has them mistake "a branch" which "knock[s] against the window" (32) for dreadful ghosts. The next morning, Mamo wakes with an infection of the eyes. LaMamo, equally experiencing the treacherous effects of Auntie Marina's stories, falls out of a tree and fractures his wrist. The narrating voice uses irony to establish a patronizing distance to the two child focalizers and thereby allows the reader to gently ridicule the superstitious pair of boys: "it was as if the ghosts they had so wanted to see were having their revenge" (34).

---

7   Ben Okri's novel *The Famished Road* (1991) constitutes a prime example of the magical realism employed by first- and second-generation Nigerian authors.

Despite these hurtful episodes, though, the twins are not yet ready to exchange the illusory stories for "the harsh daylight of reality" (23). Insofar as Mamo's adolescent 'reality' is constituted by his illness, escaping it becomes top priority: "CHEAT DEATH, BE FAMOUS" (24, capitalization in original), he notes in his "mental diary" (25). An idea of how this fame may be achieved offers itself in the character of his uncle Haruna who appears in the fictional village of Keti after the Biafran War. Although the veteran looks "like a dead man returning to life" (45), Haruna features in the many village stories as a heroic man "who had bravely given his life for his country" (45). Like Auntie Marina's fantastic tales, these stories work their magic in the twins' veins. Neglecting the earlier lesson in the delusory force of stories, they determine to follow their uncle's glorious path and become "famous as soldiers" (55) – a decision the sharp-sighted narrator can only ascribe to the irrational follies of youth. As Susanne Gehrmann notes, "the dream of winning fame through war is quickly disrupted" (229). While LaMamo will undergo the "development from a naïve small soldier into a disillusioned veteran of wars" (232), Mamo's illness prohibits that he even embarks on such an adventurous journey. Mamo's perspective emotionalizes the nation for the novel's affective online community as he begins to grow out of "the fantastic architecture" (Habila 76) of the stories that dominated his childhood days and into the "enlightenment and reality" (Ethan McLeod, *Amazon*) which satisfies the desire for a "good insight into the cultural norms" (Paula C. Aird, *Amazon*) of "African village life" (Stephanie, *Goodreads*). Confirming that he takes the ideas for his novels "[f]rom real life" (Musiitwa n. pag., also published in blog section of author's website), Habila legitimizes this reading pattern.

The main focalizer's sickle-cell anaemia creates an effect that exceeds the mere guarantee of readers' distanced pity. It is through Mamo's thoughts and perceptions that the novel produces a pattern of movement which one *Amazon* reviewer describes as "peaceful" (Lara Ade, *Amazon*). Mamo's illness, I contend, structures the novel's spatial and temporal representations and thus conveys an emotional (reading) experience of Keti's stagnant rhythms. Like – or due to – his bad health, Mamo moves in "cycle[s]" (Habila 35), both physically and mentally. A phase of illness is followed by a phase of recovery is followed by a phase of illness. Caught in this circle of illness and recovery, he always starts anew and never arrives anywhere. Accordingly, the predominant mode of representing the nation is not so much "open-ended" (Roy 9) but cyclical: Keti Community School is closed to be opened to be closed again (Habila 130, 178); the twins' father joins a political party to leave it to join it to leave it again (83, 176); and Zara, Mamo's love interest, appears to disappear to appear again (110, 226).

Compared to Adichie's novel, *Measuring Time* comes with very few temporal markers: "this year" (37), "one day" (45), "a year later" (76), or "days like this" (86) are frequently recurring phrases that make the reader float through a narrative with neither climax nor development, rendering the postcolonial nation a space of "economic stagnation" and "social misery" (Anyokwu 14). Against this backdrop, the novel's title metaphor points to the circular movement of Mamo's deliberations and Keti's everyday events. Gehrmann's suggestion that "the present continuous form of the verb underlines that [the process] of measuring is never finished" (231) substantiates my argument. Along similar lines, Roy describes the recurring motif of 'waiting' as the novel's "central narrative epistemology" (7) and quotes the following passage: "Mamo waited for something, anything to happen, and as he waited he measured time in the shadows cast by trees and walls, ... in the seconds and minutes and hours and days and weeks and months that add up to form the seasons" (Habila 139). The fact that Mamo experiences waiting as an activity in tune with nature's cycles further indicates that the motif does not so much signal the novel's constant "delay and postponement" (Roy 6) but rather the endless repetition of meaning. Through Mamo's eyes, the postcolonial nation fosters a sort of "existential despair" (Kunzru n. pag.).

The stagnant rhythm of Mamo's perspective is occasionally interrupted by inserted intratexts and considerations concerning the writing of history. The altogether four letters he receives from his fighting twin LaMamo have been read as interrogating the primacy of literacy and highlighting oral forms of historiography (Krishnan 29–30, 36). Instead of treating the letters as metafictional comments, I argue that LaMamo's troubles with literacy encourage an emotional approach to reading that invites the online audiences to rehearse their stereotypical assumptions about Africa. His letters from the trenches, "full of disconnected ideas and false grammar" (Habila 79), create both pity and horror and thereby function to consolidate the reading community's self-fashioning as superior.

Framed in terms of character development, LaMamo's successive reports from Libya, Mali, and Liberia signal the kind of personal progress that is absent from his brother's perspective. Starting out as an enthusiastic fighter for African freedom (*"we cannot continue to live like slaves even after independence from colonization"* (80, italics in original)), his second letter prompts a more disenchanted view on his former ideals: "clearly, he was no more the young, eager, hopeful; he already sounded like a veteran of many battles" (60), Mamo notes. Yet further progress is halted from now on. Similar to that of his twin, LaMamo's development begins to move in repetitive fashion, which is emphasized by two further disillusioned letters. Fighting follows fighting follows fighting and, eventually, death – ironically enough, not in one of the various African trenches but in humdrum Keti. Contrary to Mamo, though, LaMamo arrives at a form of realist representation that exceeds disenchantment and feeds on "the raw realism of someone writing from the battlefield" (Roy 12).

This form of realism provokes horror throughout: LaMamo's second letter reports on "*shooting*" and "*rape*" and "*blood*," assuring its readers that "*death is evrywhere* [sic]" (Habila 106–7, italics in original). On his arrival at a rubber plantation in Monrovia related in the third letter, LaMamo finds the same scenario of death and destruction: "*The whole country is dead, all the villages are on fire and there is no food and there are only dead bodies on the street*" (155, italics in original). The documentary style of his writing from the trenches arguably reinforces the community's notions about Africa as a place of "never-ending bloodshed and violence" (Ethan McLeod, *Amazon*). Read as a "good insight" (Paula C. Aird, *Amazon*) into contemporary Africa, LaMamo fuels online audiences' sense of alienation because he is part of the war zones he sketches. Like all the other nameless soldiers, he is a sanguinary murderer who propels the meaningless circle of combat. This becomes obvious when he shoots a major, "*the blood and brain and eyes*" splashing "*all over the place*" (Habila 60, italics in original). He only resists complete stereotyping and appears "human," i.e. "beautifully flawed" (Rebecca, *Goodreads*), because he infuses his war reports with elements of a love story. Bintou, the girl he saves from rape, allows for the reader's occasional empathy with LaMamo by telling him that he is "*different*" (Habila 163, italics in original) after the shooting.

4   Conclusion: From Imagined to Online Communities

Which role does the concept of nation play in the digital age? To what extent can we draw on the notion that Anderson famously used to describe modern nation-states and approach the affective online community as an imagined community? Does the new Nigerian novel's participation in global capitalist structures promise universal belonging to the same 'free market', or does it imply economic and imaginative exploitation? Digital platforms like *Amazon*, *Goodreads*, or *YouTube* may be understood as "creating that remarkable confidence of community in anonymity" (Anderson 36). Accordingly, they approximate the functions or effects that Anderson attributes to the eighteenth-century newspaper which enabled "an otherwise disconnected audience to think about themselves collectively in new ways" (Benwell et al. 15). Despite – or because of – their extension beyond clearly identifiable national borders, social media platforms provide virtual spaces that define belonging and membership predominantly in terms of class. Digital contexts may render a critical focus on authors' and readers' locations obsolete. However, the postcolonial scholar with an interest in uncovering and contesting unequal power relations will at least notice that the digital affect hinges on the representational power of a handful of multi-billion dollar US companies.

Works Cited

Ade, Lara. "One of the Best Reads Ever!" *Amazon*, 9 Mar. 2008, www.amazon.com/gp/customer-reviews/R21UY29FNRAYUD/ref=cm_cr_arp_d_rvw_ttl?ie=UTF8&ASIN=0393052516.

Adébáyò, Ayòbámi. *Stay with Me*. Canongate Books, 2017.

Adesanmi, Pius, and Chris Dunton. "Everything Good Is Raining: Provisional Notes on the Nigerian Novel of the Third Generation." *Research in African Literatures*, vol. 39, no. 2, 2008, pp. vii–xii.

Adichie, Chimamanda Ngozi. *Half of a Yellow Sun*. Fourth Estate, 2006.

Aird, Paula C. "Insight into Cultural Norms." *Amazon*, 26 July 2007, www.amazon.com/gp/customer-reviews/R1J2DNBF7E4LUV/ref=cm_cr_dp_d_rvw_ttl?ie=UTF8&ASIN=0393052516.

Anderson, Benedict. *Imagined Communities. Reflections on the Origin and Spread of Nationalism*. 1983. Revised edition. Verso, 2006.

Andrade, Susan Z. "Adichie's Genealogies: National and Feminine Novels." *Research in African Literatures*, vol. 42, no. 2, 2011, pp. 91–101. doi: 10.2979/reseafrilite.42.2.91.

Anyokwu, Christopher. "Inheritance of Loss: Narrative and History in Helon Habila's *Measuring Time*." *California Linguistic Notes*, vol. 33, no. 2, 2008, pp. 1–27.

Atta, Sefi. *Everything Good Will Come*. Interlink Books, 2005.

Aubry, Timothy. *Reading as Therapy: What Contemporary Fiction Does for Middle-Class Americans*. U of Iowa P, 2011.

Benwell, Bethan, James Procter, and Gemma Robinson. "Introduction." *Postcolonial Audiences: Readers, Viewers and Reception*, edited by Benwell, Procter, and Robinson, Routledge, 2012, pp. 1–23.

Bourdieu, Pierre. "The Forms of Capital." *Handbook of Theory and Research for the Sociology of Education*, edited by John G. Richardson, Greenwood, 1986, pp. 241–58.

Bryce, Jane. "'Half and Half Children': Third-Generation Women Writers and the New Nigerian Novel." *Research in African Literatures*, vol. 39, no. 2, 2008, pp. 49–67.

Cousins, Helen. "A Good Authentic Read: Exoticism in the Postcolonial Novels of the Richard & Judy Book Club." *The Richard & Judy Book Club Reader: Popular Texts and the Practices of Reading*, edited by Jenni Ramone and Helen Cousins, Ashgate, 2011, pp. 137–53.

Consumer. "You MUST Read This Book about the War in Biafra." *Amazon*, 1 May 2015, www.amazon.com/gp/customer-reviews/R67oRP3E59L99/ref=cm_cr_getr_d_rvw_ ttl?ie=UTF8&ASIN=1400095204.

Dalley, Hamish. *The Postcolonial Historical Novel: Realism, Allegory, and the Representation of Contested Pasts*. Palgrave Macmillan, 2014.

Gehrmann, Susanne. "Re-Writing War in Contemporary Nigerian Fiction: From Biafra to Present Times." *Listening to Africa. Anglophone African Literatures and Cultures*, edited by Jana Gohrisch and Ellen Grünkemeier, Universitätsverlag Winter, 2012, pp. 209–38.

Gohrisch, Jana. *Bürgerliche Gefühlsdispositionen in der englischen Prosa des 19. Jahrhunderts*. Universitätsverlag Winter, 2005.

Habila, Helon. *Measuring Time*. Norton & Company, 2007.

Howes, Sally. "An Important Postcolonial Novel." *Amazon*, 4 May 2015, www.amazon.com/gp/customer-reviews/R1DoEINF3IH0H7/ref=cm_cr_dp_d_rvw_ ttl?ie=UTF8&ASIN=1400095204.

Hron, Madelaine. "*Ora na-azu nwa*: The Figure of the Child in Third-Generation Nigerian Novels." *Research in African Literatures*, vol. 39, no. 2, 2008, pp. 27–48.

Hutcheon, Linda. *A Poetics of Postmodernism: History, Theory, Fiction*. Routledge, 1988.

Innes, C. L. *The Cambridge Introduction to Postcolonial Literatures in English*. Cambridge UP, 2007.

Jameson, Fredric. "Third-World Literature in the Era of Multinational Capitalism." *Social Text*, vol. 15, 1986, pp. 65–88.

Krishnan, Madhu. "The Storyteller Function in Contemporary Nigerian Narrative." *The Journal of Commonwealth Literature*, vol. 49, no. 1, 2014, pp. 29–45. doi: 10.1177/0021989413510519.

Kunzru, Hari. "Unparallel Lives." Review of *Measuring Time*, by Helon Habila. *The New York Times*, 25 Feb. 2007, www.nytimes.com/2007/02/25/books/review/Kunzru.t.html. Accessed 12 Nov. 2018.

McCauley, Melissa. "Wow. Just Wow." *Amazon*, 5 Oct. 2015, www.amazon.com/gp/customer-reviews/R22F2QWJGOG6OQ/ref=cm_cr_getr_d_rvw_ ttl?ie=UTF8&ASIN=1400095204.

McLeod, Ethan. "Fighting Fear and Fate for Fame." *Amazon*, 16 Apr. 2012, www.amazon.com/gp/customer-reviews/R2AYR69QGR4DAA/ref=cm_cr_arp_d_rvw_ ttl?ie=UTF8&ASIN=0393052516.

McPherson, Annika. "A Question of Perception? Transnational Lives and Afropolitan Aesthetics in Teju Cole's *Every Day Is for the Thief*." *Anglistentag 2016 Hamburg: Proceedings*, edited by Ute Berns and Jolene Mathieson, WVT, 2017, pp. 257–72.

mtnmike. "I Loved This Book." *Amazon*, 25 Apr. 2015, www.amazon.com/gp/customer-reviews/R3QWI0XBMMZ3MX/ref=cm_cr_getr_d_rvw_ttl?ie=UTF8&ASIN=1400095204.

Musiitwa, Daniel. "Helon Habila Speaks about His Writing and Winning the Windham-Campbell Prize." *AfricaBookClub.com*, 1 Apr. 2015, www.africabookclub.com/helon-habila-speaks-about-his-writing-and-winning-the-windham-campbell-prize/. Accessed 12 Aug. 2019.

Nadiminti, Kalyan. "The Global Program Era: Contemporary International Fiction in the American Creative Economy." *NOVEL: A Forum on Fiction*, vol. 51, no. 3, 2018, pp. 375–98. doi: 10.1215/00295132-7086426.

Norridge, Zoe. "Sex as Synecdoche: Intimate Language of Violence in Chimamanda Ngozi Adichie's *Half of a Yellow Sun* and Aminatta Forna's *The Memory of Love*." *Research in African Literatures*, vol. 43, no. 2, 2012, pp. 18–39. doi: 10.2979/reseafrilite.43.2.18.

Novak, Amy. "Who Speaks? Who Listens? The Problem of Address in Two Nigerian Trauma Novels." *Studies in the Novel*, vol. 40, no. 1, 2008, pp. 31–51. doi: 10.1353/sdn.0.0013.

Nünning, Ansgar. "Where Historiographic Metafiction and Narratology Meet: Towards an Applied Cultural Narratology." *Style*, vol. 38, no. 3, 2004, pp. 352–75.

Okparanta, Chinelo. *Under the Udala Trees*. Granta Books, 2015.

Okri, Ben. *The Famished Road*. Jonathan Cape, 1991.

Rebecca. "*Measuring Time* by Helon Habila: Rebecca's Review." *Goodreads*, 16 Aug. 2014, www.goodreads.com/review/show/1028323446?book_show_action=true&from_review_page=1.

Risam, Roopika. *New Digital Worlds: Postcolonial Digital Humanities in Theory, Praxis, and Pedagogy*. Northwestern UP, 2019.

Roy, Anindyo. "Auto/Biographer, Historian, *Griot*: Measures of Realism and the Writing of History in Helon Habila's *Measuring Time*." *ARIEL: A Review of International English Literature*, vol. 41, no. 1, 2011, pp. 5–26.

Samadrita. "*Half of a Yellow Sun* by Chimamanda Ngozi Adichie: Samadrita's Review." *Goodreads*, 16 Jan. 2013, www.goodreads.com/review/show/507932089?book_show_action=true&from_review_page=1.

Schulze-Engler, Frank. "Fragile Modernities: History and Historiography in Contemporary African Fiction." *Postcolonial Studies Across the Disciplines*, edited by Jana Gohrisch and Ellen Grünkemeier, Rodopi, 2013, pp. 263–82.

Selasi, Taiye. "Bye-Bye Babar." *The Lip Magazine*, 3 Mar. 2005, www.thelip.robertsharp.co.uk/?p=76. Accessed 12 Nov. 2018.

Stephanie. "*Measuring Time* by Helon Habila: Stephanie's Review." *Goodreads*, 11 July 2008, www.goodreads.com/review/show/26992968?book_show_action=true&from_review_page=1.

Strehle, Susan. "Producing Exile: Diasporic Vision in Adichie's *Half of a Yellow Sun.*" *Modern Fiction Studies*, vol. 57, no. 4, 2011, pp. 650–72. doi: 10.1353/mfs.2011.0086.

Tunca, Daria. *Stylistic Approaches to Nigerian Fiction.* Palgrave Macmillan, 2014.

Wright, Caradee. "The Brutality of It All Rocked Me to My Core." *Amazon*, 4 June 2015, www.amazon.com/gp/customer-reviews/R25VIDAQ4RDSV5/ref=cm_cr_getr_d_rvw_ttl?ie=UTF8&ASIN=1400095204.

CHAPTER 11

The British Empire and the 'Laureate of Its Demise': Postimperial Nostalgia in Jane Gardam's Old Filth Trilogy

Lukas Lammers

1   Introduction: The Decline of the British Empire in Three Parts

In January 2017, Boris Johnson, then foreign secretary, visited the Shwedagon Pagoda in Myanmar, once colonial Burma, and embarrassed the UK ambassador to Myanmar by reciting fragments from Rudyard Kipling's poem "Mandalay," half to himself, half to the surrounding crowd. The incident was caught on camera, is well known, and was criticised by some as insensitive (Booth n. pag.). Overall, however, Johnson's popularity appears to have been boosted rather than hampered by such faux pas.

Long after Kipling, but closer to Johnson, Jane Gardam published a series of interrelated novels known as the 'Old Filth trilogy.' While there is no explicit mention of "Mandalay," there are themes and references that resonate with Johnson's ad hoc performance of Kipling's poem. Gardam's admiration for Kipling not only shows in various borrowings; in the first part of the series, she also notes that she is "very much indebted to Rudyard Kipling's *Autobiography* and to his story *Baa Baa Black Sheep*" (*Old Filth* 259). Inspired perhaps by this acknowledgement, Elizabeth Lowry, in a review of the second part of the trilogy, suggests that there is an even more profound connection between the two writers. She casts Gardam as a latter-day Kipling:

> If Rudyard Kipling was the laureate of the British Empire, then Jane Gardam is surely the closest thing we have to a laureate of its demise. … Spanning nearly a century, the three novels offer a compelling, finely nuanced tableau of the end of an era and the passing of the generation that sustained it. (19)

I borrow Lowry's phrase 'laureate of the demise of Empire' for the title of this chapter to address a phenomenon that Lowry's own article does not seem to be aware of. As I see it, her comment not only attributes a perhaps rather surprising eminence to Gardam, but also hints at the curious cultural logic that makes

Gardam's novels topical in the current political climate: it seems to imply that a demise can be a mark of distinction. Drawing on the work of Paul Gilroy and Fintan O'Toole, I will elaborate on this idea to suggest that Gardam's trilogy participates in a narrative both popular and problematic which (re)imagines Britain's 'withdrawal' from the colonies as a regrettable but noble act. In a curious reversal, this narrative casts Britain in the role of a victim of imperialism – a rather astounding twist to the idea of a 'British postcolonial novel.'

Unlike many other serials, Gardam's is not a set of sequels and prequels; rather, the three parts revisit the same places, events, and characters. Tessa Hadley aptly describes the effect of this repeated return when she suggests that "[t]he method of these novels is to build their story layer by layer, as consciousness constructs memory" (19). What is more, the series offers a telling metaphor for this process of (re)construction. Following the development of a set of characters from their birth around the beginning of the twentieth century to the end of their lives in the early 2000s, and depicting in its course a significant number of funerals, the trilogy as a whole comes to resemble a collective memorial service for a generation of Britons who grew up in the aftermath of World War I, participated in a last flourishing of the Empire, partook in Britain's 'finest hour' (World War II), and whose retirement roughly coincides with Britain's decline as a world power. What makes the metaphor instructive is that it alerts us to the novels' tendency – like many memorial services – to forget or gloss over and indeed excuse the faults of the generation whose dying they mourn.

Acknowledging the success of the novels in a range of reviews across a broad political spectrum, the chapter will further suggest that Gardam's debt to Kipling is key to understanding the, to my mind, problematic appeal of the trilogy and its apparent immunity against postcolonial critique. I hope to show that it is, above all, the decision (inspired by Kipling's life and characters) to narrate recent British history from the point of view of so-called 'Raj orphans' which creates this immunity. The novels' focus on the suffering of these characters functions as an ideological lever, easing the way towards a nostalgic contemplation of Britain's imperial past while warding off feelings of guilt and shame.

Written and published over a period of ten years before the Brexit referendum, the novels anticipate a form of national nostalgia which we can glimpse in Johnson's recitation of "Mandalay" in Myanmar. Ultimately, this chapter is interested in how Gardam's trilogy makes palatable an unapologetically nostalgic perspective on parts of Britain's colonial history. I will propose to read the novels as a form of revisionist history with built-in 'insulation' against (postcolonial) critique. This revisionist account of the past has the potential to ease the postimperial pain and justify national pride vis-à-vis a globalised world in which Britain seems to have, undeservedly, lost control.

2   Postimperial Melancholia and the Heroics of Brexit

In 2005 (coincidentally a year after the publication of *Old Filth*), Paul Gilroy observed a paradoxical phenomenon in British discourses of nation and migration. He famously dubbed the phenomenon postcolonial, or, more fittingly, "postimperial melancholia" (99). According to Gilroy, the end of World War II is the crucial historical watershed at which "Britain snatched a wider cultural and psychological defeat from the jaws of its victory over Hitlerism in 1945" (90). The noted defeat is the loss of Empire, which, in this view, coincides with the end of World War II. The two events, Gilroy argues, have become inextricable in the British imaginary, so as to suggest that "Britain's continued citation of the anti-Nazi war … reveals a desire to find a way back to the point where the national culture … was, … both comprehensible and habitable" (89). This constellation is toxic insofar as the winning of the war has inhibited Britain's ability to mourn the loss of Empire and to face the violence committed in its name: "The invitation to revise and reassess often triggers a chain of defensive argumentation that seeks firstly to minimize the extent of the Empire, then to deny or justify its brutal character, and finally, to present the British themselves as the ultimate tragic victims of their extraordinary imperial successes" (94). This astute analysis is also borne out in a disconcerting way, as I show in the following sections, by Gardam's Old Filth trilogy.

Gilroy's comments have received renewed importance through the furious debates surrounding Brexit (Eaglestone; Mondal).[1] Fintan O'Toole, exploring what one might call the psychodynamics of Brexit, has recently drawn attention to similar phenomena. He documents an ongoing unwillingness to acknowledge the brutalities of colonial rule and an inability to come to terms with the loss of prestige that ensued when the Empire collapsed. Key to O'Toole's analysis is the idea of "heroic failure," the fact that "[t]he exploits that have loomed largest in English consciousness since the nineteenth century are retreats or disasters" (69). Surveying numerous examples, including the charge of the Light Brigade in 1854, the British Antarctic Expedition in 1910, and the battle of Dunkirk in 1940, he suggests that Brexit can be seen as the

---

1   I follow Gilroy in his convincing, though contestable, assumption of psychological 'needs' of a national consciousness traumatised by historical events that cut to the bone of national identity.

most recent iteration in a long history of glorified fiascos, albeit one that illustrates a radical change in the conditions under which British national identity is defined. He explains that "the original English cult of heroic failure ... arose from British power and dominance" (71). As long as cultural and political dominance prevailed, British identity could be defined through the most spectacular historical blunders. O'Toole describes this process as "an exercise in transference," arguing that "[t]he British needed to fill a yawning gap between their self-image as exemplars of liberty and civility and the violence and domination that were the realities of Empire" (72). But what happens when the required superiority wanes? With the decline of Empire, the basis for the cult of heroic failure crumbled and necessitated a revision of the stories the British told about themselves. This constellation, O'Toole argues, shapes the rhetoric of Brexiteers and helps explain how Britain and particularly England came to define themselves through self-pity: Brexit "makes sense for a nation that feels sorry for itself" (1).

Ultimately, O'Toole, like Gilroy, argues that British national identity is still rooted in a sense of unquestioned superiority as well as unacknowledged feelings of guilt and shame. Both authors suggest that these sentiments derive from Britain's former role as an empire. In O'Toole's words,

> If the point of the cult of heroic failure was to disguise the realities of colonial dominance, it required radical adjustment in the post-imperial context of British membership of the EU. It had to let in the self-pity it had always held at bay. And it did this in the most startling way: by imagining Britain itself as a colony of the EU. (79)

The reversal described here can take various forms, O'Toole argues. Resistance against the EU as a 'superstate' "could ... play itself into memories of wartime resistance movements [against Nazi Germany]," or, more powerfully, as "an anti-colonial liberation movement – the very movement that the British had previously sought to crush" (79). The Empire is turning the tables, as it were.

Having joined the group of 'victims of colonialism,' Britain creates for itself a form of 'insulation' against postcolonial critique, as Anshuman A. Mondal observes:

> Britain, for so long held to account by the forces of 'political correctness' ... for its imperial and colonial overlordship and the historical crimes perpetrated in its service, could now be positioned as itself a victim of a kind of colonial dependency and, at a (rhetorical) stroke, its colonial history could be at once evoked and obscured. (82–3)

The idea that, "at a (rhetorical) stroke," Britain's colonial history can be "at once evoked and obscured" is instructive because it captures not only the transference of colonial suffering but also the almost schizophrenic logic that makes this transference possible. In O'Toole's words, "the fundamental contradiction of Brexit is that it wants to think of itself simultaneously as a reconstitution of Empire and as an anti-imperial national liberation movement" (80). O'Toole thus updates Gilroy's observations in *Postcolonial Melancholia* and explains how allegations of violence can be (rhetorically) deflected – how an insulation can be constructed – by casting Britain as a 'vassal state' suffering colonial oppression while *simultaneously* proclaiming its right to lead the world as it did in the days of Empire. Shame is converted into self-pity and self-righteousness. From this perspective, the current state of affairs appears as a tragic reversal of Britain's (destined) historical role.

Gilroy, Mondal, and O'Toole provide ample illustrations of this reversal. Among the literary works cited by O'Toole is also Gardam's *Old Filth*. Although he refers to the novel twice (20–1 and 80), Gardam remains marginal in his argument. The following will show that the whole series merits closer inspection. While it does not anticipate any of the events directly, Gardam's trilogy illuminates the cultural moment that brought forth Brexit. It mobilises some of the same ideas discussed above, in particular the disconcerting logic of "imagining Britain itself as a colony" (O'Toole 79) and the "taking on of colonial pain" (80). Citing and imitating colonial fiction, the novels appear to be not so much writing against postcolonial theory and fiction as skipping, or forgetting, it. The trilogy's popularity suggests that such a revisionist account finds large audiences and critical acclaim.[2] I want to propose that, mainly due to its original perspective and its lightly ironic tone, it offers readers an empowering position from which it is easy to nostalgically partake in Britain's lost imperial glory and ward off feelings of guilt and shame, despite possible ethical qualms.

3   New Neighbours and 'Old Filth': Taking on the Colonial Pain

That Gardam employs irony to wrestle with Britain's imperial legacy can be seen in the very title of the first instalment which is also the nickname of the trilogy's hero, 'Old Filth.' As the connection between the real name of the character, Edward Feathers, and his nickname is by no means apparent, it invites

---

2 *Old Filth* was shortlisted for the Orange Prize (2005), voted among the 100 best books in a poll by the BBC (Ciabattari), and included in "a list of our writers' and critics' favourite 100 novels of the 21st century" by *The Sunday Times* ("100 Modern Novels to Love").

speculation. Practically, all reviews rehearse the explanation provided by Gardam in the first pages: 'Filth,' we are told, is an acronym and stands for "Failed In London Try Hong Kong" (*Old Filth* 3). The 'old' is later added as a mark of honour to acknowledge Feathers's status as a living legend at the Far Eastern Bar. Strikingly, nobody discusses what is arguably the more obvious meaning of the words. It is the literal meaning, however, which points to an instructive irony. The gap between the witty and the literal reading, I suggest, can tell us a lot about the trilogy's portrayal of the British Empire and British identity.

The second chapter of *Old Filth* introduces us to its protagonist with the following words: "He was spectacularly clean. You might say ostentatiously clean. ... His shoes shone like conkers. His clothes were always freshly pressed. He had the elegance of the 1920s" (5). This description clearly jars with the literal meaning of the character's nickname. In fact, the text, consciously or not, draws attention to this discrepancy by assuring us that "[h]is colleagues ... called him Filth, but not out of irony" (5). Readers are alerted to the possible irony but then asked to ignore it. Overall, the portrayal of Old Filth invites admiration rather than critique for an elderly gentleman who maintains the style of a bygone era: "His eyes and mind alert, he was a delightful man" (5).

The following description of Feathers's circumstances adds to this impression and hints at a colonial lifestyle: "There was no smell of old age about his house. He was rich and took for granted that it (and he) would be kept clean, fed and laundered by servants as it had always been" (6). The semi-detached mode of presentation is typical of the trilogy. Viewed from the perspective of a mostly covert, sympathetic narrator, Edward occasionally appears as a spoiled child, but he also emerges as an example of perfect British attire and manners: "Always a Victorian silk handkerchief in the breast pocket. Always yellow cotton or silk socks from Harrods" (5). To modern readers, his dress and manners may seem eccentric, but they are also reassuringly English. In the course of the trilogy, it will become clear that Feathers upholds tradition in the face of change. He owes his wealth, his confidence with servants, and his immaculate appearance to his privileges as a former judge in Hong Kong, and he is convinced that he has rightly earned them.

The literal meaning of the nickname (re-)surfaces later on. In the following passage, the elderly Edward Feathers muses about his wife Betty, who recently died of a stroke. He recalls a conversation with her when they were still young, and he was a judge in Hong Kong:

> 'Bad day?' [, Betty asks.]
> 'I condemned a man to death.'

> Silence.
> She would never have taken him in her arms from pity. ... Your job.
>> You knew there would be this to face here. You could have stayed in England.
> Instead. ....
> 'Was he guilty?'
> 'As hell.' ...
> '*Crime passionel*,' [sic] he said.
> 'Then probably he will be glad to die.'
> He said, 'You still shock me. If you had been the Judge ....'
> '.... I would have done as you did. There is not an alternative. But I would have suffered less.'
>> (But I would have wanted you to suffer more. I want you to make me resign because I disgust myself. I feel, truly, filth.) (112–3, emphasis in original)

Feathers is shown to suffer the pangs of conscience of a judge who decides about life and death, and whom his wife rebukes for feeling guilty at all. However, the passage also hints that his suffering might in fact be related, more specifically, to his involvement in the colonial enterprise ("You knew there would be this to face here."), that is, to the administering of *colonial* justice. It appears that it is *this* predicament that makes him "feel, truly, filth."

The lines – and Feathers's nickname more generally – could, then, be read as implying an ever so carefully guarded confession of guilt on behalf of the British in the colonies. Instead of a magnificent career in the 'Far East,' the character would then come to represent the 'dirty deeds' of Britain's colonial past, the 'old filth' that sticks to a postwar British identity. However, the second meaning is drowned out as quickly as it had surfaced. The episode ends with Edward's mind returning to the present: "I got out just in time, he thought when they retired and came home to the Donheads. Couldn't take much more emotion alongside the drudgery. Still can't manage emotions" (113). Indeed, the last lines illustrate Gilroy's claim about the unwillingness of British people to "work through" (90) feelings of guilt connected to the injustices and cruelties committed in the name of the Empire as well as O'Toole's point about the transference of suffering, the "taking on of colonial pain" (80). It is, after all, Feathers whose suffering readers are made to witness and empathise with, not the suffering of the condemned man. In fact, the condemned man, seen through Edward's eyes, appears only as an anonymous caricature: "his scant Oriental neck soon to be crushed bone" (*Old Filth* 113). The lines could be taken directly from a colonial novel.

In a striking instance of the novels' technique of revisiting events and places, the same episode reoccurs in the second instalment of the trilogy, *The Man in the Wooden Hat* (2009), with the exchange above being repeated verbatim. However, whereas in Part One it is presented as a flashback through a filtering consciousness (as Feathers's memories), in Part Two it is presented in the form of a dramatic dialogue. Moreover, the episode continues beyond what Edward recalled, 'adding' a conversation that might be taking place on the following day:

FILTH: Capital punishment must go.
ELISABETH: They'll take years.
FILTH: They'll have their own Judiciary by then. Someone spat at the car today when I left Court. They are changing. Lily Woo [a maid servant] took five minutes to answer the bell tonight.
ELISABETH: No, only two. But I know what you mean. Respect is fading. Well, I don't know if it was ever there. In the jewellers', the girls hardly bother to lift their heads when I go in. ... (*The Man* 194)

The passage shows that the condescending attitude towards 'the Chinese' (and other non-European inhabitants of Hong Kong) is not presented as a sign of old age, as the ramblings of an embittered old man. Instead, it is presented as a view shared among the central characters ("I know what you mean") and, thus, as common sense. It is challenged neither by the narrator nor by other characters.

The distance in this passage between the focalising characters (whose inner lives are studied with great empathy) and 'them' is characteristic. The novels continuously engage readers in a perspective from which it is 'only natural' that "they" (an anonymous mass of colonised people) will always lag behind British ingenuity and moral standards ("They'll take years"). As in the rendering of the episode in Part One, readers are left under the impression that it is really the British who are treated unfairly. They suffer because they can see the 'tragedy' (of postcolonial independence) coming, and because they are not (have never been) heeded and treated with the gratitude they deserve. Of course, the text could present such views to draw out the readers, to invite criticism. But where or in what way do the novels encourage a critical perspective?

Let us consider another central passage, in which Gardam rehearses colonial slurs and stereotypes. The passage is part of the opening of *Old Filth* and can be said to strike the keynote for the whole trilogy. At the same time, it is remarkable for its explicit reflection on one of the most important historical dates to mark the alleged end of Empire: the handover of Hong Kong from Britain to China. Here is the elderly Edward contemplating his and his wife's motives for leaving Hong Kong and moving to Dorset:

> Was it perhaps 'The Pound' that drew them to Dorset? The thought of having to survive one day in Hong Kong on a pension? But the part of Dorset they had chosen was far from cheap. Betty was known to 'have her own money' and Filth had always said merrily that he had put off making Judge for as long as possible so that he hadn't to live on a salary. And they had no children. No responsibilities. No one to come back to England for.
>
> Or was it – the most likely thing – the end of Empire? The drawing-near of 1997? Was it the unbearableness of the thought of the arrival of the barbarians? The now unknown, but certainly changed, Mainland-Chinese whose grandparents had fed the baby Miss Betty on soft, cloudy jellies and told her frightening fairy tales?
>
> Neither Filth nor Betty cared for the unknown and already, five years before they left, English was not being heard so much in Hong Kong shops and hotels and, when it was heard, it was being spoken less well. (*Old Filth* 7–8)

Feathers's blatant admiration for the 'good old days' of the British Empire and his condescending attitude towards the colonies in this passage are unsurprising. But what are readers to make of these attitudes? Focalised through the view of the endearing old gentleman, we are presented with ideas that, rendered as the comments of an overt, heterodiegetic narrator would probably strike many contemporary readers as offensive or 'politically incorrect.' By way of an experiment, we can transpose some of the phrases. Thus, Edward's thoughts about the Chinese could be rendered as a matter-of-fact comment by a narrator: 'The thought of the arrival of Mainland-Chinese in Hong Kong seems to be as frightening as the prospect of the arrival of the barbarians.' Or take the narrative about a 'British baby fed on soft, cloudy jellies and told frightening fairy tales by Chinese servants.' I suppose this part would be liable to charges of orientalist rhetoric. Similarly, a narrator complaining that 'the people speak English less well in Hong Kong today' would be considered controversial, and might in fact be identified as unreliable because the attitude towards the local culture seems so condescending and out of touch with discussions about the role of language in the process of colonisation. After all, the novel was published in 2004, not 1890.

Of course, readers are always free to reject the thoughts and comments of a character. However, while there is much praise for 'Old Filth,' the text does little to encourage criticism. None of Feathers's overtly xenophobic remarks raise concern from the novel's narrator, who does intervene from time to time. In fact, in the last sentence of the above passage, the perspective of the characters blends with that of the narrator. Edward Feathers is a staunch upholder of British traditions – and fond memories of Britain's superiority as a glorious Empire seem to be a 'natural' part of this tradition. The narrative offers a comfortable, or safe, position: it invites sympathy, but it also relays Feathers's ideas with a touch of irony. The light irony puts his more questionable comments in inverted commas, making it easier for readers to dispel any qualms concerning a rueful or nostalgic contemplation. One may have the cake and eat it too.

Another aspect of this technique can be illustrated by a shorter passage, in which Feathers's thoughts again turn explicitly to the end of Empire: "Singapore's over, like Hong Kong. Empire now like Rome. Not even in the history books. Lost. Over. Finished. Dead. Happened" (118). The lines are repeated with slight variations throughout the first part, giving them a song-like quality. They become a refrain drumming out a core theme: the British Empire is over; it is a remote phenomenon that has been unjustly neglected and deserves to be recalled with pride. One could object that neocolonialism prevails, that Singapore and Hong Kong are not "over," and that the British Empire is far from being neglected by historians; yet there is nothing in the novels that would support such a view. As I will show in the next two sections, this resistance to criticism is mainly due to the homogeneity of the cast of characters through whose eyes we see the world in Gardam's trilogy.

Before I move on to consider the choice of characters and Gardam's debt to Kipling, I want to look at the context of Feathers's remarks about the loss of Singapore and Hong Kong to reflect on the way the novels connect past and present. Incidentally, this also allows us to glimpse how the novels touch on other topics that rose to prominence in the wake of the 2016 referendum and that span out of control. Thus, we find that the train of thoughts which culminates in Feathers's melancholic turn to the colonial past is triggered by a trivial incident in present-day Britain (roughly the early 2000s). The elderly Feathers, shortly after his wife's death, is driving on a motorway to visit a childhood friend. He has not driven a car for a long time, never mind been on a motorway, and finds the experience both exhilarating and disorientating. Thus, we are plunged into the traffic:

> Lorries in strings, like moving blocks of flats, were now hurtling along. Sometimes his old Mercedes seemed to hang between them, hardly

> touching the road. Seemed to be a great many foreign buggers driving the lorries, steering-wheels left-hand side where they couldn't see a thing. Matter of time no doubt when they'd be in the majority. Then everyone would be driving on the right. Vile government. Probably got all the plans drawn up already. Drive on the right, vote on the left. The so-called left, said Filth. Not Mr Attlee's left. Not Aneurin Bevan's left. All of them in suits now. Singapore still drives on the left, though they've never heard of left. Singapore's over, like Hong Kong … (118)

The passage is one of the many moments in which Feathers is shown to feel deeply alienated by modern Britain. The sensation of fear caused by his inexperience and old age triggers a chain of complaints that sound all too familiar: the cause of his fear is displaced on foreigners who must have been 'let in' by a leftist, Europhile government that willingly participates in the destruction of British culture. The only 'British' places left seem to be the former colonies, which – the 'naivety of their inhabitants' not withstanding – appear to Feathers as more British than Britain. It is precisely the scenario that O'Toole describes as a common view of many Brexiteers. Britain is said to be losing its cultural identity due to the influence of the EU and a government that surrenders national pride and ideals to 'political correctness.' In this view, the former colonies become heterotopias in which an appreciation of Britain's former greatness has been preserved.

In the quoted passage, readers are presented with a xenophobic, anti-establishment rant that mixes feelings of personal insecurity with condemnations of the present political situation. The conclusion is that 'everything was better in the old days.' This sentiment is spelled out later when Feathers thinks, "If I had ever loved England, …, I would weep for her" (119). Presented in this form, as the confused rumblings of an old man in a stressful situation, the episode encourages readers to feel pity or laugh heartily about the deft comedy. Others might chuckle with embarrassment or even feel their laughter stifled by the apparent racism. However, the fun derives from playing along, from enjoying the ride in the old Benz which is a "[b]loody good car, strong as a tank" (119). As Feathers turns off the motorway, he only narrowly escapes a fatal accident with a "conveyor of metal from the Ruhr" (119) – a darkly comical reminder of Britain's 'finest hour.' 'Don't mention the war' – another chuckle. These are the kinds of memories and stereotypes that were also mobilised by the Leave campaign (Buckledee 25–6; Eaglestone 97–9; O'Toole 27–63;). What is striking, is the amount of sympathy and sheer space that the novels afford to such views. Partly, this is due to the fact that Gardam constructs her story as a collective remembering of a particular generation. Criticism has rightly praised Gardam for her empathetic portrayal of elderly people. What has been lost sight of is the precise makeup of this cast of characters and the implications it has for the novels' appeal to a post-imperial British imagination.

4   "You Know Kipling Had a Start like Filth?"[3] – A Generation of 'Empire Orphans'

In the introduction, I suggested that the Old Filth trilogy can be read as a memorial service to a generation. However, if we look more closely at Gardam's unique cast of characters we find that the characters are in fact socially less diverse than the term 'generation' would seem to imply. They all belong to a distinct social milieu: all male characters occupy high-ranking positions at the English Bar, and all owe their prestige and wealth to their careers as civil servants in the colonies. A statement published about three years ago by an initiative calling itself "Historians for Britain" allows us to contextualise Gardam's choice. In an article in *History Today*, the members of the initiative claim that it is important to show and remember that

> the United Kingdom has developed in a distinctive way by comparison with its continental neighbours. This has resulted in the creation of a different legal system based on precedent, rather than Roman law or Napoleonic codes; the British Parliament embodies principles of political conduct that have their roots in the 13th century or earlier; ancient institutions, such as the monarchy and several universities, have survived (and evolved) with scarcely a break over many centuries. This degree of continuity is unparalleled in continental Europe. (Abulafia 7)

It is not difficult to tell that the initiative campaigned for Britain to leave the EU. If we look at the items cited here to underscore Britain's unique position in Europe and then turn back to Gardam's novels, we find that they all feature prominently: the main characters are either lawyers or judges or their partners; the male protagonists all graduated from Oxford or Cambridge and are all partaking in the rituals and privileges of Oxbridge. Further, Feathers literally protects the monarchy when he assumes a position in the personal guard escorting Queen Mary during the Second World War, and later becomes a Queen's Counsel (QC), a senior lawyer at the Bar appointed by Her Majesty,

---

3   Gardam, *Old Filth* 170.

thus literally representing the monarchy. These aspects, it should be emphasised, are not just adornments to the story but its key concern.

If the above makes for a fairly homogenous group, the background of the characters in the trilogy is even more specific: all of them are so-called 'Raj orphans.' This, I would argue, is in fact Gardam's greatest debt to Kipling. Kipling's work and life provide the blueprint for her central characters. Readers who do not recognise the connection are helped by a passage that not only quotes from Kipling's "The English Flag" but also compares Feathers to Kipling. The scene is set at the Inner Temple in London and shows two characters, the Queen's Remembrancer and The Purveyor of Seals and Ordinances, discussing the career of the legendary Edward Feathers:

QR:	Nothing ever did go wrong for him.
PS&O:	Nothing much ever happened to him. Except success.
QR:	There's talk of a rather mysterious War, you know. Didn't fight.
PS&O:	A conchie?
QR:	Good God, no. Some crack-up. He had a stammer.
PS&O:	Pretty brave to go on to the Bar then.
	…
QR:	And there was something else. Someone gave him a push upstairs somewhere. Or out East. There's always something a bit dicey about that circuit.
	…
QR:	What do the likes of us know, creeping round the Woolsack at Home and round the Inns of Court?
PS&O:	'What should they know of England Who only England know.'
QR:	Kipling. You know Kipling had a start like Filth? Torn from his family at five. Raj Orphan.
PS&O:	Kipling didn't do too badly either. (169–70)

What Feathers and Kipling have in common, then, is that they both grew up as Raj orphans, that they suffered from this experience, and that – despite their "crack-up" (170) – they went on to become outstanding Britons. The passage makes it clear that the characters' admiration for Kipling and Feathers derives precisely from the fact that they turned failure into achievement. The passage therefore emerges as a perfect example of what O'Toole calls heroic failure, that supposedly quintessentially British quality. What is more, it grounds the men's (and by implication the nation's) suffering and success in the colonial experience.

Born at a colonial station in British Malaya, Feathers is sent 'Home' at a young age. His foster mother, Ma Didds, we soon learn, was "a sadistic disciplinarian" (Lowry 19) who traumatised him. In another strand of the story, it transpires that Feathers's wife, Elisabeth, experienced a similar shock. She was raised in a Japanese internment camp during the Second World War, where her missionary parents were executed. Unearthing layer after layer of memories, the trilogy gradually reveals how Feathers and other Raj orphans suffered from the harsh treatment at the hands of their foster parents, as well as from being abandoned by their parents. The revelation of these traumatic events becomes the central quest readers are invited to embark on as the childhood memories return to the aging characters. Gardam's depiction of children in the trilogy, particularly their emotions, is impressive and points to her previous success as an author of children's books. It creates significant sympathy for the characters (particularly Edward Feathers) by engaging readers in the views of the young protagonists.

By focusing on Raj orphans, Gardam illuminates a neglected part of colonial history. Drawing attention to the destiny of this group of people certainly deserves praise, and it is not my intention to dispute the significance of this history or to relativise the suffering inflicted on this group. What I find troubling is the way in which this effort of uncovering a history of suffering sidelines the plight of people from the colonies. Although the novels do not shy away from exposing flaws in the colonial enterprise, the suffering that we are made to witness is invariably the suffering of the privileged British characters. The potential effect of this bias is evident in a passage from the second part of the trilogy, *The Man in the Wooden Hat*, in which Edward, who has just proposed to Elisabeth, expresses his horror of being left alone:

> 'Elisabeth, you must never leave me. That's the condition. I've been left all my life. From being a baby, I've been taken away from people. Raj orphan and so on. Not that I'm unusual there. And it's supposed to have given us all backbone.' 'Well, I [Elisabeth] know all that. I am an orphan, too. My parents suffered.' 'All our parents suffered for an ideology. They believed it was good for us to be sent Home, while they went on with ruling the Empire. We were all damaged even though we became endurers.' (32)

The passage leaves the impression – which is also conveyed by the trilogy at large – that colonialism was something that took place elsewhere but, curiously, only seems to have left a mark on people from the imperial centre. Building and maintaining the Empire, the novels suggest, involved a lot of suffering – the gradation in the above passage rises to a perfect climax. And yet those who were colonised do not feature at all in this equation.

Feathers's suggestion that the British have "suffered for an ideology" recalls Kipling's (in)famous poem "The White Man's Burden." However, since Gardam's novels were written in the lead-up to the 2016 referendum, it seems more pertinent to recall O'Toole here. His comments on the transference of suffering in debates about Brexit allow us to see the main characters as "taking on [the] colonial pain" (O'Toole 80). The effect(iveness) of Gardam's emotional investment in the main characters can, I believe, be glimpsed in a review of Gardam's first novel. In *The Spectator*, John Mortimer echoes Edward's and Elisabeth's complaints: "One of the least attractive results of our great days of empire was that parents, serving in its outposts, would send their children to school in England and not see them again for three or four years" (n. pag.).[4] Focusing readers' empathy on white British characters who were traumatised as children here mutes the suffering of colonised people and thus enables an untarnished, nostalgic contemplation of, in Mortimer's telling phrasing, "our great days of empire."

The most revealing comment, however, occurs towards the end of Mortimer's article. Quoting from *Old Filth*, Mortimer revels in the atmosphere created by the novels:

> The state of mind of the typical Raj orphan, or indeed the Raj itself, is summed up by Filth's friend Pat who says, 'Most of them grew up never to like anyone, but they didn't moan because they had this safety-net, the empire. Wherever you went you wore the crown and wherever you went you could find your own kind. There are still thousands around the world who think they own it' [*Old Filth* 56].
>
> The words may console us for the loss of empire; the illusion of ruling the world has now passed to the other side of the Atlantic. This harsh judgment does not wholly apply to Old Filth, who doesn't seem to hate people. And by the end of this book we've grown to like the poor old orphan quite a lot. (n. pag.)

There is a striking conflation in Mortimer's comment – one that the novels themselves arguably encourage. The "typical Raj orphan" comes to stand for

---

4 *The Spectator*'s editor at the time of publication was no other than Britain's current Prime Minister, Boris Johnson. Whether coincidentally or not, the ideas outlined in the following analysis arguably tally with Johnson's unconcerned attitude towards British colonialism and its connection to Brexit.

"the Raj itself." Mortimer's reading illustrates the ease of the metonymical slip and, thus, the significance of Gardam's choice of central characters. What is more, the comment spells out what may well be the most potent appeal for many British readers ("us"): "The words may console us for the loss of empire." Mortimer's use of 'us' and 'we' implies a strong sense of community. The novels appear to cater to a longing for a time when, in the words of Edward Feathers's best friend, as a British person, "[w]herever you went you wore the crown and wherever you went you could find your own kind." I therefore maintain that it is also telling that, despite the ironic ring of the character's remark (its hyperbolic phrasing), the potential irony is completely lost in Mortimer's reading.

5   Conclusion: "Malaya's My Country"

In the introduction, I noted that it has been some time now since Gilroy diagnosed Britain with 'postimperial melancholia.' Brexit and the recent rise of a new British nationalism suggest that Britain may have entered another phase of the ailment described by Gilroy. Gardam's trilogy offers an opportunity to 'mourn the profound change' and especially the 'loss of imperial prestige,' without however working through the problems that Gilroy's analysis implies. Put simply, the novels offer to reconcile British people with a controversial part of their past and allow them to contemplate the 'end of Empire' as well as some of its darker sides from a position of relative moral superiority. Fond memories of the British Empire are 'insulated' against critique by presenting them from the point of view of characters who, as children, have been traumatised by their experiences as Raj orphans. Their biggest achievement appears to be that they have overcome their trauma, built a successful career at the English Bar, and, ultimately, become part of the system that they blame for their suffering – British colonialism. Those who rule the Empire are those who take on the pain and, therefore, seem to deserve our sympathy.

In his trailblazing analysis of post-imperial Britain, Gilroy, in 2005, had observed a "totemic power of the great anti-Nazi war" as well as a "mysterious evacuation of Britain's postcolonial conflicts from national consciousness" (89). While World War II appears simply to retain its 'totemic power,' it has become increasingly difficult to 'evacuate' memories of Britain's colonial and postcolonial conflicts, thanks mainly to a host of postcolonial writers who have 'written back to the centre' and brought to the fore the less benevolent, often cruel sides of British rule. It is against this background that Gardam's trilogy appears disconcerting. The novels do not attack or refute postcolonial fiction and criticism; instead, they appear to have simply forgotten about it. More worryingly, they may encourage readers to set it aside.

The community imagined in these books is one of, to quote from the first part once again, "perfectly international people" (*Old Filth* 7). The phrase is another example of the trilogy's pervasive use of irony (here invoked by the qualifier "perfectly"). However, as with the name of its central character, the critical potential inherent in irony is quickly eclipsed. These people really do consider themselves to be "perfectly international," and there is nothing in the novels' content or form to contradict them. To be "perfectly international" does not mean embracing multiculturalism; it means that these people once ruled the world and are therefore 'at home' in the world. Being British, in this sense, means being "perfectly international." However, socially and ethnically, the characters are 'British' in a much more narrow sense: they are white, upper-middle-class, involved in running the Empire, and have British-born parents, who themselves were part of the colonial apparatus.[5] When the narrator assures us at one point that "Filth's country had never been England" (*The Man* 272) this echoes other passages (some discussed above), which endow the central character with an air of cosmopolitanism. A passage towards the end of the first novel, however, reveals that Feathers ultimately considers himself to be British. It shows the eponymous hero towards the end of his life, in a hospital, in England:

> Whatever would the young make of him today? ... He found them repellent. And homosexuals repellent, if he were honest. And divorce repellent. Blacks – here he was disturbed by a cluster of different coloured people surrounding his bed. These are not the black people of the Empire, he thought, and then realised that that was exactly what most of them were. 'Any of you chaps Malays?' he asked. 'Malaya's my country. *Malaysia* now, of course. And Ceylon's Sri Lanka, Lanka's what my friend Loss called it, and he should know. It was full of his uncles. ...' (*Old Filth* 226–7, emphasis in original)

---

5 An exception to this rule is the roguish Terry Veneering (focus of *Last Friends*) who has a working-class background and is in many ways Feathers's antipode. To discuss this aspect is beyond the scope of this paper. Suffice it to say that Veneering ultimately facilitates an engagement with Feathers's more radically conservative positions. Despite their antagonism, they have much in common (both are orphans, embark on a successful career in the colonies, and eventually settle in Dorset as well-off retirees).

Feathers's racism could of course (again) be explained away as ironic by arguing that he is depicted as confused or senile. However, the passage is congruent with the overall drift of the novels. The fact that he claims "Malaya" as 'his country,' and then corrects himself to say, "*Malaysia* now, of course" gives him away. The slip of the tongue hints at more than just Feathers's negligent attitude towards political correctness. It tells us something about the trilogy's idea of Britishness. When Feathers rejects England as his home, he lays claim to a British imperial identity instead. It is British Malaya, rather than independent Malaysia, which he considers to be 'his country.' What is eclipsed in the slip of the tongue – and indeed by the trilogy as a whole – is both the former colonies' long struggle for independence and the struggle of those who migrated to 'the mother country' to be accepted as British. The Empire, it seems, is somehow still alive. It still lives in the idea of Britishness represented by this 'generation' of "perfectly international people" whose views we are asked to sympathise with. The trilogy concludes not with a funeral but with a metaphorical union. Two of Feathers's friends discover their love for each other in old age and close the narrative by walking to an allegorical, if not an actual, wedding. The trilogy ends with the telling line, "And so they made their way towards the Resurrection" (*Last Friends* 239). The Empire may have died, but in this phantasmagoria, there is still a chance of resurrecting it, at least in spirit.

Works Cited

"100 Modern Novels to Love; Elena Ferrante, Sarah Waters, Colson Whitehead and Colm Toibin – Just the Tip of the Iceberg in Our List of Great 21st-century Reads." *Sunday Times* [London, England], 7 Apr. 2019, p. 4.

Abulafia, David. "Britain: Apart from or a Part of Europe?" *History Today*, vol. 65, no. 5, 2015, p. 7.

Booth, Robert. "Boris Johnson Caught on Camera Reciting Kipling in Myanmar Temple." *The Guardian*, 30 Sept. 2017, www.theguardian.com/politics/2017/sep/30/boris-johnson-caught-on-camera-reciting-kipling-in-myanmar-temple. Accessed 15 July 2020.

Buckledee, Steve. *The Language of Brexit: How Britain Talked Its Way Out of the European Union*. Bloomsbury Academic, 2018.

Ciabattari, Jane. "The 100 Greatest British Novels." *BBC Online*, 7 Dec. 2015, www.bbc.com/culture/story/20151204-the-100-greatest-british-novels. Accessed 15 Jul. 2020.

Eaglestone, Robert. "Cruel Nostalgia and the Memory of World War II." *Brexit and Literature. Critical and Cultural Responses*, edited by Robert Eaglestone, Routledge, 2018, pp. 92–104.

Gardam, Jane. *Last Friends*. Abacus, 2014.

Gardam, Jane. *Old Filth*. Chatto & Windus, 2004.

Gardam, Jane. *The Man in the Wooden Hat*. Chatto & Windus, 2009.

Gilroy, Paul. *Postcolonial Melancholia*. Columbia UP, 2005.

Hadley, Tessa. "Thank God for Betty." *London Review of Books*, vol. 32, no. 5, 2010, pp. 19-20.

Kipling, Rudyard. "Mandalay." *The Collected Poems of Rudyard Kipling*, edited by R. T. Jones, Wordsworth Editions, 1994, pp. 431–2.

Kipling, Rudyard. "The English Flag." *The Collected Poems of Rudyard Kipling*, edited by R. T. Jones, Wordsworth Editions, 1994, pp. 233–5.

Kipling, Rudyard. "The White Man's Burden." *The Collected Poems of Rudyard Kipling*, edited by R. T. Jones, Wordsworth Editions, 1994, pp. 334–5.

Lowry, Elizabeth. "Decline and Falter." *The Times Literary Supplement*, 24 May 2013, p. 19.

Mondal, Anshuman A. "Scratching the Post-imperial Itch." *Brexit and Literature. Critical and Cultural Responses*, edited by Robert Eaglestone, Routledge, 2018, pp. 82–91.

Mortimer, John. "Orphan of the Raj." *The Spectator*, 6 Nov. 2004, www.spectator.co.uk/2004/11/orphan-of-the-raj/. Accessed 15 July 2020.

O'Toole, Fintan. *Heroic Failure: Brexit and the Politics of Pain*. Head of Zeus, 2018.

CHAPTER 12

'Bastardizing' National Belonging: Derek Walcott and Joseph Conrad

Kathrin Härtl

1   Joseph Conrad, "that Bastard"

In *White Egrets*, a poetry collection from 2010 by the late Caribbean poet Derek Walcott, the untitled forty-sixth poem starts provocatively with a curse and then delves into an impressive description of a Caribbean landscape: "Here's what that bastard calls 'the emptiness' – / that blue-green ridge with plunging slopes, the blossoms, / like drooping chalices, of the African tulip, the noise / of a smoking torrent" (*Egrets* 150, lines 1–4). By contrasting lush descriptions of Caribbean culture and landscape with a bastard's images of "emptiness," Walcott's poem provides a strong critique of the concept of the 'tabula rasa,' a frequent trope in colonial discourse.[1] While the former colonizers and conquerors claimed the 'New World' as a blank space which called for a European cultural imprint, it was actually the colonizing and conquering powers that violently produced a 'blank slate' by eradicating the Caribbean peoples, their languages and cultures. Thus, Michel de Certeau concludes that colonial writings "use the New World as if it were a blank 'savage' page on which Western desire will be written. It will transform the space of the other into a field of expansion for a system of production" (xxv–xxvi). Derek Walcott contemplates on the trope of the blank slate in various poems.[2] He reappropriates the "blank page" (*Life* 97), for example, in his autobiographical poem *Another Life* in order to introduce an 'adamic' quality to his and his fellow poets' works, and he finally claims, "We were blest ... / with Adam's task of giving things their names" (152). These verses dismiss European and imperialist representations of the Caribbean and celebrate Caribbean self-representations as a liberation from any European tradition. It is therefore not only the poet's decision

---

1   Bill Ashcroft neatly summarizes the origin of the 'tabula rasa' in John Locke's empiricism and its use in colonial discourse: "The unformedness of colonial space is the geographic metaphor of the savage mind. Both consciousness and space form childlike innocence which is the natural surface of imperial inscription" (*Post-Colonial Futures* 39–41).
2   For example, in *Another Life* (1973), *Omeros* (1990), and in "The Sea Is History" (*Poetry* 253–6).

to aestheticize the Caribbean landscape in contrast to the colonialist trope of emptiness. Rather, Walcott's poetics use the representation of landscape to express the ongoing political liberation from Great Britain in the second half of the twentieth century when most of the Caribbean gained political independence. However, Walcott brings the colonialist trope back into play by referring to "the emptiness." But who exactly is "that bastard" who uses this trope and to whom Walcott refers in the very first verse of his poem?

The poem connects the concept of "emptiness" with one specific author: "The image / is from Conrad" (*Egrets* 150, lines 9–10). I argue that by attributing "the emptiness" to the famous writer Joseph Conrad and using an image from *Heart of Darkness*, his most notorious texts of late imperialist English literature, Walcott incisively comments on concepts of national literature and the Anglophone literary influence on Caribbean literature. More specifically, it is the double act of naming Conrad *and* himself "bastard" that this chapter establishes a point of departure to analyze how Walcott develops his understanding of national belonging and literature in the Caribbean and the extraordinary role of Joseph Conrad in this concept.

In *White Egrets,* Walcott quotes Conrad's infamous trope of European aggression towards a supposedly empty African jungle in *Heart of Darkness*. Here, first-person narrator Marlow reports: "Once, I remember, we came upon a man-of-war anchored off the coast. ... In the empty immensity of earth, sky, and water, there she was, incomprehensible, firing into a continent" (Conrad, *Darkness* 16). The use of this Conradian image creates a powerful counterpoint to the descriptions of the Caribbean landscape and urban spaces in the first part of Walcott's poem. The poem transfers Marlow's imperialist view of the African coast to the description of the Caribbean. The notion of the "vicious talent" in the concluding verses of Walcott's poem express the powerful yet negative impact of Conrad. Conrad's works, Walcott's lyric persona suggests, are virulent "poison ... as well as a genuine curse" (*Egrets* 150, lines 15–7) for Caribbean literature.

Calling Conrad a "bastard" infers that for Walcott the imagination of Conrad as author serves as a despicable example of European colonization through literature. Conrad's trope of "emptiness" figures as a cultural symbol for the imperial power of the English language, literature, and its abuse.

Yet Walcott uses the term "bastard" to describe his relation to his Anglo-Caribbean heritage. In terms of literary tradition, he is "this neither proud nor ashamed bastard, this hybrid, this West Indian" ("Twilight" 9). I will show that concepts of the nation and national belonging are intertwined with acts of naming and other performative speech acts which Walcott and Conrad use in their self-representations as authors. Both are preoccupied with questions of legitimacy in their works. Walcott and Conrad legitimize why they write in English and discuss for whom they speak and write. Both write under the flags of British Empire but also in the light of its decline, and it is this decline that questions their national belonging as writers.

Conrad's own hybrid perspective on Englishness and the English language, as well as divergent evaluations of his work by his contemporaries make him an ambivalent addressee of Walcott's curse. Ironically, Walcott uses a Polish exile, who did not write in his native language as his metonym for the colonizing English literary voice that denigrates colonial spaces. By simultaneously placing Conrad in the curious position of a metonymic figure for English literature *and* drawing on Conrad's work intertextually within his own poetic play, Walcott questions Englishness and European literary traditions in post-1950 Caribbean poetry. In his poetry and essays, Walcott refrains from binary oppositions. Instead, he creates a new understanding of transnational poetics. Accordingly, this chapter examines the tension in Walcott's poetics between European traditions, the choice of literary language, and the establishment of a Caribbean notion of belonging and national language. I argue that Walcott develops the figure of the "bastard" as an authorial image to discuss the question of the nation-state in the Caribbean with reference to terms such as genealogy, legitimacy, and hybridity in order to situate his literary achievements in relation to both the 'Great Tradition' of English literature, as epitomized by Joseph Conrad, and to a distinctly Caribbean poetics.

This chapter analyzes Walcott's poetics in a selection of his essays and poems in the critical and historical context of his contemporaries, V. S. Naipaul and Kamau Brathwaite, in order to illustrate different attitudes towards nation and language within this specific generation of Caribbean writers. I propose that Walcott's own complex attitude towards the literature and language of the colonizer emerges in the curse on Conrad. Placing Walcott's figure of the "bastard" in the context of early postcolonial theory on hybridity, I will reveal unexpected affinities between Conrad and Walcott which unsettle essentialist concepts of nation and belonging.

2 Walcott, the Caribbean 'Nation', and Language

Walcott's stance on the relationship between concepts of the nation and literature in the postcolonial Caribbean is closely connected to his poetics and more specifically to his poetic language since he chose to write predominantly in English. In a 1986 interview, Walcott states that "there are always images of erasure in the Caribbean – in the surf which continually wipes the sand clean, in the fact that those huge clouds change so quickly" (qtd. in Hirsch 74). At first sight, Walcott's various uses of the blank page read as a repetition of European imaginations of the New World lacking any culture, but as Paul Breslin puts it, "[n]onetheless, Walcott's description of 'erasure' should not be confused with [James Anthony] Froude's notorious libel of Caribbean nothingness. For to describe a surface as 'erased' is to be aware that something was once written there, though it is no longer visible" (17). For Walcott, the emptiness of the white page is no primordial state but is preceded by a process of erasure expressed in the cyclical trope of the oceanic ebb and flow. By contrast, J. A. Froude's representation of the Caribbean in his travelogue *The English in the West Indies* (1888) encapsulates the imperial concept of the colony as a cultural *terra nullius*: "There are no people there in the true sense of the word, with a character and purpose of their own" (347). Such erasures of Caribbean culture and political entities over the last centuries led to European imaginations of a political, historical, and cultural void in the Caribbean. Reflecting on this discourse of alleged want, Caribbean writers expressed conflicting ideas of the 'nation' in the Caribbean archipelago during the period of decolonization, while a discussion about the role of the English literary tradition and especially the use of the English language evolved simultaneously. The point of departure was the idea that not only culture and literature were English imports but that the discourse of nationalism itself was a "derivative discourse" (Chrisman 184–6).[3] Benedict Anderson, for instance, proposes that anti-colonial nationalist movements developed only by the contact of native intelligentsia with Western culture and with European models of the nation (116). Consequently, scholars such as Eric Hobsbawm perceived the Caribbean and other "Third-World" anti-colonial nationalist desires and the establishment of literature only as poor products of mimicry (Sivanandan 46). Yet the complex history of nationalisms in the Caribbean, which began well before the twentieth century, dismisses fixed notions of the nation-state and clear temporal and causal interdependencies due to the complex entanglements of colonial powers and diasporic peoples and languages. The history of Haiti and its process of independence are a case in point. Anti-colonial national movements, cultural theories of the Caribbean, and nationalist ideas by Caribbean theorists such as Édouard Glissant or Brathwaite are subject to various influences that are not only limited to Western concepts. The different names the Caribbean was given over the course of time, with their "onomastic significance" (Collier 225), are indicative of various and sometimes mutually exclusive conceptions of the

---

3 See Chrisman for a critical discussion of this concept.

nation. These acts of naming exemplify the complex relationship between language, colonialism, and nationalism in the Caribbean (225).

Concerning the question of literature, language, and Caribbean self-consciousness, V. S. Naipaul and Kamau Brathwaite are two contemporary writers that scholars often juxtapose with Derek Walcott. Walcott's *White Egrets* and the description of "that bastard" and a "vicious talent" (*Egrets* 150) has been read as a critique of Naipaul and his infamous pessimistic view on the Caribbean as a hybrid and therefore not a genuinely innovative culture in the travelogue *The Middle Passage* (1962). Here, Naipaul rewrites Froude's claim that "[h]istory is built around achievement and creation; and nothing was created in the West Indies" (20). While Naipaul considers Caribbean culture as consistently dependent on other cultures and laments this mimicry, Walcott understands mimicry as an essential core of innovation: "these forms originated in imitation, if you want, and ended in invention" (*Caribbean* 9).

Consequently, in the forty-sixth poem in *White Egrets* Walcott critiques Naipaul's view on the Caribbean (Kirsch n. pag.).[4] Conrad also emerges in Naipaul's discourse on literary language in the Caribbean. In opposition to Walcott, Naipaul perceives himself as a legitimate heir to Conrad: "And I found Conrad – sixty years before, in the time of a great peace – had been everywhere before me" (Naipaul, "Conrad's Darkness" 18). Naipaul uses Conrad's tropes (specifically the trope of darkness) not as an ambivalent curse or an illegitimate succession but as his confident inheritor.[5] While the literary feud between Naipaul and Walcott is indicative of a Caribbean self-confidence that reflects on Caribbean literature and its representation without direct reference to the European, metropolitan 'center,' the English literary tradition nevertheless plays a significant role in literary texts of both authors. Walcott's and Naipaul's understandings of a Caribbean 'national' literature depend on the English literary tradition.

Brathwaite, for example, develops a different understanding of literature and language. The concept of the use of English as an expression of imperial power is Brathwaite's point of departure for his term 'nation language.' He states that Caribbean languages and their histories of creolization can also be the core of a nation, whereby he undermines supposedly monolingual

---

4 Derek Walcott's critique on Naipaul centers on Naipaul's rather pessimistic view on the Caribbean and his multiple use of the Conradian trope of darkness to describe colonized spaces, as he makes a pun on Naipaul's name and quotes him in "The Spoiler's Return": "I see these islands and I feel to bawl, / 'area of darkness' with V. S. Nightfall" (*Poetry* 304).

5 For a discussion on Naipaul's relationship to Joseph Conrad, see Nixon 183–7, Döring 88–9, and Härtl 103–5.

European concepts of the nation (5). Brathwaite defines nation language as the interplay of different languages produced by the history of slavery, calling it "the kind of English spoken by the people who were brought to the Caribbean, not the official English now, but the language of slaves and labourers, the servants who were brought in by the conquistadors" (5–6). In contrast to Standard English, Brathwaite suggests, nation language is not primarily a language of letters but derives from oral traditions. Specifically, Brathwaite focusses on its (West-)African origins (13) and its linguistic influences on the "language of the conquistador" (8) in the Caribbean. The fact that he declares English as a literary language to be incapable of representing Caribbean nature, culture, and experience is of importance. Nation language abdicates the rhythm and meter of the English language, prototypically the pentameter: "The hurricane does not roar in pentameter" (10). Although Brathwaite diagnoses in Walcott's poem "The Schooner *Flight*" one of the first occurrences of nation language (10), he identifies Walcott as a contrasting figure to his own understanding of language and literature (Breiner 44). The choice of language is therefore always a matter of national consciousness in the Caribbean and derives from the assumption that "language itself was *inherently* the key to that control" (Ashcroft, *Caliban's Voice* 2–3, emphasis in original) which enables self-empowering expressions of Caribbean consciousness. While Brathwaite highlights that the choice of language is an act of resistance, Walcott chooses to write in English and explains his departure from writing in Creole:

> I began to feel that I was doing that effort out of some kind of national duty and I missed the excitement that I would have had in writing in English. Then I sort of reminded myself that what was important was not the language but the tone of the language and that speaking in English with the right tone would have been the same as speaking in Creole. ... I feel that I have never gone away from the sound of my own language: I am not saying the vocabulary but the sound, the tone. (qtd. in Fumagalli 278)

By suggesting that writing in Creole is a "national duty" Walcott refers to Brathwaite's nation language. Both his own use of English and his excessive intertextual references to canonized texts of the European tradition, ranging from Homer to T. S. Eliot, thus stand in deliberate opposition to Brathwaite's notion of nation language. Walcott uses a different way of discussing the nation and literature in his poetics.

Walcott's transnational poetics culminate in his ambivalent use of the term "bastard," for cursing as a mode of expression in postcolonial discourse refers back to Shakespeare's famous Caliban, who has become a recurring trope in critical thought about Caribbean consciousness. In *The Tempest*, Caliban tells Prospero, "You taught me language, and my profit on't / Is, I know how to curse. The red plague rid you / For learning me your language" (Shakespeare 1.2. 364–6.). The famous trope of Caliban, with his ability to speak and therefore to curse, is a negotiation of the question whether the colonizer's language is a potential tool for subversion for the postcolonial subject (Retamar 24). Being capable of using the colonizer's language in order to curse, and thus being capable of a performative speech act, questions the power relations established by language. Walcott's use of Caliban as a trope for postcolonial authorship transfers the issue of power relations from language to literature (Ashcroft, *Caliban's Voice* 16–8). The persona's insult at the beginning of the poem in *White Egrets* therefore requires further analysis. Why is the author-figure of Joseph Conrad the target of the persona's curse?

3   Joseph Conrad on Language and Nationality

The relation between cultural belonging and literary language has been an issue not only in Walcott's poetics but also in Conrad's work. Some seventy years earlier, Conrad's use of English as a literary language was rather controversial. This becomes evident in Virginia Woolf's obituary on Conrad: "Suddenly, without giving us time to arrange our thoughts or prepare our phrases, our remarkable guest has left us; and his withdrawal without farewell or ceremony is in keeping with his mysterious arrival, long years ago, to take up his lodging in this country" (493). Woolf's statement situates the universalistic notion that everybody is "a stranger in the earth" (*The New Oxford*, Psalm 119) in the context of canonical and 'national' literature. As Woolf will later conclude, Conrad, who until his death had a "strong foreign accent," is not only a "stranger in the earth" but also a "stranger in England" despite having been granted British citizenship (493). Yet, as F. R. Leavis said, the "guest," who "took up his lodging" in England, rose to become one of the "great English novelists" (18). While Leavis does not withhold that Conrad "brought a great deal from outside," he nevertheless claims "for us, who have *him* as well as the others, there he is, unquestionably a constitutive part of the tradition, belonging in the full sense" (18, emphasis in original). It is precisely Conrad's choice of becoming a British citizen that his Englishness equates with a "belonging in the full sense." This argument deconstructs concepts such as national belonging and patriotism although it seeks to affirm exactly those terms. Nationality, in this sense, is not a matter of language or belonging but a matter of choice and submission. But this stance stands in strong opposition to the idea of a 'great tradition' and the establishment of an English canon, an aim Leavis pursued with his book. In addition to Leavis describing Conrad as an exemplary English writer, other contemporaries discussed his position in the English literary canon at the beginning of the twentieth century. Ford Madox Ford remarked in 1911, "I have thought very often that Conrad is an Elizabethan," (77) while others stressed his foreignness.[6] In a review of Conrad's fiction in 1908 the matter of belonging becomes the essential point of argument to dismiss his literature. Language is centrally at issue:

> Mr Conrad, as everybody knows, is a Pole, who writes in English by choice, as it were, rather than by nature ... A writer who ceases to see the world coloured by his own language – for language gives colour to thoughts and things in a way that few people understand – is apt to lose the concentration and intensity of vision without which the greatest literature cannot be made. ... Mr Conrad, without either country or language, may be thought to have found a new patriotism for himself in the sea. His vision of men, however, is the vision of a cosmopolitan, of a homeless person. (Lynd 210–1)

Robert Lynd refers here to a typical nationalist concept: the 'natural' relationship between 'mother tongue' and national belonging. It is no matter of choice but a matter of essence: a national consciousness is closely related to one's language, without it, it is impossible to express, as it were, one's essence fully in any other language; therefore Conrad and his texts are cursed to be "homeless" and "cosmopolitan".

However, if "Conrad," despite his curious position in English literature, is used as a paradigmatic example of 'English Literature,' it becomes obvious that the concept of a 'literature of a nation state' had already been contentious at the beginning of the twentieth century. The name "Conrad" subverts any homogenizing, unified insular idea of English literature. Since Józef Teodor Nałęcz Konrad Korzeniowski changed his name to the Anglicized version "Conrad," as a metonym his name negates essentialist concepts of national literature. Thus, Conrad creates his "English" author figure by an act of self-naming.[7]

Yet Conrad (as well as Walcott) chose to talk about cultural belonging and language in terms of heritage and biology. In the "Author's Note" of *A Personal*

---

6 For an extensive discussion of the early critical reception of Conrad and his 'Englishness,' see McInturff.
7 The role of the changing authorial signature of Conrad is discussed at length in Smith 39–81. Frederick R. Karl gives an overview of the various modes, spellings, abbreviations, and changes that Conrad used with regards to his name (20).

Record Conrad gives an account of a conversation with a friend about his linguistic origins:

> [W]e talked of ... the characteristics of various languages ... and it is on that day that my friend carried away with him the impression that I had exercised a deliberate choice between French and English. ... The truth of the matter is that my faculty to write in English is as natural as any other aptitude with which I might have been born. I have a strange and overpowering feeling that it had always been an inherent part of myself. English was for me neither a matter of choice nor adoption. ("Author's Note" iv–v)

Conrad goes to great lengths to stress the 'naturalness' of his language acquisition, although it is obvious that the faculty to specifically "write in English" is a cultural practice. While Walcott highlights the cultural divergence between roots and routes,[8] Conrad evades the establishment of his route to England also by his rejection to begin his autobiography with his birth place: "Could I begin with the sacramental words, 'I was born on such a date in such a place?' The remoteness of the locality would have robbed the statement of all interest" (xx). Not only his birthplace but also his actual 'native' language, Polish, remains unmentioned in the "Author's Note." Further into the note, Conrad turns his case around and complicates the issue:

> And as to adoption – well, yes, there was adoption; but it was I who was adopted by the genius of the language, which directly I came out of the stammering stage made me its own so completely that its very idioms I truly believe had a direct action on my temperament and fashioned my still plastic character. (v)

Adoption comes into play, nevertheless. The concept of adoption represents Conrad's attempt of putting down 'roots' in English literature. Generally, the main characteristic of adoption (as well as baptism) is a speech act that must be executed by an authority. Conrad claims, not unlike Walcott ("Twilight" 9), that language itself achieves agency – and gives the authorial self, in this case Conrad, its name as an English author. Whereas Walcott establishes his hybrid origin by presenting his roots as well as his routes, Conrad devalues the 'natural'

---

8   My use of "roots and routes" alludes to James Clifford's *Routes* (1997), in which he examines the intertwining of these presumably incompatible concepts in his prologue by referencing Amitav Gosh's autobiographic traveller figure (1–2).

parent by using the concept of adoption and stresses cultural kinship as being preferable and even necessary to become part of a national community.

The matter of belonging is further disrupted in the next paragraph. Here, Conrad closes his remarks on nationality with another trope, namely the trope of colonization: "There was something in this conjunction of exulting, almost physical recognition, the same sort of emotional surrender and the same pride of possession, all united in the wonder of a great discovery" ("Author's Note" vi). This paragraph strikes as odd since the matter of agency remains ambiguous. Conrad experiences the "wonder of great discovery," and thereby adopts the language of exploration and colonization. Simultaneously, he figures as a colonized, because he surrenders to the hegemony of the English language (Härtl 80). The process of colonization replaces the agency Conrad had handed over to English as a language, although – and this shows Conrad's ambivalence towards his position as an English writer – he presents himself at the same time as colonizer and colonized.

Conrad struggles with the relationship between language and nation-state and although he seems to fashion himself as a legitimate heir of English literature and culture by adoption, he states in a famous letter: "Both at sea and on land my point of view is English, from which the conclusion should not be drawn that I have become an Englishman. That is not the case. Homo duplex has in my case more than one meaning" (*Letters* 389). Conrad's awareness of being a *homo duplex* and his differentiation between essence and perspective allow the reader to question the relationship between language and nation-state.

4   Walcott and the Nation

In "A Far Cry from Africa" (1960), Walcott's poem about British atrocities during the Mau-Mau Uprising, he creates for himself a persona as a cursing Caliban: "I who have cursed / The drunken officer of British rule, how choose / Between this Africa and the English tongue I love? / Betray them both, or give back what they give?" (27–8, lines 28–31). The cursing persona of *White Egrets* who defies Conrad's "emptiness" relates the trope of Caliban to the usage of English as a literary language. Walcott establishes this notion of identity regarding language and nation in the essay "What the Twilight Says" (1970): "so that mongrel as I am, something prickles in me when I see the word 'Ashanti' as with the word 'Warwickshire,' both separately intimating my grandfathers' roots, both baptizing this neither proud nor ashamed bastard, this hybrid, this West Indian" (9). This statement provides Walcott's authorial self with an eminent literary heritage by the allusive spaces it refers to: "Ashanti" and "Warwickshire." It creates a lineage from Shakespeare on the one hand and West African orature on the other hand in order to disclose a literary past that is marked by two profoundly different literary modes. Walcott establishes his literary past with two points of departure and two resulting routes of the Atlantic triangular trade. The phrase "grandfathers' roots" alludes to the Victorian discourse of hybridity that, as Robert Young notes, stems from the botanical discourse of cultivating and crossbreeding species (*Colonial Desire* 9). "Roots," in this understanding, describes Walcott's genealogy in the mode of floral procreation. The trope of the botanical hybrid, a naturalized and territorial idea of 'origin' and identity, is also present in other texts, for example in "A Far Cry from Africa": "I who am poisoned with the blood of both, / Where shall I turn, divided to the vein?" (27, lines 26–7). Nevertheless, in both texts, Walcott turns this naturalized idea of different breeds into a cultural matter, namely that of language and literature, by explicitly referring to literary spaces and to language. For Walcott, hybridity is no reason for being proud or ashamed; rather, in this case, he avoids comment on how to evaluate the entanglements of European and African heritage in his poetics and evades common classifications as being 'pan-African' or 'Eurocentric.'

The performative speech act of baptism in "What the Twilight Says" ("both baptizing this … bastard") highlights the cultural genesis of this hybrid subject. Walcott produces a literary lineage for his literary author-persona, and the powerful act of baptism further highlights the necessity of legitimation that seems to be obligatory in order to give this author-persona a possibility to speak. There is no authority mentioned, but the act baptizes the persona of the text; the words themselves perform a naming process where, oddly enough, the given name does not play a role. Nevertheless, the poem creates an authorial self by a sequence of attributes: "bastard, this hybrid, this West Indian." Thus, just as in the case of Conrad, it is the English language that baptizes the speaker in "What the Twilight Says" as an author and therefore legitimizes him.

In his autobiographical long poem *Another Life* "this bastard, this hybrid, this West Indian" fashions himself as the illegitimate heir of English literature: "I had entered the house of literature as a houseboy, / filched as the slum child stole, / as the young slave appropriated / those heirlooms temptingly left / with the Victorian homilies of *Noli tangere*" (77, emphasis in original). By referring to himself as a slave who appropriates "those heirlooms," the persona establishes the master-slave trope that is not only important for the postcolonial theory of writing back and rewriting but also for intertextuality in general (Terada 78). In addition, Walcott anticipates theories of hybridity from various postcolonial critics, such as Homi Bhabha. Bhabha understands hybridity as the discourse that arises in the moment of contact between colonizers and colonized in a (former) colony. Hybridity incites complex processes which enable the colonized to resist and to subvert the hegemonic discourse inscribed on them. For Bhabha, hybridity happens when the colonial power loses its hegemony of meaning. In the moment of enunciation, the voice of the colonial power becomes the Other; it becomes different. Therefore, the process of subversion is at the core of the speech act of the colonizing force:

> It is precisely in that ambivalent use of 'different' – to be different from those that are different makes you the same – that the Unconscious speaks of the form of otherness, the tethered shadow of deferral and displacement. It is not the colonialist Self or the colonized Other, but the disturbing distance in-between that constitutes the figure of colonial otherness – the white man's artifice inscribed on the black man's body. (Bhabha 44–5)

Walcott's use of the hybrid as a mode of representation is not so much a general cultural critique, but he employs hybridity as a productive term in his poetics by introducing the bastard as a trope of an author who takes advantage of his colonial past and employs his mode of writing in the colonizer's language as an act of self-legitimization. In "The Muse of History," he declares that Caribbean literature is not supposed to be seen as "literature of revenge" nor as "literature of remorse" (37). Although colonialism is "[t]he common experience of the New World" (36), the result is not to understand Caribbean writings only by means of this narrative but as a reaction to this experience. Nevertheless, Walcott considers his poetics as an intertextual play with various European writers, including Conrad, in an ambivalent way. By analyzing Walcott's writing it becomes apparent that Conrad stands for English colonial literature on multiple occasions. In his essay "Leaving School," he tellingly writes: "we had worshipped Foxy, and hated to see him go ... Our last English headmaster, he had been a lonely man, devoted to parades, fond of sailing and Conrad's prose, proud of the benignity of his Empire" (25).[9]

---

9 Conrad is introduced in *Another Life* almost identically: "I saw history through the sea-washed eyes / of our choleric, ginger-haired headmaster, / beak like an inflamed hawk's, / a lonely Englishman who loved parades, / sailing, and Conrad's prose" (70). However, the different intertextual allusions in *Another Life* show Walcott's divergent relation to Conrad (33–6). Other poems where Conrad is explicitly mentioned are, for example, *The Fortunate Traveller* and "Volcano" (Härtl 4, 25).

5 Conclusion

Walcott's use of Joseph Conrad as a metonym of imperialist literature in *White Egrets* develops multiple layers of interpretation, as well as a complex position towards language and English literary tradition. This becomes apparent by analyzing his representation of an authorial self in his critical essays. How is Joseph Conrad's position to be read given that Walcott claims "bastard" for his own authorial representation?

In conclusion, I want to come back to the last verse of the poem of *White Egrets*: "This verse / is part of the emptiness, as is the valley of Santa Cruz, / a genuine benediction as his is a genuine curse" (150, lines 15–7). Walcott situates his verse in Conrad's emptiness and in the Caribbean landscape. By this, his position between the English literary tradition and Caribbean national consciousness becomes liminal. This liminality deconstructs the simple dialectics of benediction and curse that the poem ends with. Thus, in the case of English as a literary language, this chapter has shown how both authors seem to feel the need to legitimize (for different reasons) their use of that language. The crucial but ambivalent role of the English language as a tool for establishing or abdicating national literature becomes evident while looking at these authors. Even though he curses Conrad and presents him as his antagonist, Walcott creates a bond with Conrad at the same time by quoting him by name. He perpetuates the canonization of Conrad by referring to him as "bastard," as another allegedly illegitimate heir of English literature.

Works Cited

Anderson, Benedict. *Imagined Communities. Reflections on the Origin and Spread of Nationalism*. 1983. Verso, 2006.

Ashcroft, Bill. *Caliban's Voice. The Transformation of English in Post-Colonial Literatures*. Routledge, 2009.

Ashcroft, Bill. *On Post-Colonial Futures: Transformations of Colonial Culture*. Continuum, 2001.

Bhabha, Homi. *The Location of Culture*. Routledge, 1994.

Brathwaite, Edward Kamau. *History of the Voice: The Development of Nation Language in Anglophone Caribbean Poetry*. New Beacon Books, 1984.

Breiner, Laurence. "How Shall the History of West Indian Literature Be Told?" *Journal of West Indian Literature*, vol. 11, no. 1, 2002, pp. 39–47.

Breslin, Paul. "Derek Walcott's 'Reversible World': Centers, Peripheries, and the Scale of Nature." *Callaloo*, vol. 28, no. 1, 2005, pp. 8–24. doi: 10.1353/cal.2005.0005.

Certeau, Michel de. *The Writing of History*. Columbia UP, 1988.

Chrisman, Laura. "Nationalism and Postcolonial Studies." *The Cambridge Companion to Postcolonial Literary Studies*, edited by Neil Lazarus, Cambridge UP, 2004, pp. 183–98. doi: 10.1017/CCOL0521826942.010.

Clifford, James. *Routes: Travel and Translation in the Late Twentieth Century*. Harvard UP, 1997.

Collier, Gordon. "The Caribbean." *English Literatures Across the Globe: A Companion*, edited by Lars Eckstein, Fink, 2007, pp. 224–55.

Conrad, Joseph. "Author's Note." *The Mirror of the Sea and A Personal Record*. 1908–09. Edited by Zdzisław Najder, Oxford UP, 1988, pp. iii–x.

Conrad, Joseph. *The Collected Letters of Joseph Conrad: Volume 3. 1903–1907*, edited by Frederick R. Karl and Laurence Davies, Cambridge UP, 1988.

Conrad, Joseph. *Heart of Darkness*. 1899. Edited by Owen Knowles, Penguin Classics, 2007.

Döring, Tobias. *Caribbean-English Passages: Intertextuality in a Postcolonial Tradition*. Routledge, 2002.

Ford, Ford Madox. "Joseph Conrad." *Critical Essays of Ford Madox Ford*, edited by Max Saunders and Richard Stang, Carcanet, 2002, pp. 76–90.

Froude, James Anthony. *The English in the West Indies or The Bow of Ulysses*. 1888. Cambridge UP, 2010.

Fumagalli, Maria Cristina. *The Flight of the Vernacular: Seamus Heaney, Derek Walcott and the Impress of Dante*. Rodopi, 2001.

Härtl, Kathrin. *The Common Bond of the Sea. Derek Walcott und Joseph Conrad*. Fink, 2019.

Hirsch, Edward. "The Art of Poetry (1986)." *Critical Perspectives on Derek Walcott*, edited by Robert D. Hamner, Lynne Rienner, 1997, pp. 65–84.

Karl, Frederick Robert. Introduction. *The Collected Letters of Joseph Conrad: Volume 3, 1903–1907*, edited by Robert Karl, Cambridge UP, 1988, pp. xxiii–xxxii.

Kirsch, Adam. "Full Fathom Five. Derek Walcott's Seascapes." *The New Yorker*, 3 Feb. 2014, www.newyorker.com/magazine/2014/02/03/full-fathom-five-2. Accessed 11 Nov 2020.

Leavis, Frank Raymond. *The Great Tradition*. New York UP, 1969.

Lynd, Robert. "Daily News." 1908. Reprinted in *Conrad: The Critical Heritage*, edited by Norman Sherry, 1973, pp. 210–2.

McInturff, Kate. "'The Heritage of Perception': Nation and Deracination in Early Conrad Criticism." *Conradiana*, vol. 37, no. 3, 2005, pp. 275–92.

Naipaul, V. S. *The Middle Passage*. 1962. Vintage, 2002.

Naipaul, V. S. "Conrad's Darkness." *The New York Review of Books*, 1974, pp. 16–21.

Nixon, Rob. "Preparations for Travel: The Naipaul Brothers' Conradian Atavism." *Research in African Literatures*, vol. 22, no. 2, 1991, pp. 177–90.

Retamar, Roberto Fernández, et al. "Caliban: Notes towards a Discussion of Culture in Our America." *The Massachusetts Review*, vol. 15, no. 1/2, 1974, pp. 7–72.

Sivanandan, Tamara. "Anticolonialism, National Liberation, and Postcolonial Nation Formation." *The Cambridge Companion to Postcolonial Literary Studies*, edited by Neil Lazarus, Cambridge UP, 2004, pp. 41–65. doi: 10.1017/CCOL0521826942.003.

Shakespeare, William. *The Tempest*. 1623. Edited by Stephen Orgel, Oxford UP, 2008.

Smith, David, "The Hidden Narrative: The K in Conrad." *Joseph Conrad's Under Western Eyes: Beginnings, Revisions, Finals Forms*, edited by David R. Smith, Archon Books, 1991, pp. 39–81.

Terada, Rei. *Derek Walcott's Poetry: American Mimicry*. Northeastern UP, 1992.

The New Oxford Annotated Bible with Apocrypha: New Revised Standard Version, edited by Michael D. Coogan, et al., Oxford UP, 2010.

Walcott, Derek. "A Far Cry from Africa." *The Poetry of Derek Walcott. 1948–2013*, selected by Glyn Maxwell, Farrar, Straus and Giroux, 2014, pp. 27–8.

Walcott, Derek. *Another Life*. 1973. Edited by Edward Baugh and Colbert Nepaulsingh, Lynne Rienner, 2009.

Walcott, Derek. "Leaving School." *Critical Perspectives on Derek Walcott*. 1965. Edited by Robert Hamner, Lynne Rienner, 1997, pp. 24–32.

Walcott, Derek. *Omeros*. Farrar, Straus and Giroux, 1990.

Walcott, Derek. *The Fortunate Traveller*. Farrar, Straus and Giroux, 1981.

Walcott, Derek. "The Muse of History." *What the Twilight Says: Essays*. 1974. Faber & Faber, 1998, pp. 36–64.

Walcott, Derek. *The Poetry of Derek Walcott. 1948–2013*, selected by Glyn Maxwell, Farrar, Straus and Giroux, 2014.

Walcott, Derek. "The Schooner *Flight*." *The Poetry of Derek Walcott. 1948–2013*, selected by Glyn Maxwell, Farrar, Straus and Giroux, 2014, pp. 237–52.

Walcott, Derek. "The Sea is History." *The Poetry of Derek Walcott. 1948–2013*, selected by Glyn Maxwell, Farrar, Straus and Giroux, 2014, pp. 253–6.

Walcott, Derek. "The Spoiler's Return." *The Poetry of Derek Walcott. 1948–2013*, selected by Glyn Maxwell, Farrar, Straus and Giroux, 2014, pp. 303–8.

Walcott, Derek. "*Volcano*." *Collected Poems 1948–1984*. Farrar, Straus and Giroux, 1986, p. 324.

Walcott, Derek."What the Twilight Says." *What the Twilight Says: Essays*. 1970. Faber & Faber, 1998, pp. 3–35.

Walcott, Derek. *White Egrets. Weiße Reiher*. 2010. Translated by Werner von Koppenfels, Hanser, 2012.

Woolf, Virginia. "Joseph Conrad." *Times Literary Supplement*, 14 Aug. 1924, p. 493.

Young, Robert. "The Overwritten Unwritten. Nationalism and Its Doubles in Post-Colonial Theory." *(Un)writing Empire*, edited by Theo d'Haen, Rodopi, 1998, pp. 15–36.

Young, Robert. *Colonial Desire: Hybridity in Theory, Culture, and Race*. Routledge, 1995.

Index

agency   89, 124, 136, 143, 147, 161–2, 187, 231–2
Aboriginal peoples   132, 134–6, 140
Adichie, Chimamanda Ngozi   185
   Half of a Yellow Sun   186–8, 190–3, 195, 198
advertisement   30, 51, 113, 122
affect, affective   78, 114, 120, 187–90, 192, 194, 196–7, 199–200
   capital   187
   digital   188, 200
   modes of historical knowledge   189
   national   6
   online community   188, 189, 190, 192, 194, 196–7, 199
   perspective   189
   response   190
Africa, African   13, 25, 30, 32–3, 36–7, 40, 76, 83–4, 95–6, 156, 170, 173, 175, 187, 192, 195, 197–9, 223–4, 228, 232–3
   -American   156
   diaspora   96
   East   25, 30, 32
   pan-   173, 233
   West   76, 228, 233
Afropolitan, Afropolitanism   13, 173, 186
Agboluaje, Oladipo   13–4
agency   89, 124, 136, 143, 147, 161–2, 187, 231–2
Akashvani —   see: All India Radio
All India Radio   115
Amazon   187–8, 190–2, 197, 199
America, American   1–3, 13, 27, 33–4, 93, 103, 105, 115, 123, 138, 142, 156, 158–60, 170, 187, 194
   English —   see: English, American
Anderson, Benedict   5, 9–10, 23, 58, 112, 170–1, 186–7, 199, 226
anglophone Caribbean   32, 80
anticolonialism   25, 174, 226
"Apology to Australia's Indigenous People"   132–3, 135–7, 141
archive   77, 79, 81–2, 89
Arnold, Matthew, "Dover Beach"   99–100, 102, 104
art   11, 13, 76–8, 112, 114, 145–6, 169–70, 180–2
Ashcroft, Bill   6, 9, 223, 228–9

Asia, Asian   13, 57, 83, 97, 153
   British   97
   South   13, 57
assimilation   141–2, 145
austerity   102
Australia, Australian   3, 11, 28, 112, 132–48
   landscape —   see: landscape, Australian
Australia (Luhrmann)   132–48
Australianness   134, 137–40
autobiography   13, 172, 204, 231

Balibar, Etienne   9, 58
BBC   208
belonging   5–6, 41, 50, 52, 86–7, 89, 151, 190, 199, 223–5, 229–32
Benjamin, Walter   171
Berman, Bruce   13
Bhabha, Homi   9, 234
Bhamra, Gurminder K.   7
Bharat Mata —   see: Mother India
Bharatiya Janata Party   1, 5, 123–5
Bhave, Vinoba   57
Biafra   188–90, 192, 194, 197
Bildungsroman   186, 192, 196
Billig, Michael   9, 113, 120
Blake, William   98–9, 101
   "Jerusalem"   98
   "London"   101
blindness   177, 180–2
body, representations of   181, 190–1, 234
Bollywood   111, 116, 120–1, 123
borders, bordering   2, 4–5, 10, 190, 199
Bourdieu, Pierre   35, 113, 187
Brathwaite, Kamau   225–8
Brexit   1–3, 11, 15, 17, 97–8, 100, 205–8, 214, 218–9
Bringing Them Home-report   132, 136
British: colonialism   27, 62, 133, 218–9
   colony   29, 32
   Crown   76, 80
   East India Company —   see: East India Company
   Empire —   see: empire, British
   identity —   see: identity, British
   India   114, 117

Malaya — see: Malaya;
  Raj 115, 218–9 — see also: Raj orphan
Britishness 97, 137, 221
Britpop 96–7
broadcasting 11, 56, 115–21
Burma, colonial 204
Bush myth 138–40, 146

calypso 75–89
calypsonian 76–82, 84–6
campaign (election, political) 2, 29, 32, 43, 45, 47, 51–2, 97, 122–3, 133, 214–5
Canadian national identity — see: national identity, Canadian
Canadianness 158–62
canon, canonization 63, 65, 68–9, 95, 97, 172, 176, 228–30, 235
capital (Bourdieu) 187, 194
Capital (Lanchester) 104
capitalism, capitalist 10, 13, 58, 93, 102, 104–5, 151, 160, 187–8, 199
  print 58
Caribbean 32, 75, 77, 80, 84, 223–9, 234–5
  consciousness 228–9
  culture 223, 226–7
  landscape — see: landscape, Caribbean
  literature 224, 227, 234
  national consciousness 235
  poetry 223, 225
  postcolonial 76, 80, 225
Carlyle, Thomas 98
censorship 77
Ceylon 220
Chrisman, Laura 12–3, 226
class 3, 9, 13–4, 29, 33, 44, 50, 58, 62, 76, 87, 94, 112, 122, 152, 154, 173, 187–94, 200, 220
Clifford, James 231
code-switching 55
Cole, Teju 169–83
  "A Quartet for Edward Said" 173
  Blind Spot 181–2
  "Blind Spot" 180
  Every Day Is for the Thief 69, 71–9, 183
  Open City 172–4, 176, 181
  "The History of Photography Is a History of Shattered Glass" 177
colonial space 114, 223

colonialism 7–11, 27, 62, 79, 81, 83–4, 93–4, 133, 135, 171, 207, 217–9, 227, 234
colonized 12, 94, 146, 227, 232, 234
colonizer 225, 232
common mwananchi and *common wananchi* 42–3, 47–51, 53
Commonwealth 126, 149, 201
community 9, 25, 28, 34, 42, 44–8, 50–2, 58–66, 69, 80, 92, 111–2, 123, 137, 141, 154, 158, 160, 170, 186, 188, 189–99, 219–20, 232
  online 188–92, 194–7, 199
  speech 28
condition of England genre 92–3, 97–8, 103–4, 106
Conrad, Joseph 223–5, 227, 229–35
  A Personal Record (cited as "Author's Note") 231–2
  Heart of Darkness 224
  The Collected Letters of Joseph Conrad, Vol. 3, 1903–1907 232
consciousness, national — see: national consciousness
continent, -al, -s 4, 10, 13, 215, 224
coronationalism 1, 4–6, 8
cosmopolitanism 1, 156, 159–60, 163, 182–3, 186, 220, 230
COVID-19 4–5, 7–9
creole 26–7, 32–5, 227–8
Crown Colony 78, 85, 87
crown dominion — see: dominion, crown
cultural imperialism 36
culture, national — see: national culture
culture, state — see: state culture

decolonization 11, 26–7, 29, 35–7, 84, 93–4, 226
democracy, democratic, democratization 1, 4, 6, 8, 13, 42, 47, 58, 66, 78, 81, 85–6, 88–9, 119, 121, 159–60, 175
dialect 23, 25–6, 28–9, 32–3, 35–7, 59–60, 62
dialectic 78, 106, 235
dictatorship 3
diglossia 31–3
discourse 9, 24, 40, 43, 47, 50, 52–3, 60, 68, 78, 105, 111, 112, 117, 123, 135, 137–8, 140, 154, 156–8, 160–3, 171, 175, 189, 191, 193, 206, 223, 226–8, 233–4

INDEX

anti-terrorism 117
derivative 12
hegemonic 40, 43
nativist 117
of nationalism —see: nationalist
   discourse; public 123
racist 40
discourse analysis 43, 111
diversity 9, 14, 16, 24–8, 30–1, 35–7, 40–5,
   47–9, 51–2, 57, 60, 62–3, 65–6, 83, 85,
   95, 100, 115, 119–20, 151, 153, 156–8,
   161–2, 215
dominion 115
   crown 133, 137
Doordarshan 115–6, 120–1
doxa (Bourdieu) 113
drama 13, 120–1, 145, 153, 211

East India Company 114
education 11, 57, 59, 68, 82, 85–6, 89, 114, 123,
   144, 170, 187, 192–4, 196
   emotional 195
   higher 29, 31, 34
   political 43
   re- 132, 134, 136–7
   Western education 191
election campaign — see: campaign
empire 10, 11, 16–7, 92–7, 99–102, 105–6, 114,
   162, 204–10, 212–3, 215, 217–21, 225, 234
   British 16–7, 92–7, 99–102, 105–6, 204,
      209, 212–3, 219, 225
   Mughal 114
empiricism 32, 223
England 1, 86, 92–4, 97–106, 134, 139, 207,
   210, 212, 214, 216, 218, 220–1, 229, 231
English landscape — see: landscape, English
English (language): American 26–7, 34
   Kenyan 31
   Jamaican 33–5
   Standard 24, 32–5, 228
   Standard variety of 27, 33
   varieties of 27
Englishes 25–9, 32, 34–7, 40 —see also:
   postcolonial Englishes, World
   Englishes
Englishness 92–8, 100, 103, 106, 225,
   229–30
Enlightenment, European 13

epos, epic 121, 133–7, 141, 146
ethnicity 3, 9–10, 13, 23–5, 27–9, 35, 40, 42,
   44–5, 47, 49–50, 58, 83, 86, 119, 139–40,
   142, 156, 160, 220
Eurocentrism 233
Europe, European 2, 7, 10–2, 23, 25, 36, 40–1,
   52, 76, 83, 97–8, 100, 103–4, 136, 141, 175–
   6, 191, 211, 215, 223–9, 233–4
European Union, EU 1, 2, 7

father, -s 144, 197
   fore- 23
   grand- 140, 144, 232–3
   language of one's 232
Fichte, Johann Gottlieb 24
film (movies) 102, 104, 111, 116–20, 122–3,
   133–5, 137–43, 145–7, 151, 162, 180
film (photography) 177
First Nation 162
flag 82, 86, 120–2, 124, 155, 188, 216, 225
Ford, Ford Madox 230
foreign, -er, -s 2–3, 5, 10, 27, 61, 84, 114, 118–9,
   123, 174, 193, 204, 214, 229–30
Foucault, Michel 111, 113
Froude, James Anthony, *The English in the*
   West Indies 226–7

game studies 152–3
Gandhi, Indira 121
Gandhi, Mahatma 57–8, 61, 65,
   67, 115
Gardam, Jane 204–6, 208–9, 211,
   213–9
Gaskell, Elizabeth, *North and South* 93
gaze, photographic 169–72, 176–7
Gellner, Ernest 9, 58, 117
gender 14, 44, 114, 123, 151–3,
   160, 188
genre 64, 92–3, 96–7, 106, 134, 140, 153, 155,
   158, 171–3, 175, 182–3
Gikandi, Simon 93–4, 98, 106
Gĩkũyũ 43, 46–7, 49
Gilroy, Paul 1, 94, 97, 99, 105–6, 205–8,
   210, 219
globalization 1, 4, 152, 163
Goffman, Erving 113
Goodreads 187–8, 192, 197, 199
griot 76–7, 84

Habila, Helon, *Measuring Time*   187–8, 195–9
Hall, Stuart   112, 116, 160
Harvey, PJ   92, 97–106
Haugen, Einar   24–5
Hausa   77, 190
hegemonic masculinity   151, 162
Herder, Johann Gottfried   23
heritage   33, 51, 79–81, 85–6, 102, 112, 115, 117, 119, 137, 142, 224, 231, 233
   film   102
heteronormativity   152, 157, 159, 162
Hindi, Hindi language   57–63, 65–9, 111, 115–6, 118–9, 121
   cinema   111
   literature   59–60, 62–6, 69
Hindu   1, 3, 13, 59–61, 68, 111, 114–21, 123–25
   nationalism — see: nationalism, Hindu
Hindustan, Hindustani   57, 67, 117–8, 121
Hindutva   119, 121, 124
historical novel   13, 186–7, 195
history, historiography   4, 7–8, 10, 13, 23–4, 26, 33, 43–4, 51, 53, 58–61, 63–4, 66, 69, 75–84, 86–7, 89, 93–5, 97–9, 101, 105–6, 112–5, 118, 121, 132–5, 137, 139–40, 147–8, 152, 154, 156, 160, 169–70, 175–7, 183, 186–7, 189–90, 195, 198, 205–8, 212–3, 215, 217, 223, 225–8, 234
Hitlerism   206
Hobsbawm, Eric   9, 113, 226
Holy Family, the   132, 134–5, 138, 141, 147
home   5, 7, 15, 59–60, 63, 76, 85–7, 89, 115, 119, 120, 132, 136, 141, 158–9, 169, 175–6, 183, 189, 193, 210, 216–7, 220–1
   -less   230
homogeneity   9–10, 23–4, 27–9, 41, 45–8, 50–3, 58, 60, 62, 66–7, 69, 92, 114, 119, 125, 213, 216, 230
Hong Kong   209, 211–4
Huizinga, Johan, *Homo Ludens*   152
Humboldt, Wilhelm von   24, 37
Hutcheon, Linda   195
hybridity   10, 95, 225, 233–4

iconography   102, 115, 118, 121
identity: Australian   134, 136–7
   British   207, 209–10
   Canadian   164
   Indian   130
   Jamaican   77

identity politics   40–1, 53, 133–4, 147, 153–5
ideology   4, 8–9, 13, 24–6, 29, 31, 34–7, 40, 53, 57–8, 63, 67–8, 77–8, 89, 104–5, 112–3, 116, 121, 123, 151–3, 156–7, 160–2, 170–1, 174–5, 187, 189, 205, 217–8
   (of) language   4, 24–6, 29, 31, 34–7, 40, 53, 57–8, 63, 67–8
Igbo   188–91
   -Ugwu, -Ukwu   169, 189
Imagined Communities (Anderson)   9, 125, 170, 186, 235
imagined community (Anderson)   9, 58, 170, 186–7, 189
imperialism   10–1, 36, 88, 93–4, 99, 106, 134, 151–2, 156, 162, 170, 175, 205, 223–4, 235
   Trinidad   88
independence   11–3, 25, 27–8, 33, 50, 57–8, 60, 65, 67, 75–89, 115, 120, 135, 138, 147, 160, 171, 189, 198, 211, 221, 224, 226
India, Indian   1, 5, 7, 10–2, 27, 57–69, 93, 95, 111, 113–25
   civilization   57, 60–3, 65–9
   Partition   67, 115
indigeneity, indigenous   28, 29–32, 36, 58, 61, 77, 132, 134–7, 139, 141–3, 145, 147
   languages   28, 29–32, 36, 58
   peoples   11, 132, 136, 139, 141, 147–8
inheriting   4, 68, 93, 171, 227
institution, total — see: total institution
intermediality   176
intertextuality   141–2, 146, 176, 225, 228, 232–4
Ireland, Irish   11

Jamaica, Jamaican   11, 26, 28, 32–6, 77
   English — see: English, Jamaican
   identity — see: identity, Jamaican
   national identity — see: national identity, Jamaican
James, Marlon, *A Brief History of Seven Killings*   33
John, Elton   97–8
Johnson, Boris   3, 5, 204–5, 218
journalism   4, 13, 123, 151, 173, 189

Kenya, Kenyan   26, 28–32, 35–7, 40–53
Kenya*n: 40–3, 50
   Talking Kenya*n   29, 40–1, 50
Kenyan English — see: English, Kenyan

INDEX

Kenyan General Election 2013   40–5, 47, 52
Kenyatta, Uhuru   42–4, 46–7
Khari Boli   59
kinship   23, 64–5, 86, 144, 232
   colonial   86
   cultural   232
Kipling, Rudyard   204–5, 213, 215–16, 218
Kiswahili   41, 43–6, 48–50, 53

Lagos   169, 171–2, 174, 179–80, 182–3
Lanchester, John *Capital*   104
landscape   98–100, 102, 106, 138, 140, 181, 223–4, 235
   Australian   138, 140
   Caribbean   223–4, 235
   English   98–100, 102, 106
language: ideology —   see: ideology, language
   literary   225, 227–9, 232, 235
   of the masses   113 —see also: masses, the
   planning   25
   politics, politics of   26, 36–7, 53, 60
   standard variety of a   24–5, 27
   usage, use, user, performance   26–7, 29, 32–3, 35–7, 40–1, 43, 50–1, 53, 61 —see also: vernacular, vernacular languages
   variation   39
Lazarus, Neil   10
Leavis, F. R.   93, 229–30
Leitkultur   24
LGBTQ*, GLBT   153, 158
lingua franca   25, 27, 29, 31
linguistics, postcolonial —   see: postcolonial linguistics
Locke, John   223
Lord Brynner   79–85, 87–8
Luhrmann, Baz   132–7, 139, 141–2, 144, 146–7
Lynd, Robert Wilson   230
lyric persona   224
lyrics   78–9, 89, 92, 97–8, 100–6, 117–8, 123

Malaviya, Madan Mohan   67
Malaya   217, 219–21
Malaysia   220–1
"Mandalay" (Kipling)   204–5
masculinity   158 —see also: hegemonic masculinity
Mass Effect   150–63
mass media   32

masses, the   58, 62, 65, 78, 80, 105, 112–3, 115, 124
   agency of   124
   ignorant   105
   language of   113
   mouthpiece of   80
   voice of   78
media, mediacy, mediation, medium   25, 27, 32, 41–3, 45, 49, 52–3, 85, 97, 120, 125, 151–3, 157, 162, 171, 176–7, 179–83, 187, 190, 193 —see also: mass media, social media
melodrama   141, 147, 150, 189
metadiscourse   50
metafiction   194–5, 198
meta-medial   177, 179, 182
metrolingualism   56
metropolis, metropolitan area   30, 94, 99, 106, 158, 170, 227
migration, migrant   2–3, 7, 9–10, 13, 24, 26, 94, 97, 105, 133, 137, 146, 154, 157, 172, 206, 221
milieu   215
mimicry   100, 226–7
Modi administration, Modi government — see: Modi, Narendra
Modi, Narendra   1, 3, 12, 122–4
Mondal, Anshuman A.   206–8
monolingual bias, monolingualism   23–6, 28, 35–6, 40, 42, 52–3, 227
mother, -hood   68, 86, 95, 114–5, 117–9, 135, 138–9, 142–5, 147, 192, 194, 217
   Australia   135
   Britain   137
   country   28, 80, 221
   England   86
   grand-   59
   India, *Bharat Mata*   114–5, 117–20
   -land   68, 134
   tongue   36–7, 45, 49, 50, 68, 230
movies —   see: film
Mughal Empire —   see: empire, Mughal
Mukherjee, Pranab   68
multicultural Australia   132–3, 135, 137, 140, 147
multiculturalism   1–2, 95, 133, 135, 137, 152, 159–61, 163, 220 —see also: multicultural Australia
multidialectal   26, 28–9, 35–7

multilingual, multilingualism 25–6, 28–30, 35–7, 40
museum 103, 169–71, 183
music 11, 13, 26, 33, 76–8, 86, 89, 92, 95–7, 100–4, 106, 113, 115, 117–8, 120, 123, 142, 180
  reggae 34, 77
  ska 96
music video 101–4, 117–8, 122
mwananchi, common and *common wananchi* 42–3, 47–51, 53
myth, myth-making, mythology 6, 9, 23, 92, 94, 112–3, 115, 117, 119, 120–1, 134–5, 137–40, 146, 160, 163, 180

Nagari 57, 59, 67
Naipaul, V. S. 225, 227
Nairn, Tom 113
Nairobi 30, 41, 44, 48–9, 51–3
narrative 2, 10, 12, 29, 35, 42, 50, 53, 75–6, 79, 85, 92, 94, 111, 113, 115, 118, 133, 135, 137–9, 141–4, 146–7, 150, 152–8, 161, 163, 171–2, 174, 176, 179–80, 183, 186, 192, 194–6, 198, 205, 212–3, 221, 234
nation 2–7, 9–10, 12–3, 23–5, 27–9, 31, 33, 35–7, 40–7, 49–53, 57–60, 62–4, 66–9, 75–7, 79, 81–2, 84–9, 92, 94, 96–7, 105, 111–20, 122, 124–5, 132, 135–8, 147, 158–9, 161–2, 170–2, 186, 188–9, 192, 195–9, 206–7, 224–8, 230, 232
  Australian 132, 136, 147
  Indian 13, 57, 59–60, 62, 67, 111, 113–5, 117–8, 120–1
  Jamaican 35
  Kenyan 13, 42, 45–6, 52–3
  new 13, 28, 67, 85–7, 137, 161
  postcolonial 12, 28, 75, 87, 186, 189, 195, 198, 226
nation-building 5, 25, 28, 31, 33, 37, 52, 58, 76–7, 79, 81, 86, 117–8, 138
nation language 227–8
nation-state 6–7, 10, 12, 23, 27, 35–6, 40, 84, 112, 158, 161, 170–1, 199, 225–6, 232
national consciousness 235
national culture 3, 31, 68, 79, 93, 111–3, 115–6, 124, 159, 169, 206
National Health Service, NHS 6
national identity: Australian 133–4, 137–9, 147
  Canadian 158–9
  English 92
  Indian 68, 111–2, 115–6, 125
  Jamaican 34
  Kenyan 41–3, 48, 51
national literature 67, 224, 227, 229–30, 235
national narrative 35, 75, 95, 135, 137–9, 147, 192, 195–6
National Sorry Day 133
nationalism: Australian 133–6, 147
  anti-colonial 11
  British 219
  cultural 175
  emotional 186, 188–9, 194–5
  European 175
  ethno-linguistic 24
  Hindu 1, 3, 13, 115, 118, 124–5
  Indian 13 117, 121
  linguistic 5
  in museums 169–70
  methodological 25–7, 29, 36
  populist 1, 3–4, 8, 11
  postcolonial 10, 12, 14
  religious 13
  state 111, 115, 119
  studies 9–10
  vaccine 8
  Western 9, 171
nationalist discourse, discourse of nationalism 60, 68, 105, 161
nationality 95, 153–4, 229, 232
native language 27, 49, 225
native-speakerism 29
neocolonialism 187, 213
neoliberalism 97, 104–5, 152, 160–1, 163
new Nigerian novel 186–8, 199
news 1, 3, 7, 34–5, 116, 120
  -paper, -s 3, 194, 199
Nigeria 13–4, 169–70, 172, 174–5, 179–80, 183, 186–93, 195–6, 199
nostalgia 1, 92–3, 95–6, 99, 102, 106, 159, 169, 204–5, 208, 213, 218
Nyerere, Julius 25

Odinga, Raila 42, 46–7
Olick, Jeffrey 136
'one nation, one language' 23–5, 29, 35–7, 40, 43, 50, 52

INDEX

online community — see:
    community, online
online reviews   187
Orientalism   61, 162, 173, 180, 212
othering, Other   4–5, 10, 13, 28, 95,
    120–1, 156–8, 160–1, 163, 175, 179–80, 183,
    223, 234
O'Toole, Fintan   1, 205–8, 210, 214, 216, 218
outback   134, 138–40, 146

Partition of India   67, 115
pastoral   92, 98–103, 106
People's National Movement (PNM)   79
performance, performativity   10, 13, 45, 76–7,
    96, 100, 103–4, 111, 115, 136, 161, 204, 224,
    229, 233
Persian   57, 62–3
photography   101, 103–4, 145, 169, 171, 176–7,
    179, 181–4
'piccaninny'   145–6
poetry   13, 23, 63–4, 104, 112, 223, 225, 227
political correctness   207, 214, 221
politics   1–2, 7, 10, 12–3, 29, 40–2, 52–3, 57,
    60, 67–8, 78, 84, 97, 111, 115, 121–2, 136,
    141, 147, 152–5, 173, 190, 195
    high   111, 121–2
    identity — see: identity politics
    of regret   136
polylingualism   40–1, 50, 52–3
pop culture, popular culture   10, 81, 111–5,
    116, 119, 121–5, 152
popular music   77, 92, 95–7
postcolonial: Africa   1
    Caribbean   76, 225
    critique   205, 207
    conflict   219
    Englishes   25–8, 32, 35–7, 40
    India   111
    justice   149
    linguistics   36, 40
    literature   186
    melancholia   1, 92, 94–101, 103, 105, 208
    nation — see: nation, postcolonial
    nationalism —see: nationalism,
        postcolonial
    speech community   26, 35–7
    space   40, 87, 98
    studies   9–12, 75, 186

subject   10, 229
theory   7, 23, 25–6, 40, 208, 225, 233
tradition   184, 236
world   1, 10
writers   219
writing   186
postcolonialism   9–11, 78
postimperial melancholia   206, 219
post-independence   83–4
    euphoria   189
    India   57, 65, 67
    language politics   60
    polity   67
    states   171
Powell, Enoch   95
Premchand   57–8, 62–3
primordialism   13, 226

queer, queerness   150–5, 157–62
queer studies   153–4

race   3, 7, 9, 14, 80, 87, 98, 150, 153–4, 156–7,
    160–1, 188
racism, racist   2, 10, 95, 98, 139–40, 145, 147,
    153, 156–7, 160, 214, 221
radio   11, 30, 34–5, 52, 79, 115–6, 122
Raj — see: British Raj
'Raj orphans'   205, 216–9
realism   195–6, 199
    allegorical   188–9
    disenchanted   188, 195
    magical   196
raw   196, 199
reconciliation (Australia)   132–7, 143–
    4, 146–8
refugees   2, 7, 10, 24
reggae music — see: music, reggae
religion   3–4, 13, 44, 57, 61–5, 69, 83, 114, 119,
    123, 154, 171
representation   5, 6, 10, 111, 141, 145–6, 151–4,
    156–8, 161–2, 170–2, 192–3, 195–7, 199–
    200, 223–4, 226–7, 234–5
    self-   170, 223–4
reviews, online — see: online reviews
role-playing games, RPGs   151, 154–5, 161–2
romance   13, 155–7, 159
root, -s, -ed   57, 61, 69, 76, 78, 160, 207,
    215, 231–3

245

Rudd, Kevin   132–3, 135–7
rural   29–32, 34, 46, 100, 102, 134, 139, 147, 191
rural-urban distinction   32 —see also: urban-rural divide
Rushdie, Salman   95
Ruto, William   44

Said, Edward   93, 173, 175, 180
scapegoat, scapegoating   2, 5, 100, 105
Scotland, Scottish   11–2
Sebald, W. G., *Austerlitz*   176
Selasi, Taiye   186
self-fashioning   187
self-representation —   see: representation, self-
sexuality   145, 150–5, 157–8, 160, 174, 189–92, 220
Shakespeare, William: sonnets   76
    The Tempest   229, 233
Sheng   30–2, 35, 43, 48–9, 51–2
Shukla, Ramchandra   57, 59–69
Shwedagon Pagoda   204
ska music —   see: music, ska
skin colour   5, 141, 154, 156
skinhead scene   96
Smith, Anthony D.   9, 113, 115
sobriquet   81–2
social   2–3, 5–6, 9–10, 12, 23–4, 26–31, 33, 35, 37, 44–5, 49, 53, 61–2, 65, 67, 76–8, 83, 86, 93–4, 104–5, 111, 114, 118, 133, 142, 153–4, 156–8, 170, 175, 187, 192, 194, 198–9, 215, 220
    construction, constructionist   9, 111
    distancing   5
    engineering   170
    media   2–3, 187, 199
societal, societies, society   1, 7, 13–4, 25, 29–30, 34, 40–3, 48, 58–9, 62, 64–6, 78, 83–4, 87, 117–8, 133, 141, 147, 152, 173
sociolinguistic variation   26
sociology of literature   200
song   23, 64–5, 76, 78–80, 85, 89, 92, 96–106, 111, 114, 116–9, 122–4, 135, 139–40, 213
space, -s   30, 40, 85, 87, 93–4, 98–9, 106, 114, 122, 134, 138, 141, 152–3, 162, 187, 196, 198–9, 214, 223–5, 227, 233
    national   127, 185
    postcolonial   40, 87, 98

speech act   43, 45, 47, 231
    performative   224, 229, 233
speech community —   see: community, speech
Standard English —   see: English, Standard
standard variety of English —   see: English, standard variety of
state ceremonies   120
state culture   112, 115–6
state nationalism —   see: nationalism, state
Stolen Generations, the   132–4, 136, 147
Sud, Nikita   13
Swadeshi movement   115, 117
Swahili   25, 29–32, 41, 43, 49
    Kiswahili   41, 43–6, 48–50, 53
    Vi-Swahili   43, 48–50, 53

tabula rasa   93, 223
Talking Kenya*n —   see: Kenya*n
Tandon, Purushottam Das   67
Taupin, Bernie   98
television, TV   2–3, 11, 45, 102, 104, 115–6, 122, 192
Tempest, Kate   92, 97–8, 100, 103–6
territory   9, 28, 60, 62–3, 65
Tiffin, Helen   6, 9
Tiranga   120–1, 124
Tobago, Tobagonian   79, 86–8
Torres Strait Islanders   136
total institution   113
transnationalism   1–2, 4–5, 8, 13, 26, 160, 225, 228
trauma   136, 191, 206, 217–9
travel: literature   173
    writing   173, 175, 180, 182
travelogue   169, 172, 175–6, 179, 226–7
Trinbago, Trinbagonian   75–81, 83–5, 87–9
Trinidad and Tobago   75–8, 80, 82–9
Trinidad, Trinidadian   82, 84–5, 87–8
    imperialism —   see: imperialism, Trinidad
Trump, Donald   1–3, 5, 123

underlexicalization   193
UK Independence Party   2
UN (United Nations)   12
United Kingdom, UK   1–3, 6–7, 11–2, 88, 204, 215

unity   6, 43–8, 52–3, 61–2, 65, 67, 69, 112, 115, 119–20, 136
  cultural   112
  'diversity in unity'   47
  national   43–5, 48, 53, 119, 136
  'unity despite diversity'   44, 47
  'unity in diversity'   115, 119–20
urban   29–33, 48–50, 52–53, 58, 94, 98–9, 122, 224
urban-rural divide   29 —see also: rural-urban distinction
Urdu   57, 59, 63, 67

Valluvan, Sivamohan   4, 10
vernacular, vernacular languages   42, 48, 58, 60, 63, 114
videogames   150–3, 157, 160–2
violence   1, 11, 42, 47, 101, 105, 111, 122, 124, 177, 199, 206–8

Vi-Swahili —   see: Swahili, Vi-

Walcott, Derek   223–9, 231–5
Wales, Welsh   11
wananchi, common and *common mwananchi*   42–3, 47–51, 53
war   5, 11, 92, 94, 101, 118, 133, 137, 150, 188–9, 191–2, 195–7, 199, 205–6, 214–17, 219
Ward, Russel   138
Weinreich, Max   23
West Indies, West Indian   78, 224, 226–7, 233
Woolf, Virginia   180, 229
World Englishes   25–7, 37
World Health Organization   5, 8

xenophobia   94–5

YouTube   3, 79, 122, 188, 199

Printed in the United States
by Baker & Taylor Publisher Services